The Technique of
ORCHESTRATION

PRENTICE-HALL MUSIC SERIES

Douglas Moore. Editor

THE TECHNIQUE

of

PRENTICE-HALL, INC.

KENT WHEELER KENNAN

Professor of Music
The University of Texas

ORCHESTRATION

Englewood Cliffs, N. J.

L. C. Cat. Card No.: 52–8604

Current printing (last digit)
22 21 20 19 18 17 16

PRINTED IN THE UNITED STATES OF AMERICA

90032–C

PREFACE

THE basic material of orchestration has long since been stated in such monumental treatises as those by Berlioz, Rimsky-Korsakoff, and Forsyth, and in a number of excellent books of more recent vintage. Nevertheless, there are several reasons why a new book on the subject would seem to be in order at this time.

In the first place, instruments and orchestral practice are constantly changing, with the result that even the best orchestration books sooner or later become outmoded in certain respects. For example, discussions of the woodwinds used to bristle with lists of unplayable trills, whereas recent improvements in the construction of instruments have made many of these trills quite practical. And pedal timpani, which not too many years ago were mentioned as a comparative rarity, are now included in every professional orchestra. We need, then, to bring information on orchestral instruments up to date.

In the second place, a good deal of the available material on orchestration is based on European practice and does not necessarily hold true in this country. This book, being American in orientation, aims at preparing students in this country for the actual situations they will meet when they are called upon to make practical use of their knowledge of scoring.

Thirdly, many of the most complete and scholarly works on orchestration were conceived as reference books and consequently are not well suited to teaching needs. They tend to include a mass of historical and technical detail that the student cannot possibly absorb at a time when his attention must be devoted to practical fundamentals.

The present volume attempts to present these practical fundamentals as clearly and concisely as possible, in units that can be digested easily. After a brief introduction to the orchestra as a whole, the instruments of each section are taken up individually and then in combination; finally the sections are combined. No attempt has been made to give a detailed account of the construction of instruments, and historical background has been included only where it seemed essential to an understanding of the modern instruments—or of scores of an earlier period. Although the main emphasis has been on the full-fledged symphony orchestra, most orchestration classes include students who are majoring in music education and will have to work with smaller, less skilled, and often oddly assorted orchestral groups. For the benefit of these students, certain problems involved in scoring for school orchestras are mentioned from time to time, and a short chapter is devoted to that subject.

The material in this book has been used in orchestration classes at the University of Texas for the past two years. As a result of this testing through actual use, certain portions of the original version were rewritten and re-tested. The author therefore feels confident that the material as presented here can be readily understood.

Obviously, it is important that orchestration students gain a knowledge of various *styles* of scoring. But a sense of style must come from an acquaintance with the scores themselves; without such an acquaintance no amount of reading on the subject would mean much. Consequently, that aspect of orchestration has not been discussed in this book but has, instead, been left in the hands of the individual teacher, to be included as scores of various periods are studied. Some of the author's ideas concerning this phase of the work are included in the "Suggestions for the Use of This Book" that follow.

So many people have been of help in the preparation of this volume that a complete acknowledgment of indebtedness cannot very well be attempted. The author is especially grateful to Joseph Blankenship, Frank Elsass, Bernard Fitzgerald, Albert Gillis, John McGrosso, Alfio Pignotti, Angel Reyes, Homer Ulrich, James Williams, and other colleagues in the music department at the University of Texas who have read portions of the manuscript or contributed information; to Dr. Kenneth Hjelmervik, Director of Music Education in the Baltimore Public Schools, and to Karl Van Hoesen of the Eastman School of Music for suggestions concerning the material on school orchestras; to Harvey C. Biskin of the San Antonio Symphony for his valuable help with the chapter on percussion instruments; to Dr. Bjornar Bergethon of New York University, Dr. Paul Pisk of Redlands University, and Louis Lane of The Cleveland Orchestra for their detailed examination of the book and for their excellent suggestions; to Mrs. Janet McGaughey for proofreading; and to Dean E. W. Doty for his sympathetic encouragement and practical assistance.

KENT KENNAN

SUGGESTIONS FOR THE USE OF THIS BOOK

CERTAIN changes in the order of material in this book are possible. Some of these are the following:

Chapter XI (Special Problems in Transcribing Piano Music) might be taken up earlier—at any point after Chapter IV—depending on whether or not the material in it is needed in connection with the particular assignments given.

Chapters XIII and XIV, on percussion instruments, could be introduced after Chapter IX. The same is true of Chapter XV (chiefly about the harp).

The section in Chapter V on the piccolo, English horn, bass clarinet, and contra bassoon might be delayed until later instead of being presented along with the material on the other woodwinds.

The section in Chapter IV on string harmonics (always a difficult subject for the student) might also be taken up later as a separate project, after the student has had more time to become familiar with the workings of stringed instruments and when he is not so busy absorbing the more basic information.

Since much of the most important material on orchestration can be learned through a study of symphonic scores, it would seem best to equip the student for score reading as quickly as possible. With that end in mind, the author recommends moving fairly rapidly through the first nine chapters of this book, rather than dwelling very long on any one of them. Once the student has acquired enough knowledge of all the instruments to undertake score reading, it is always possible to return to individual instruments or sections for more concentrated work.

As far as the choice of music for score study and listening is concerned, the author feels that shorter works are preferable—at least in beginning orchestration courses, where time is generally at a premium. The student can grasp the essential characteristics of Mozart's orchestration about as well from the Overture to *The Marriage of Figaro* as he can from the C major Symphony (*Jupiter*) for example, and the choice of shorter works allows for the study of more scores of various styles within the allotted time. As a *minimum* program of score study, one work from each of the following groups is suggested:

(1) Haydn, Mozart, Beethoven
(2) Tchaikovsky, Rimsky-Korsakoff, Wagner
(3) Debussy, Ravel
(4) Richard Strauss

There are, of course, many other composers (including contemporaries such as Stravinsky, Hindemith, and Bartók) whose music could also be included if time permitted. Following are a few of the many scores that might be used for class study and listening:

Mozart, Overture to *The Marriage of Figaro*
Beethoven, *Leonore* Overture No. 3; *Egmont* Overture; *Coriolanus* Overture
Weber, *Oberon* Overture; *Der Freischütz* Overture
Tchaikovsky, *Romeo and Juliet*
Rimsky-Korsakoff, *Capriccio Espagnol*
Wagner, Prelude to *Die Meistersinger;* Prelude to *Parsifal;* Prelude and Love Death from *Tristan and Isolda;* Overture to *Tannhäuser*
Debussy, *Prelude to The Afternoon of a Faun*
Ravel, *Bolero*
Strauss, *Till Eulenspiegel; Don Juan; Death and Transfiguration*
Stravinsky, *Fire Bird* Suite

In this list, shorter works of the composers represented have been chosen wherever possible, for reasons mentioned earlier. As for longer or more involved works which would be particularly instructive for score study, a few of the possibilities that come to mind are these:

Berlioz, *Fantastic Symphony*
Mussorgsky-Ravel, *Pictures from an Exhibition*
Tchaikovsky, Symphonies No. 4, 5, and 6
Franck, Symphony in D minor
Brahms, the Symphonies

Debussy, *Iberia; La Mer*
Ravel, *Daphnis and Chloe* Suite No. 2
Stravinsky, *Petrouchka; The Rite of Spring*
Hindemith, *Mathis der Maler*
Bartók, Concerto for Orchestra

In planning this book, the author had in mind a year's course in orchestration. When the book is used for a course of only a semester's length, a detailed covering of all the material in it may not be feasible. The decision as to what material to stress and what to pass over lightly (or omit altogether) must rest with the individual teacher and will be determined by the particular needs of his students. For example, students majoring in music education will need to know the practical problems connected with scoring for school orchestras but will, in all probability, never encounter a contra bassoon or a celesta in their work. Student composers, on the other hand, will need to know these instruments well enough to write for them but are likely to have little immediate use for the material on school orchestras. And the embryo musicologists will have more reason than the other students to learn about such instruments as the viola d'amore and the basset horn. Thus the matter of emphasis, in the use of this book, can be determined only in the individual teaching situation.

Actual music to be used for the exercises in scoring is not included in this volume but is available in *Orchestration Workbook,* also published by Prentice-Hall, Inc.

Kent Kennan

TABLE OF CONTENTS

LIST OF ILLUSTRATIONS

Chapter 1

INTRODUCTION

HOW DOES one go about learning orchestration?
In the first place, there is a certain amount of factual information that must be acquired. Under this heading would come the following:

Names of instruments and orchestral terms (including Italian, French, and German equivalents, because many scores are printed in these languages);
Order of instruments on the page;
Ranges of instruments;
Proper notation (including transpositions and special clefs);
General technical abilities and limitations of each instrument (This does not necessarily involve the ability to *play* the instruments);
Principles of combining and of balancing instruments; and
Characteristics of various "schools" of scoring.

This material can be learned from classroom explanations, from books, from talks with orchestral players or demonstrations by them, and from a close study of orchestral scores.

But there is another type of information which, in a sense, cannot be taught and which can be learned only by careful and frequent listening (along with score-reading) over a considerable period of time. In this category might be listed a knowledge of these things:

The characteristic tone quality of each instrument;
The sound of various instruments in combination; and
The sound of special effects.

The point here is that tone colors cannot really be described adequately in words. It is all very well to read in an orchestration book that the clarinet is "dark" in its lower register, but until one has

1

actually heard the sound in question and impressed it on his "mind's ear," he has no real conception of that particular color for purposes of orchestration. Not everyone seems to be equally endowed in the matter of aural memory and aural imagination, but these qualities can be sharpened by practice.

Of course, once this information has been acquired, it must be applied in actual exercises in scoring—transcriptions of piano music, of songs, or of music for solo instrument with piano. Students who are composers will want to go on and write directly for orchestra. That is obviously the ideal situation, in that the musical ideas are conceived with the orchestral instruments in mind. But we cannot very well expect all students to be composers. Besides, the ability to *transcribe* for orchestra is one of the most usable and important skills to be gained from an orchestration course.

It is assumed that students who are studying orchestration from this book have already had a thorough training in harmony. The writer's experience indicates that poor scoring on the part of students is more often the result of a failure to understand harmonic and general musical structure than of a faulty knowledge of orchestration. In spite of the fact that integration has been preached *ad nauseam* of late, many students seem to feel that their work in harmony has nothing to do with orchestration (or with their other musical courses). But unless the principles of good voice-leading, spacing, and doubling are applied in an arrangement, no amount of clever orchestration will make it sound well; and without an understanding of harmonic content and form, intelligent scoring is impossible. It is of the greatest importance, in orchestrating, to think in terms of *lines* rather than of isolated notes. Otherwise the total result will be confused and the individual players' parts will be unmusical and ungrateful to play.

Finally, it cannot be stressed too strongly that accurate workmanship, attention to detail, and a practical approach are all parts of successful orchestration. Anyone who has witnessed an orchestra rehearsal where time was wasted and tempers strained because of mistakes in the players' parts will know how costly and serious inaccuracy can be. As for "attention to detail," there are a thousand small points involved in scoring—points which may seem trivial but which, taken all together, make the difference between scoring that "comes off" in performance and scoring that does not. This all ties in, of course, with a practical approach, which involves the ability to achieve the maximum effect with the simplest means. Orchestration is not a nebulous sort of business conditioned by "artistic inspiration" but an intensely real and down-to-earth technique which requires, among other things, a large amount of common sense.

Although the terms *orchestration* and *instrumentation* are sometimes used as being synonymous, it might be well to point out a distinction in meaning which is generally made by musicians and which is observed in this book. Orchestration has to do with the actual process of scoring music for orchestra. Instrumentation, on the other hand, usually refers to a study of individual instruments—their construction, history, abilities, and so on. Sometimes the word is also used in connection with the list of instruments required for a particular piece of music, as when we speak of "the instrumentation" employed in an orchestral work. Of course anyone who sets out to learn orchestration must, in the process, learn a good deal about instrumentation. There is, then, a certain amount of overlapping between the two terms, in the sense that the second is included (at least partially) in the first.

In order to gain a general perspective before concentrating on individual instruments and sections of the orchestra, we are going to take time in this chapter for a brief look at the orchestra as a whole. "Orchestra" here means symphony orchestra, of course; but even that term is rather lacking in precision because symphonic groups vary considerably in size and make-up. The table on page 4 lists the orchestral instruments and shows approximately how many of each might be found in orchestras of various sizes. Parentheses around a number mean that the instrument in question may or may not be included.

The celesta and piano, though not regular members of the orchestra, may be used with any of these groups and, like the harp, are "extras" which do not belong to any one of the four sections shown.

Orchestras even larger than the "large orchestra" described here are sometimes called for (by Stravinsky and Richard Strauss, among others). In such cases woodwinds in fours are generally required: piccolo, three flutes, three oboes, English horn, E♭ clarinet, two B♭ clarinets, bass clarinet, three bassoons, and contra bassoon. In order to supply this instrumentation, most of the major orchestras in this country have extra woodwind players on call.

		Small Orchestra	Medium-sized Orchestra	Large Orchestra
Woodwind Section	Piccolo		(1)	1
	Flute	1	2	2
	Oboe	1	2	2
	English Horn			1
	Clarinet	1	2	2
	Bass Clarinet			1
	Bassoon	1	2	2
	Contra Bassoon			1

(Large Orchestra woodwind: or 3, 3, 3, 3)

		Small Orchestra	Medium-sized Orchestra	Large Orchestra
Brass Section	(French) Horn	1 or 2	4	4 to 6
	Trumpet	(1)	2 or 3	3
	Trombone	(1)	3	3
	Tuba		1	1
Percussion Section	Percussion	2*	3*	4 or more*
	Harp	(1)	(1)	(1) or (2)
String Section	1st Violins	4 to 8	8 to 12	12 to 16
	2nd Violins	3 to 6	6 to 10	10 to 14
	Violas	2 to 4	4 to 8	8 to 12
	Cellos	2 or 3	3 to 6	6 to 10
	Double Basses	1 to 3	3 to 6	6 to 10

* These figures indicate the number of percussion players, including the timpanist.

As for the ways in which the woodwind, brass, and string sections of the orchestra may be combined, certain general possibilities might be pointed out:

Strings and woodwinds;

Strings and brass;

Woodwinds and brass; and

Strings, woodwinds, and brass.

Of course each section may also play by itself. When sections are combined, they may take the same musical material or different material. Sometimes only one instrument of a section is used, along with part or all of another section. If all the instruments of the orchestra— or most of them—play, the combination is known as a *tutti* (the Italian word for "all").

The fourth section, the percussion, is most often used for rhythmic support of other instruments, although now and then it can perform on its own to good effect.

The order in which the instruments are listed above is a standard one which is always employed in modern scores. If an instrument is not included in a score, it will not be listed on the page, but those instruments which *are* used will still follow the standard order. In most scores, all the instruments to be used are included on the *first* page, whether they play at that point or not, but on succeeding pages instruments which do not play may be omitted from the listing. When a solo instrument is involved (as in a concerto), its part is normally placed directly above the strings. The same is true of piano, celesta, and choral parts. The examples in Chapter XVI show the appearance of a page of orchestral score.

A note of explanation is necessary concerning the system used in indicating ranges throughout this book. The limits of the *extreme possible* range are shown in open notes, the limits of the practical or commonly used range in black notes. The reason for this distinction is that nearly every one of the orchestral instruments has notes at the bottom and/or the top of its range which, because of technical difficulties or doubtful intonation or both, are little used and then only under certain conditions. It must be remembered, though, that there is no sharp dividing line between the practical registers and the extreme possible registers, particularly since players and instruments vary. Consequently it is extremely difficult to fix exact limits for each practical range.

Suggested Assignment

Know:
  (1) The four sections of the orchestra.
  (2) The names (in English) of the instruments included in each section.
  (3) The number of each instrument commonly included in the "medium-sized" orchestra.
  (4) The plan used in indicating ranges throughout this book.

Chapter II

THE STRINGS

The Violin

Italian: Violino	French: Violon	German: Violine
(Plural) Violini	Violons	Violinen

Ex. 1

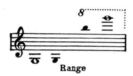

Range

The violin's four strings are tuned to the following pitches:

Ex. 2

These are known as the "open" strings—that is, the strings as they are when not stopped by the fingers. A chromatic scale upward is obtainable on each string by stopping the string at the appropriate points. Normally a note is played on the nearest string below it; for

example, the note  would usually be played on the D string.

However, the G string might be chosen in certain cases in order to maintain the particular color of that string throughout a passage or to avoid a change of position. This same principle is sometimes used in connection with the D and A strings. Although notes more than a 10th above the pitch of each open string are seldom used on any one of the three bottom strings, the top string is necessarily called upon for very high notes.

Normally, the choice of string rests with the player, a particular string being indicated only in cases where a choice other than the normal one is involved. The strings are sometimes designated by Roman numerals, starting with the E string as "I" and working down. Thus, "on the G string" is often indicated by "IV" placed above the first note to be taken on that string and followed by a dotted line to show how far the direction is to apply. Another way of indicating the same thing is to write *sul G* (literally, in Italian, "on the G") above the passage. The German equivalent is *G Saite, Saite* meaning string.

As for the colors of the various strings, the G string is characteristically full, rich, and rather dark in quality. From about upward, its tone becomes curiously intense, as if charged with a suppressed emotion. The D string is less dark and full, the A considerably brighter, and the E especially brilliant and penetrating.

Each of the following examples illustrates the use of a particular string of the violin. Of course not all melodies lie entirely on one string, as these do; the great majority, in fact, require changes from one string to another.

EXAMPLES SHOWING THE USE OF PARTICULAR STRINGS OF THE VIOLIN

Ex. 3

(a) E string:
Classical Symphony   PROKOFIEFF

(b) A string:
Third Symphony   HANSON

Eastman School of Music Publication; Carl Fischer, Inc.

(c) D string:
Second Symphony SIBELIUS

(d) G string:
First Symphony BRAHMS

Stringed instruments may be either bowed or plucked. For these two effects the Italian words *arco* (bow) and *pizzicato* (picked or plucked) are used. *Pizzicato* is usually abbreviated to *pizz.* and written above the staff, over or near the first note of the passage concerned. When the player is to return to the use of the bow, the word *arco* is written in above the staff. These directions are important and must be included by the orchestrator. However, since the normal method of tone production on stringed instruments is by means of the bow, *arco* need not be included unless there has been a pizzicato passage just previously. For example, if a work starts out with a bowed passage, no *arco* direction is needed. It is not customary to use dots (to indicate short notes) in pizzicato passages; if the pizzicato direction is there, the notes will automatically be short (though pizzicato notes that are not too high can be made to ring somewhat—especially if *vibrato* is used). Usually, the easiest notation of time values is employed, rests being omitted wherever possible. For instance, write

narily best not to write pizzicato passages for the violin above about

; higher notes played pizzicato are so thin and lacking

in resonance as to be ineffective for ordinary purposes. It is important to remember that there is a limit to the speed with which successions of pizzicato notes can be performed, also that very rapid changes from arco to pizzicato (or *vice versa*) are awkward—and impossible beyond a certain speed. Changes of this sort which must be made with scarcely any rest between the last arco note and the first pizzicato note are somewhat easier if the last arco note can be taken "up-bow" so that by the end of the bow-stroke the player's hand is close to the strings and in position to play in pizzicato fashion. Left-hand pizzicatos, though not uncommon in solo violin literature, are seldom used in orchestral parts. The usual indication is a small cross above the note.

There are a few names for particular parts of stringed instruments, which come up frequently in orchestration work. The *fingerboard* is the part of the instrument on which the fingers stop the strings. The *bridge* is a small piece of wood that keeps the strings raised and in place above the main body of the instrument. Parts of the bow which are often referred to are the *frog*—or *nut* or *heel*—which is the portion nearest the player's bow hand, and the *point* or *tip* at the opposite end. Special effects involving these and other terms are discussed later on.

A *vibrato* is normally used in playing stringed instruments and is produced by an oscillating motion of the hand on the fingerboard. Without a vibrato the tone is "white" and lacking in expressiveness and warmth (although this very sound is occasionally used for a particular effect in orchestral music). Because a vibrato cannot be produced on an open string,[1] players usually avoid the open strings in slow, *espressivo* passages where the difference in tone quality would be too apparent. A further disadvantage in such cases is that the open strings tend to ring and to be louder than stopped tones. Of course the alternative to playing an open tone is to take the same pitch as a

---

[1] Except by artificial methods, usually involving sympathetic vibration between the open string and another string fingered with vibrato at the pitch of the open string.

Studio Gilmore, Austin, Texas

Double Bass   Violoncello

       Viola   Violin

10

stopped tone on a lower string, though this is obviously not possible with the lowest open string of each instrument. The symbol for an open string is an "O" above the note (not to be confused with the symbol for a natural harmonic, which is smaller and perfectly round; harmonics will be discussed in a later chapter). The numbering of the fingers in string writing may be mentioned in passing, because it is invariably confusing to pianists. The index finger is "1"; the middle finger is "2"; and so on. Since the thumb does not figure in the stopping of the strings, no symbol is needed for it.

One frequently hears string players speak of taking a passage "in first position" or in some other position. Perhaps a few examples will serve to explain this concept of "position," which is basic to string technique. If the player's left hand is placed on the D string (choosing that at random) with his first finger on E and the other fingers ready to play F, G, and A (or F♯, G, and A, or other chromatic variations of these basic pitches), he is said to be "in first position on the D string." If he were in first position on the A string, his first finger would rest on B (or B♭, or in rare cases B♯). For second position on the E string, the first finger would rest on G; for third position on the G string, it would be on C, in each case with the other fingers on (or over) the three notes immediately above. The first, third, and fifth positions are easier and more natural than the second and fourth and are consequently chosen more frequently. Positions higher than the fifth are seldom used on the three lower strings (except in solo writing), but higher positions are often needed on the E string. Although players can shift rapidly from one string to an adjacent one or from one position to another, sudden or repeated jumps *across* strings make for awkward string writing, as do sudden or repeated changes from one position to a distant position. A fingering chart for first position on the violin is given on page 12.

A point to remember, especially in writing for players of limited ability, is the fact that the higher the player goes on a string, the closer together the notes lie on the fingerboard and the harder it is to play perfectly in tune. Because higher positions are not so often necessary on the three lower strings, the chief point of difficulty is in passages high on the top string. These can be written with safety for a professional group, but they are an almost certain invitation to disaster in a school orchestra. As a general rule it is safest not to go beyond third

position in scoring for school groups.   (See Chapter XVIII for further
comments on this subject.)

Fingering Chart

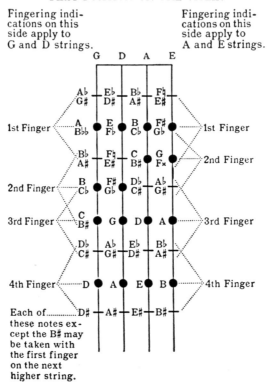

FIRST POSITION ON THE VIOLIN

Fingering indi-
cations on this
side apply to
G and D strings.

Fingering indi-
cations on this
side apply to
A and E strings.

FINGERBOARD OF THE VIOLIN

Double, Triple, and Quadruple Stops

Although the violin is predominantly a single-line instrument, it is
capable of playing two, three, or four notes at a time, provided that
each note can be taken on a separate string and that the pitches involved can be fingered at once.   If any of the notes can be played on
open strings, that will make the fingering problem much easier for
the player.   It is obvious that two pitches cannot be played at the same

time on the same string.   For example, [musical notation] is impossible as

a double-stop on the violin because both notes would have to be taken on the G string. But [♪] is quite easy, since the A can be played on the G string and the F♯ on the D string, the bow being drawn across both strings at once. The double stop [♪] is even easier, because the D can be played on the open D string and the B on the A string. Of course the notes of a double stop must be playable on *adjacent* strings. The following may be considered practical upward limits for double stops involving intervals up to an octave (practical, that is, for the professional orchestra violinist of average ability):

Ex. 4

| 2nds | 3rds | 4ths | 5ths | 6ths | 7ths | 8ves |
| maj. min. | maj. min. | perf. aug. | dim. aug. perf. | maj. min. | maj. min. | |

Of these intervals, 6ths are probably the most successful as double stops. Octaves, 5ths, and 4ths present a certain problem of intonation, since the slightest deviation from the correct pitch in either note is more apparent to the ear than it would be in such intervals as the 6th and 3rd, where the mathematical ratio between notes is more complex. Perfect 5ths, by the way, are played with one finger stopping both strings (assuming that open tones are not involved). Unisons, though rare, are possible and are sometimes introduced for the sake of added resonance and volume. They almost always involve an open string; that is, they are generally written on one of these three pitches:

For example, in [♪] one of the A's would be played on the open A string, the other on the D string. Intervals larger than an octave are also possible in certain cases. Sometimes even such widely spaced double stops as [♪] are used. Unwieldy as this may look to the pianist's eye, it is actually very simple, since the A is an open note and the D presents no problems. For purposes of orchestral writing, quick successions of double stops are generally impractical, though short successions of 6ths or 3rds are not out of the question. Usually, however, such passages are better arranged *divisi* (with the string group divided).

As for triple and quadruple stops, those which include at least one open string are the easiest and the most resonant, but certain other chord arrangements which contain no open note are also possible. Because of the curvature of the bridge, four notes cannot be played at exactly the same time. However, in quadruple stops the bow can be drawn so quickly over the strings that the effect is that of a four-note chord only slightly arpeggiated or broken. Examples 7 and 8 show the more commonly used three-note and four-note chords play- able on the violin. (According to Forsyth, a complete catalog of all the chords possible on the violin would amount to nearly 1500 com- binations!) The method used here in listing chords which contain no open notes may need a word of explanation. Instead of actually writing out all the possibilities in connection with each chord pattern, we have merely indicated them in the following manner:

Ex. 5

This particular example means that three-note chords arranged in this pattern are playable on every half-step within the limits shown:

Ex. 6

This and other upward limits given must not be thought of as hard and fast points above which the chords become impossible. All the patterns are possible in still higher positions, but at that level they become so difficult as to be impractical for normal orchestral use. The limits shown here are therefore intended merely as guides for practical usage.

Notice that the predominant intervals in these chord arrangements are 5ths and 6ths. Notice, too, that four-note chords which contain

open notes in the middle with stopped notes on the outside are generally impractical and are therefore not included.

THREE-NOTE CHORDS FOR THE VIOLIN (PARTIAL LIST) *

Ex. 7

Note: Accidentals are written separately for each chord.

* This list has been limited to major and minor triads and dominant-type seventh chords
(or incomplete forms of these chords).

FOUR-NOTE CHORDS FOR THE VIOLIN (PARTIAL LIST)

Ex. 8

Note: Accidentals are written separately for each chord.

Although double stops may be used effectively in sustained chords and at a low dynamic level, there is not much point in writing triple and quadruple stops except in fairly loud passages, usually in sharply detached chords where an extra degree of volume or accent is wanted. It is, however, possible to sustain the top note or the two top notes of a three-note or four-note chord:

Ex. 9

Even inner notes may be sustained, though that possibility is not of much practical use. Since the main objective in triple and quadruple stops is usually added resonance, those which contain one or more open tones are ordinarily the most effective, as well as the most comfortable to play.

Certain other string effects, although not technically triple or quadruple stops, depend on the same principle. For instance, in these passages

Ex. 10

the player's fingers remain fixed on the quadruple stop

while the bow produces the particular effect called for.

Examples 17(b) and (h) at the end of Chapter III illustrate the use of "multiple stops" (a term that may conveniently be used to apply to double, triple, and quadruple stops).

EXAMPLES OF PASSAGES FOR THE VIOLIN

Ex. 11

(a) G minor Symphony   MOZART

Allegro assai

(b) Third Symphony

BEETHOVEN

(c) Overture to *Oberon*

WEBER

(d) *Capriccio Espagnol*

RIMSKY-KORSAKOFF

(e) Fifth Symphony

TCHAIKOVSKY

(f) *Death and Transfiguration*

STRAUSS

(g) *The Rite of Spring*

STRAVINSKY

THE VIOLA

Italian: Viola	French: Alto	German: Bratsche
Viole	Altos	Bratschen

Ex. 12

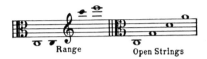

Range   Open Strings

If the material on the violin has seemed lengthy and detailed, there may be some consolation in the thought that much of it applies to the other stringed instruments as well. In the case of the viola, the chief differences to be considered are: (1) its greater size as compared with the violin; (2) its characteristic tone color; (3) its range; and (4) the use of the alto clef (viola clef).

It is not surprising that the uninitiated concert goer is apt to confuse the viola with the violin. Although the two look quite similar from a distance, the viola is actually somewhat larger and heavier,[2] and the distance between notes on the fingerboard is slightly greater than in the case of the violin. As for the characteristic quality of the instrument, someone once commented that the sound of the viola is to the sound of the violin what the flavor of duck is to the flavor of chicken. It is unfortunate that this attractive "gaminess" of tone is sometimes minimized in an effort to make the viola sound like the violin, whereas there is no reason why the viola should not be allowed to assert its own distinctive personality.

For those who have not used the C clefs before, a note of explanation is necessary here. The alto clef, 𝄡 , puts middle C on the middle line of the staff. The open strings of the viola, then, are C, G, D, and A, reading from bottom to top. Since the viola's normal register is from an octave below middle C to about a 12th above it, the use of the treble clef would require frequent leger lines below the staff, while writing in the bass clef would involve an even more terrifying array of leger lines above the staff. The alto clef provides a solution to the problem by placing middle C in such a

---

[2] There is more variation in size among violas than among the other stringed instruments. Many violas are slightly larger than the one shown on page 10.

location that the average viola part can be kept within the staff. If the part goes unusually high and stays there for some time, the treble clef is usually used. As a rule, it is not wise to change clef for the sake of one or two notes; players prefer to read a few leger lines rather than to shift their thinking from one clef to another too often. Viola parts in scores intended for high school use had better not go

above .

What has been observed about the quality of the strings in the case of the violin applies in a relative way to the viola. There are the same darkness and body to the lowest string, the same comparative brilliance to the top string, and the same gradations between these extremes in the two middle strings.

Too often in orchestral scoring the violas are given rather undistinguished parts—chordal figurations, sustained harmony tones, afterbeats, and the like. (This is particularly true in older music.) Actually, however, they are capable of doing everything the violins can do, discounting differences of range, of course. As we move on to a view of the string group as a whole, it will become more apparent how valuable the viola is as a bridge between the violin and the cello.

The same patterns available as multiple stops on the violin are possible on the viola a 5th lower. However, quadruple stops in the higher positions are a bit more difficult and less effective than on the violin and are better avoided. Examples 13 and 14 show the more usable triple and quadruple stops on the viola.

THREE-NOTE CHORDS FOR THE VIOLA (PARTIAL LIST) *

Ex. 13

(Chords containing two open notes)

(Chords containing one open note)

(Chords containing no open note)

Note: Accidentals are written separately for each chord.

* This list has been limited to major and minor triads and dominant-type seventh chords (or incomplete forms of these chords).

FOUR-NOTE CHORDS FOR THE VIOLA (PARTIAL LIST)

Ex. 14

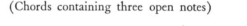

(Chords containing three open notes)

(Chords containing two open notes)

(Chords containing one open note)

(Chords containing no open note)

Note: Accidentals are written separately for each chord.

EXAMPLES OF PASSAGES FOR THE VIOLA

Ex. 15

(a) Prelude to *Tristan and Isolda*

WAGNER

(b) *Romeo and Juliet*

TCHAIKOVSKY

(c) Fifth Symphony

TCHAIKOVSKY

(d) *Till Eulenspiegel*

STRAUSS

(e) *Daphnis and Chloe* Suite No. 2

RAVEL

Permission for reprint granted by copyright owner, Durand et Cie, Paris, France; Elkan-Vogel, Co., Inc., agents for the U.S.A.

THE VIOLONCELLO (CELLO)

Italian: Violoncello	French: Violoncelle	German: Violoncell
Violoncelli	Violoncelles	Violoncelle

Ex. 16

The complete name violoncello (not vio*li*ncello!) has been more or less abandoned today in favor of the shortened form, cello. Although the instrument is too large to be held as the violin and viola are and must rest on the floor (secured by a "spike" at the bottom), it operates on basically the same principles as the smaller stringed instruments, except for some differences in fingering necessitated by the fact that the notes are farther apart on the fingerboard. The open strings have the same letter names as the open strings of the viola but are an octave lower.

The normal clef for the cello is the bass clef. However, in order to avoid the use of many leger lines in passages which lie in the upper part of the compass, the tenor clef, 𝄡 , is often used. This clef places middle C on the fourth line and must not be confused with the alto clef, which is never used by the cello. If the part goes so high as to require the continuous use of leger lines even in the tenor clef, then the treble clef will probably be substituted. One might argue that bass and treble clefs would be sufficient. That is perfectly true. But when a passage lies between, say, the F below middle C and the F above middle C, the tenor clef will keep the notes on the staff, whereas either bass or treble clef would require leger lines. In any case, tradition and common practice dictate that the cello shall use the tenor clef for most of its higher passages. An old and fortunately obsolete custom ruled that when the treble clef was used immediately following the bass clef, the notes in the treble were to be written an octave higher than the sounds desired. Such a system appears completely pointless. It is mentioned here only because it occasionally turns up (as late as Tchaikovsky and Dvořák) and proves confusing to the uninitiated score reader.

The cello has a reputation, amply deserved, for mellowness and warmth of tone. The two bottom strings (the C string in particular) are rich and full-bodied; passages played on them have a way of sounding grave and somehow reflective. The D string is brighter, with a warm and ingratiating quality, while the A string possesses a vibrant, singing tone all its own. Melodies played on it take on a strongly *espressivo,* almost passionate, quality that becomes more intense and poignant as one goes higher on the string. The upper limit of use is particularly hard to fix here. Virtuoso solo work occa-

sionally calls for notes even higher than the top G given as the
highest possible note; but for orchestral use it is best not to write
above  , and even notes in that area are rather difficult
from the standpoint of intonation. In school orchestras, the cello sec-
tion had better not be written above  .

Much of the time, the cellos constitute the bass voice of the string
group (often with the double basses sounding an octave lower). However, they may be used as a tenor or baritone voice, or even on the
melody if it does not go too high.

There are a few small limitations concerning double stops on the
cello: Avoid 2nds and 3rds unless one of the notes is open. Octaves
and major 7ths (with both notes stopped) are difficult but possible.
Triple and quadruple stops based on the following patterns are all
practical as long as the top note is no higher than  .

Ex. 17

This is by no means an exhaustive list but includes the chord arrangements most frequently encountered in orchestral cello parts.

The cello section is frequently called upon to play broken-chord
patterns such as the following, which (like those on page 17) are simply
multiple stops in which the notes are sounded consecutively instead
of at approximately the same time.

Ex. 18

(a) *Scheherazade*

RIMSKY-KORSAKOFF

Allegro non troppo

Cello

(b) Symphony in D minor

FRANCK

Allegro

Cello

(c) Fourth Symphony

MAHLER

Cello

fff

Revised edition, copyright, 1943, by Boosey & Hawkes, Inc. By permission of the copyright owner.

EXAMPLES OF PASSAGES FOR CELLO

(See also the double bass examples, which include passages for cellos and basses sounding in octaves.)

Ex. 19

(a) Third Symphony

BEETHOVEN

Allegro con brio

p

cresc.

(b) Fifth Symphony

BEETHOVEN

Andante con moto

(In unison with Violas)

p dolce

f   *p*

(c) Fourth Symphony

BRAHMS

Andante moderato

p
espress.

(d) *Don Juan*

STRAUSS

♩=76
senza espr.

p

(e) Third Symphony

HARRIS

Copyright, 1940, by G. Schirmer, Inc.

THE DOUBLE BASS

Italian: Contrabasso	French: Contre basse	German: Kontrabass
Contrabassi	Contre basses	Kontrabässe

Ex. 20

The double bass is known by a variety of other names: contra bass, string bass, bass viol, or simply bass. ("Bass violin" is an amateurish misnomer.)

We now encounter for the first time an instrument that does not sound as written. The double bass sounds an octave lower than written, or, to state the case conversely, the notes must be written an octave higher than they are intended to sound. A glance at the lower range of the instrument will explain the need for such an arrangement. If the part were written at actual or "concert" pitch, leger lines would be in continuous use, and the result would be cumbersome to write and awkward to read.

The double bass in standard use today has four strings, which are tuned in 4ths rather than in 5ths. The five-string bass, which is still much used in Europe but is rarely seen in the United States, tunes its fifth string to a C below the low E. In this country, the device commonly used for making these low notes possible is an extension to the fingerboard of a four-string bass. The bottom string can then be tuned down to C instead of E. In most professional orchestras at least two or three basses have this extension, and in some orchestras the whole bass section is equipped with them. School orchestras, on the other hand, seldom include a bass with an extension. For-

tunately, notes below the low E do not occur very often; and where
they do, they can often be played an octave higher without any
serious damage to the effect. This "extended" low register of the
instrument is valuable for dark color effects and for finishing out
phrases that dip below the low E. But as a general rule, the double
bass sounds much better when it is not kept too low. It has more
incisiveness, more sense of definite pitch, in its upper and medium
registers. Then, too, it has a way of sounding low even when the part
appears to be moderately high.

Because of its great size and the ponderousness of its technique, the
instrument has some limitations of performance as compared with its
smaller relatives. For one thing, it is less agile. Though rapid running passages are possible, they should not be too long or too frequent.
Besides being rather strenuous for the player, they are apt to sound
strangely "fuzzy" and unsatisfactory. In order to ease the technical
problem and make for a clearer effect, the basses are sometimes given
a simplified form of what the cellos—and possibly the lower woodwinds—are playing:

Ex. 21

Of course it is not necessary, or even advisable, that the basses play
constantly; in fact, their effectiveness is often in inverse ratio to the
amount they play. Therefore, a possible solution, in case the passage
at hand seems unsuited to their technique, is simply to give them a rest.

One point to remember in writing for the double bass is that triple
and quadruple stops are completely out of the question. A few
double stops—those involving one or two open strings—are possible
but so ineffective as to be scarcely worth using. Where two notes must
be played by the basses, it is usually better to divide the section. Most
of the other effects discussed in connection with the violin, viola, and
cello are possible on the double bass. Pizzicato passages are frequent
and especially effective, because they provide support without heaviness
and give a welcome relief from the bowed sound.

The basses are seldom called upon to play by themselves—that is, with no other instruments playing. Their tone is apt to be a bit dry and lacking in "focus," and they do not have the *espressivo* possibilities of the cellos. But they frequently take melodic passages an octave below the cellos. Their lower register is dark, almost ominous in quality, while the upper two strings are somewhat clearer and brighter in color.

EXAMPLES OF PASSAGES FOR DOUBLE BASS

(Since the double bass sounds an octave lower than written, passages in which the cellos and basses are *written* in unison will sound in octaves.)

Ex. 22

(a) Fifth Symphony

BEETHOVEN

(b) Symphony in B minor (*Unfinished*)

SCHUBERT

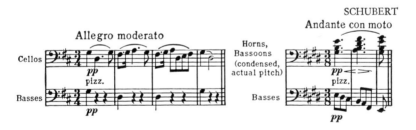

(c) *The Elephant* (from *The Carnival of Animals*)

SAINT-SAËNS

Permission for reprint granted by copyright owner, Durand et Cie, Paris, France: Elkan-Vogel Co., Inc., agents for the U.S.A.

(d) *Death and Transfiguration*

STRAUSS

(e) *Daphnis and Chloe* Suite No. 2

RAVEL

Permission for reprint granted by copyright owner, Durand et Cie, Paris, France; Elkan-Vogel Co., Inc., agents for the U.S.A.

(f) *Symphonic Metamorphosis of Themes by C. M. von Weber*

HINDEMITH

Reproduced by permission of Schott & Co., Ltd., London.

So far we have discussed only the more elementary material on the individual stringed instruments. There is a good deal to be learned about combining these instruments to make up a string orchestra, as well as about matters of bowing and special effects. These are the subjects to be taken up next.

In the meantime, it should be apparent even from this brief discussion that writing for strings is a rather special technique. What looks easy to the pianist may prove surprisingly awkward for the string player, while there are fine string parts that would be totally impractical for woodwind or brass instruments.

Know:

(1) Open strings and ranges (possible and practical) of the stringed instruments.

(2) Correct notation in alto and tenor clef.

(3) Transposition used by the double bass.

(4) Indications for the use of a particular string.

(5) General principles involved in writing double, triple, and quadruple stops.

(6) Italian, French, and German names for the stringed instruments.

SUGGESTED LISTENING

Because passages for the violins are so abundant and familiar, and because the violins are heard prominently in the music for suggested listening given at the end of Chapter IV, they are not included here.

VIOLAS

Wagner, Prelude to *Tristan and Isolda,* measure 90.

Tchaikovsky, *Romeo and Juliet,* letter G;[3] Fifth Symphony, 3rd movt., letter E.

Strauss, *Don Quixote,* measure 18, etc.; *Till Eulenspiegel,* measure 179 (*Gemächlich*).

Ippolitov-Ivanov, *Caucasian Sketches: In the Village.*

Ravel, *Daphnis and Chloe* Suite No. 2, figure 158.

Britten, *The Young Person's Guide to the Orchestra,* Variation F.

Instruments of the Orchestra (Victor, 20522 A).

CELLOS

Beethoven, Third Symphony (*Eroica*), beginning.

Schubert, Symphony in B minor (*Unfinished*), 1st movt., 2nd theme.

Brahms, Third Symphony, 3rd movt.; Fourth Symphony, 2nd movt., measure 41.

Saint-Saëns, *The Swan* from *The Carnival of Animals* (solo cello).

Wagner, *Tristan and Isolda,* beginning of Prelude; *Love Death,* measure 9.

Glinka, Overture to *Russlan and Ludmilla,* 2nd theme, measure 81.

Strauss, *Don Quixote,* Variation 5.

Elgar, *Enigma Variations,* Variation 12.

Mahler, Fourth Symphony, 3rd movt., beginning and at figure 9.

Harris, Third Symphony, beginning.

Hanson, First Symphony, beginning.

Villa-Lobos, *Bachianas Brasileiras* No. 1, for eight cellos.

Bloch, *Schelomo* (virtuoso writing for solo cello with orchestra).

Britten, *The Young Person's Guide to the Orchestra,* Variation G.

Instruments of the Orchestra (Victor, 20522 A).

---

[3] Throughout the "Suggestions for Listening" in this book, only the *beginning* point of each passage is indicated, by means of a measure number or a rehearsal letter or figure.

Since the double bass section seldom takes a musical idea entirely by itself, most of the examples that follow involve octave or unison doublings with other instruments.

Beethoven, Fifth Symphony, 3rd movt., beginning; also beginning of Trio; Ninth Symphony, 4th movt., measure 8.

Franck, Symphony in D minor, beginning.

Saint-Saëns, *The Elephant* from *The Carnival of Animals*.

Goldmark, *Rustic Wedding* Symphony, beginning.

Strauss, *Also Sprach Zarathustra,* fugue in the *"Von der Wissenschaft"* section (involves four desks of basses, each desk playing a separate part); *Death and Transfiguration,* 16 bars after letter D.

Mahler, Fourth Symphony, 3rd movt., figure 9 (basses playing *pizzicato* notes).

Stravinsky, *The Rite of Spring,* 1 bar after figure 121.

Respighi, *Pines of Rome,* beginning of Part IV (*Pines of the Appian Way*) (bottom string tuned down to low B).

Britten, *The Young Person's Guide to the Orchestra,* Variation H.

Instruments of the Orchestra (Victor, 20522 A).

Chapter III

THE STRING ORCHESTRA

THERE ARE a good many reasons why the strings may well be considered the most important section of the orchestra:

(1) As a group they possess an enormous pitch range; the orchestrator has at his command the entire compass from the highest note of the violin to the lowest note of the double bass.

(2) Strings are very versatile technically. Rapid scale passages, slow *cantabile* melodies, short detached notes, long sustained tones, skips, trills, and chordal figurations are all practical and effective.

(3) The vibrancy and warmth of the string tone make it especially useful. The strings can produce a particular *espressivo* quality not obtainable in the other choirs of the orchestra. And the tone is one that does not pall easily.

(4) There are fewer problems of *blend* in the string section than in the other sections of the orchestra.

(5) The *dynamic* range of the string section is unusually wide. Although neither strings nor woodwinds can equal the brass in the matter of sheer power, a full string section is able to produce a good resonant *fortissimo*. At the other end of the dynamic scale, the string choir can reduce its tone to an almost inaudible *pianissimo*.

(6) Unlike the woodwind and brass instruments, which must be given rests from time to time in order to allow the players to breathe and rest their lips, the strings are able to play continuously for longer periods if necessary. This is not to say that they should be asked to play indefinitely without resting, but the problem is not nearly so acute as in the case of the wind instruments.

(7) The strings are sometimes spoken of as "the backbone of the orchestra." This description is based in part on the points listed above but also on traditional usage. Since the early days of the orchestra, the strings have been called upon to carry the greatest burden of the

playing. That is, if one were to count the number of measures played by the woodwind, brass, and string sections, respectively, in a large number of scores, it would be found that in each work the strings played the greatest number of measures, with the woodwind section ranking second, and the brass ranking third.

The number of players in each string group is not specified in scores (except in rare cases where an extra-large string section is called for). Ordinarily the full complement of strings is implied—that is, 16 first violins, 14 second violins, 12 violas, 10 cellos, and 8 to 10 double basses. But in actual practice a good many orchestras do not include this many string players, as the table on page 4 has indicated. When scores written especially for "small orchestra" are played, the size of the string section is reduced. Also, because the orchestra of Haydn and Mozart's day included fewer string players than our modern orchestra does, many conductors prefer to use only a portion of each string group in performing music of the classical period.

Normally, the members of each string group play a single melodic line in unison. But it is possible to divide each group into two or more parts, each part playing different notes. In that case the Italian word *divisi,* usually shortened to *div.,* is placed next to the passage, most often above the staff. In the case of division into more than two parts, the number of parts is indicated as follows: *div. a 3* or *div. a 4,* etc. (See Appendix A for the equivalents of these terms in other languages.) Ordinary *divisi* passages (two parts) are very frequent; more than two parts are less often used, while the use of more than four is apt to be risky if one is writing for anything less than a full string section or for players of limited ability. In ordinary *divisi* writing, the two parts can usually be written on the same staff. If they involve the same time values, a single stem may be used for both—provided, of course, that the *div.* indication is present so that the two notes will not be taken for a double stop. But if the time values in the two parts are different, then separate stems will be necessary—that is, stems up for the upper part, stems down for the lower part. When the two parts cannot conveniently be written on the same staff (for example, when they cross repeatedly) two staves are used. In that case, the *divisi* direction is sometimes put at the edge of the page, preceding the divided part. (All these points can be seen illustrated in the examples of string scoring that follow.) With divisions into three or more parts, the parts may be arranged in whatever way is most convenient—two or more to a staff or each part on a separate staff. Any or all of the string groups may be divided, though the basses are divided less often than the other string groups. After a *divisi* passage, when the string group is to play in unison again, the expression *unisono,* shortened to *unis.* is used. *Non divisi* (*non div.*) is commonly written in above passages that could be played *divisi* but are meant to be played by the use of double stops.

Dynamics must be indicated below each staff. This is extremely important and sometimes difficult to impress upon the beginning orchestrator. Whereas the pianist can gain a complete idea of the music he is playing from the page before him and can adjust dynamics and the weight of individual voices accordingly, the orchestral player sees only his own part. He cannot tell from it whether he is playing an important musical idea that should be brought out or a subordinate voice that must be kept in the background. Therefore, he must be told exactly how loudly to play at all times. It is quite possible that while he is playing *ff,* another instrument in the orchestra will be marked *mf* or even *pp* in order to achieve the proper effect. Crescendos, diminuendos, and any other dynamic changes, along with such directions as *espressivo* or *marcato,* must likewise be written in beneath each part they apply to.

Since matters of *tempo* necessarily apply to all the instruments at the same time, one tempo marking at the top of the page, above the woodwinds, and one lower down, just above the strings, are usually sufficient in the score. But these tempo indications (including any *ritardandos, accelerandos,* or similar markings) are included by the copyist in each part, when the players' parts are extracted from the score.

A brief reminder on a few points of notation might be in order here: Notes below the middle line of the staff have stems up; those above the middle line have stems down; notes *on* the middle line may have stems either up or down. In groups such as eighths or sixteenths, the direction of the stems is determined by the position of the majority of the notes in the group. Notice that in orchestral writing, instrumental rather than vocal notation is used.

Ex. 1
  (a)

not
  (b)

Notice, too, that it is unnecessary to have a separate bar-line for each staff. Simply draw one long bar-line through all the parts of each section. Be sure to "line up" the parts so that the notes which are to sound together are in a straight line, vertically, on the page. Whole notes go at the beginning of the measure, but whole rests should be placed in the middle. Nowadays, the whole rest ▬ may be used with any time signature to indicate a full measure of rest.

On the first page of a score, the names of instruments are normally written out in full; but after that, abbreviations are commonly used. In the case of strings, those most often seen are: "Vl." or "Vln." or just "V." for Violin (followed by "I" or "II" for "first" or "second"); "Vla." for Viola, or "Vle." (the Italian plural abbreviated) for Violas; "V-Cello" or "Vc." for Violoncello; and "D. Bass," "D.B.," "C.Bass," or "C. B." for Double Bass. The usual method of bracketing the violins and the whole string section can be observed in the examples that follow.

POSSIBLE ARRANGEMENTS IN SCORING FOR STRING ORCHESTRA

In order to make our first work in scoring for strings as uncomplicated as possible, a short phrase from a Bach chorale [1] has been chosen as an example:

Ex. 2. *Jesu, meine Freude*

BACH

---

[1] This chorale excerpt is from an *a cappella* motet. With the exception of Example 3, the arrangements shown here are not in accordance with Bach's own practice as seen in his cantatas.

Certain obvious arrangements of the strings suggest themselves immediately: first violins on the melody, second violins on the alto part, violas on the tenor, and cellos on the lowest voice. The double basses may either rest or be given the same *written* part as the cellos, which means that they will sound an octave lower than the cellos. Using the latter choice, the scored version would look like this:

Ex. 3

This is the most usual arrangement of the strings and one which will sound very satisfactory, either with or without double bass.

The range of a voice is obviously a factor in deciding what instrument shall take it. For example, in this Bach excerpt the tenor line could not be taken by violins because it goes down to an F♯, one half-step lower than the violins can play. Nor could the bass voice be taken by viola, because of the notes below the viola's low C.

Since no dynamics or tempo indications are included in the original Bach version, we are forced to invent our own. Dynamic markings could be anything from *ppp* to *fff,* depending on the mood and general conception we give to the excerpt. Various dynamic levels have been used in the scorings shown and a tempo marking of *Adagio* chosen arbitrarily. We might decide that the music should be either *legato* or *molto marcato;* but that question will have to be put aside temporarily, as it involves problems of bowing which are being reserved for the next chapter.

Suppose we feel that the chorale melody (the upper part) in *Jesu, meine Freude* should be brought out a bit in relation to the other voices. The effect could be achieved very easily by marking the first violins a little louder than the other instruments. Or, we could arrive at an

effect of greater "weight" and resonance on the melody by giving it
to both first and second violins. In that case, we have a new problem:
There are three voices left which must somehow be taken by *two* sections, the violas and the cellos. (It seems best to use the double basses
only for the part they played in the first version.) The obvious solution here is to divide either the violas or the cellos to give two parts.
If we divide the violas, the arrangement is as follows:

Ex. 4

With a full viola section this version would sound all right; but in
school and other nonprofessional groups, viola sections are apt to be
"understaffed," and when they are divided in half there is simply not
enough body in each half to balance the rest of the strings. In such
a case, the balance could be improved by marking the violas a degree
louder than the other sections, as shown in parentheses.

The other solution here is to divide the cellos:

Ex. 5

In this version the division is somewhat compensated for by the fact that the upper cellos are in their high, vibrant register where they will come through rather prominently.   If this upper part stayed high, it might well be written in tenor clef, in which case separate staves would be used for the two halves of the cello section, as in Example 6.

If the particular color of violas were wanted on the melody, that arrangement could be used.   Because the tenor part in our example is too low for violins, the alto is the only line left that they could play. First and second violins together would be too heavy for the alto, so that either first or second violins should be given rests in this case.   There is nothing wrong with letting a section rest.   But a more effective solution might be to put violas and first violins on the melody (in unison) for greater weight and for mixed color:

Ex. 6

Half the cellos doubled in unison with violins on the melody would add poignancy and intensity to the tone.   That would take the upper half of the cellos rather high, but not unreasonably so for a professional group.   It should be pointed out, though, that this arrangement of the strings is by no means a common one, and that in many pieces of music it would be inappropriate or impractical (or both) to give the cello the melody, particularly at its original pitch.

Ex. 7

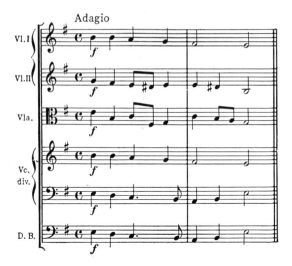

Of course it would be possible to use all the cellos on the melody, but in that case the double basses would have to play the bass at its original pitch by themselves. While that arrangement would be satisfactory if the bass section were large, it is a bit safer to retain half the cellos on the bass line and to write the double basses so as to sound an octave lower. One might suppose that dividing the double basses in octaves (on the bass and its doubling an octave lower) would work out well. In actual practice it does not; the effect is disappointing and is almost never used in orchestral scoring.

Versions Using Octave Doublings of the Three Upper Voices

In having the double basses play the bass voice an octave lower than in the original, we amplified the original version slightly. Similarly, the top voice (when it is the melody) may be doubled an octave higher than in the original. The effect is somewhat more brilliant. It is also possible to fill in the octave at the top by doubling the alto and tenor voices an octave higher as well. These two versions are shown in Examples 8 and 9.

Ex. 8   Ex. 9

As a rule, the effect of doubling only the alto or only the tenor an octave higher is not good because of the gaps of open 4ths and 5ths that are apt to result. In other words, it is normally best to double both alto and tenor or neither, at the octave, in scoring a four-voice composition of this sort. Doubling of inner voices an octave *lower* than the original is usually out of the question because of the muddiness that results when voices are spaced close together low in a chord.

In some music, the same objection would apply to a doubling of the melody an octave lower. In our Bach example, however, the effect of doubling it at the lower octave is not too thick; in fact, that arrangement actually improves the spacing by filling in some unnecessarily wide gaps between the tenor and bass voices. This possibility is demonstrated in Examples 10 and 11. Example 11 also makes use of upper-octave doublings of the soprano, alto, and tenor voices; and, as in the preceding versions, the double basses have been written so as to sound an octave lower than the bass in the original. Although the layout of the divided violin sections is different in Examples 9 and 11, respectively, the sound of the combined violin sections will be approximately the same in each case.

Ex. 10   Ex. 11

The last version is obviously the fullest, the most resonant. This is not to say that it is necessarily the "best." In fact, in orchestration one can scarcely use the term "best." There are usually many ways of scoring a given passage, and the way chosen will be the one that seems the most effective in context. Personal taste naturally enters in here, too. Granted that there are "poor" ways of scoring any given piece of music, the student who asks whether his way is "the right way" has simply failed to realize the exciting range of possibilities open to him in orchestrating. The versions of the Bach excerpt given here are not the only ones possible; but they demonstrate the most likely and usable arrangements.

Of course not every piece of music falls conveniently into four clear-cut and continuous voices, as our chorale example did. There are other, more complicated types of texture which will require different approaches and other techniques in scoring. These will be taken up in later chapters.

REMARKS ON THE OVERTONE SERIES AND ON SPACING AND DOUBLING

Students who are using this book as a text will normally embark on their first project in scoring for strings after reading this chapter, and there are some points concerning spacing and doubling which they will need to keep in mind. Although these are points which they will presumably have covered in their harmony courses, the author has found that a brief review of them is often helpful.

Since we shall want to refer to the overtone series presently in connection with spacing and with string harmonics and at many other points later on in connection with wind instruments, a short commentary on that subject seems in order here.

All musical instruments make use of a vibrating body (a string, an air column, etc.) which vibrates not only as a whole, to produce the main tone or "fundamental," but in halves, thirds, fourths, and so on. These fractional vibrations produce pure sounds of higher pitch and much weaker intensity which are normally heard as part of the composite tone. Example 12 shows a fundamental (C) with its first fifteen overtones.

Ex. 12

(Notes that do not correspond exactly with our equally tempered scale are shown in black.)

The terms "partials" and "harmonic series" are often used in connection with overtones, but they include the fundamental, whereas the term "overtone" does not. The first overtone, then, is the second partial. In the preceding example the notes have been numbered on the basis of partials; that is, the fundamental is numbered "1," and so on. Certain partials come out more strongly in some instruments than in others, with consequent differences between the respective tone qualities of the various instruments.

Normally, spacing of harmony is modeled in a general way on the harmonic series: the wide intervals are put at the bottom, the smaller intervals in the upper part of the chord. Usually it is best to leave a clear octave at the bottom, although if the chord is not too low it may be possible to begin with a 5th at the bottom:

Ex. 13

If notes are put close together in the lower portion of a chord, a thick, muddy effect results; therefore, avoid putting the 3rd of the chord too low—say below  (assuming the chord to be in root position).

In scoring music written originally in open spacing, it is often a wise idea to fill in the gaps between the upper parts by means of octave doublings—in effect to convert the open structure to close. For example,

Ex. 14

(a)

might become

(b)

While open spacing is frequently used for the strings and is not out of the question for the other instruments, close spacing is, as a general rule, more effective in the orchestra.

Even in music written in close structure it sometimes becomes necessary to add a "filler" part; that is, an extra voice which is introduced in order to fill in gaps between voices (most often between tenor and bass). Such a voice may double other voices part of the time, then branch off to fill in gaps where necessary; or it may take an independent line of its own, possibly doubling chord tones at times but not actually playing the same line as any of the other voices. In the following excerpt from *America* a possible filler part is shown in small notes:

Ex. 15

However, students will probably do well to avoid fillers except in cases of absolute necessity. Such parts are usually not very strong or interesting from a linear standpoint, and if used indiscriminately they tend to detract from the clarity of the other voices and to bring about a muddy texture. Besides, beginning orchestrators often have difficulty in maintaining good voice-leading in the orchestral parts, and the addition of an extra voice that may rove at will only complicates the problem.

Sometimes the top voice of a closely spaced chord is doubled an octave higher, leaving a gap of an octave at the top (as in Example 8). In such cases the effect is perfectly good, and there is no objection to the octave gap.

When a primary triad (I, IV, or V) is in first inversion, the bass should not be doubled in the upper parts, as a rule. The same applies to 7th chords in any inversion:

Ex. 16

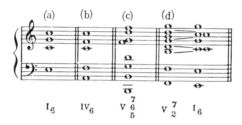

(Of course the bass may always be doubled an octave *lower*.) Notice that in (d), above, proper voice-leading demands that certain notes be doubled in the tonic chord. When an "active" tone (such as the seventh scale degree) is taken by a particular instrument, the resolution of that tone must obviously occur in the same instrument.

It should perhaps be added that this material on spacing and doubling does not always apply in twentieth century music. Certain composers, Stravinsky in particular, have achieved fresh and intriguing effects by a deliberate use of unusual spacings and doublings. But the principles stated here will apply to most of the assignments to be done in connection with this book.

Following are examples that show some of the many possibilities in arranging the strings. In most of these, other instruments in addition to the strings are playing.

EXAMPLES SHOWING VARIOUS POSSIBILITIES IN ARRANGING THE STRINGS
Ex. 17

(a) C major Symphony (*Jupiter*)   MOZART

(b) Fifth Symphony   BEETHOVEN

(c) Fourth Symphony   BRAHMS

(d) Fourth Symphony   TCHAIKOVSKY

(e) Second Symphony   SCHUMANN

(f) Symphony in E minor (*New World*)   DVOŘÁK

(g) *Prelude to The Afternoon of a Faun*

DEBUSSY

(h) *The Rite of Spring*

STRAVINSKY

A. Know:

(1) Number of players in each string group (in a full orchestra).

(2) Order and arrangement of the strings on the page.

(3) Customary abbreviations of names of stringed instruments.

(4) Directions for the division of a string group into two or more parts.

(5) Proper placing and use of indications for dynamics and tempo.

(6) Principles of good spacing and doubling.

B. Select a short phrase from a Bach chorale (or from another composition in four-part harmony) and score it in six different ways for strings. Use the various arrangements of *Jesu, meine Freude* given in this chapter as models. Be sure to indicate dynamic markings. It is not necessary to indicate bowing in this assignment, however.

(*Music for suggested listening is listed at the end of Chapter IV.*)

BOWING AND SPECIAL EFFECTS

THE TERM "bowing" may mean the actual motion of the bow over the strings, or it may mean the indications in a string part which tell the player how the music is to be bowed. Using the word in the latter sense, bowing includes: (1) slurs over each group of notes to be taken in the same bow; (2) down-bow marks (⊓) or up-bow marks (∨) at points where the use of one or the other is preferable; (3) such indications as dots or accent marks over the notes to suggest the type of bowing appropriate; and (4) actual words, such as *spiccato*, to indicate the exact type of bowing to be used. The directions *arco* and *pizzicato*, which have been discussed earlier, might also be listed under the heading of bowing.

Beginning students of orchestration invariably feel "put upon" when they are asked to include bowing in their scores. Their usual reaction is, "Why not let the string player worry about that problem? He knows more about it than we do." There are several answers to this attitude. For one thing, a passage may be given a number of different interpretations depending on how it is bowed; and although the player may know more about bowing than the budding arranger, he does not know, without bowing marks, just what effect the arranger intended. In other words, bowing is an integral part of the music and should not be left to chance. A glance at any orchestral score will confirm the fact that slurs to indicate bowing are always included, simply as a matter of standard practice. It may be objected that the conductor or the players will probably make some changes in the bowing anyway. This is perfectly true, even in the case of standard symphonic literature. Nevertheless, the original bowing will give an idea of the basic conception of the music. Also, planning of the bowing for all the groups of the string section at the same time brings about a uniformity of effect which is very important and which would be hard to achieve if each group were allowed to choose its own bowing.

There is a point that needs to be clearly understood at the beginning: in string music the slur does not normally indicate broad phrase outlines as it does in piano music; instead it is used to show which notes are to be taken on the same bow. For instance, in the following example the first four notes are taken on one bow; then the bow reverses direction to take the next two notes and again to take the last three.

Ex. 1

(a)

Allegro moderato

The same passage might have been bowed in several other ways, three of which are shown here:

(b)   (c)   (d)

In the last version, where no slurs are shown, the player would use a separate bow (that is, change the direction of the bow) for each note. It should be emphasized that no break in sound need occur when the bow changes. (However, a separation between notes *may* be made if desired.)

There are a few scores in which phrasing rather than bowing is indicated at certain points in the string parts—usually in long sustained melodic lines. In such cases the actual bowing to be used is decided upon by the conductor or the players. Occasionally phrase marks are included in addition to bowing slurs in order to insure an even, connected effect. But the vast majority of scores rely solely on bowing slurs to project the musical structure of the string parts.

Some factors that influence bowing are the dynamics and tempo involved, the general effect desired, and such technical considerations as the need for a down-bow or an up-bow at certain places.

As for dynamics, the amount of bow "used up" varies in a general way with the volume of tone produced. Consequently, the player can take more notes per bow in a soft passage than in a loud one. But that does not mean that all soft passages should be slurred in long groups and all loud passages played with separate bows. It is perfectly possible to change bow frequently in a soft passage, even to the point of playing rapidly moving parts with a bow to a note:

Ex. 2. Overture to *The Marriage of Figaro*

MOZART

And a reasonable number of notes may be taken on one bow even in a *fortissimo:*

Ex. 3. *Mathis der Maler*

HINDEMITH

Reproduced by permission of Schott & Co., Ltd., London.

The influence of tempo on bowing is fairly obvious. The faster the tempo, the more notes the player can take comfortably on each bow.

In describing the difference between a slurred effect and a separately bowed effect, it might be said that the first is smoothly flowing, while the second gives a greater sense of articulation to each note. Fast running passages in which each note is separately bowed are particularly vigorous and "sparkling." Of course a passage need not be all bowed or all slurred. Interesting combinations of the two effects are illustrated in the following brief examples:

Ex. 4

   (a) First Symphony

BEETHOVEN

Allegro molto

   (b) C major Symphony (*Jupiter*)

MOZART

Allegretto

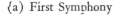

In plotting bowing, it is often necessary to bring the player out on a down-bow or an up-bow at a particular point. For example, down-bows are in order for heavily accented notes and are even preferable for strong beats in a measure. On the other hand, an anacrusis (up-beat) is best given to an up-bow, in order that the strong beat that follows may be taken down-bow. Crescendos are somewhat easier on an up-bow. Also, a "group-staccato" bowing, to be described presently, is exclusively an up-bow stroke, while the *jeté* must be performed on a down-bow. The signs for up-bow and down-bow ($\vee$ and $\sqcap$) are put in, above the notes, only at points where the player would not be apt to choose that bowing automatically. For instance, it is a convention that the first note of a passage will be taken down-bow unless an up-bow mark is shown (or unless the first note is obviously an up-beat requiring an up-bow). But in any case where the proper bowing cannot be anticipated at a glance, it should be clearly indicated at the beginning of the passage. It is usually superfluous to include alternate down-bow and up-bow signs throughout a passage, since the player must change from one bow to the other, of necessity, and the slurs will tell him where to change. The important thing is to get him started on the right bow, and the rest should follow automatically.

There is another small technical point that influences bowing: if a jump from one string to a nonadjacent string is involved, the notes in question obviously cannot be taken *legato*.

TYPES OF BOWING

Perhaps no aspect of orchestration offers more chance for controversy than does the labeling of various types of bowing. There is disagreement on this subject not only among orchestration books but among players themselves. In the first place, the terminology involves a hodge-podge of languages, and there are sometimes two or three different names in each language for a particular type of bowing. To complicate matters still further, descriptions of certain bowings differ from book to book and from player to player. And it should be pointed out that the period and style of the music influence the interpretation of bowing marks. For example, dots over the notes in a passage by Haydn might call for one type of bowing, while the same indication in a contemporary score might suggest another type.

As a result of all this confusion, it is very difficult to write in an authoritative way on the subject of bowing types. All one can do is to attempt to use the terms and definitions accepted by the greatest number of string players.

The most important types of bowing are the following:

(1) *Legato*[1] :

Ex. 5. *Don Juan*

Groups of notes are slurred together, and the total effect is as smooth as possible.

(2) Separate bows[1] :

Ex. 6. Prelude to *Die Meistersinger*

Though each note is bowed separately, the notes are still connected.

(3) *Spiccato* (*sautillé*):

Ex. 7. Overture to *The Magic Flute*

This is a light, middle-bow stroke in which the bow bounces off the string, taking one note to each bow. It is used very frequently in orchestral playing but is not practical if the dynamic level is to be louder than about *mf*. The usual indication consists of dots over the notes, though occasionally the word *spiccato* is written in.

---

[1] These are not, strictly speaking, *names* for particular types of bowing but are used here for the sake of convenience in order to describe two very common bowing arrangements.

(4) *Jeté* (*ricochet, saltando* [2]):

Ex. 8

(a) *Capriccio Espagnol*

RIMSKY-KORSAKOFF

(b) *Fire Bird* Suite

STRAVINSKY

The *jeté* (meaning "thrown" in French) is a down-bow stroke which sounds a group of notes—most often repeated notes—very rapidly. The notation usually consists of dots under a slur.

(5) *Détaché:*

Ex. 9. Symphony in B minor (*Unfinished*)

SCHUBERT

The notes are bowed separately, but there is a slight separation between notes caused by a brief stopping of the bow at the end of each stroke. However, the bow does not leave the string. Three gradations of this stroke are possible: *grand détaché,* in which the entire length of the bow is used; *détaché moyen,* in which about a third of the bow is used; and *petit détaché,* which must be played at the point of the bow. The faster the tempo, the smaller the portion of the bow that can be included in the stroke. Often there are no special marks in the music to indicate *détaché* bowing; the player simply chooses that type of bowing as being appropriate to the music. At other times, dots over the notes are included as the signal for the *détaché* effect, particularly where a pronounced separation between notes is desired.

---

[2] There is considerable confusion over the use of the word *saltando* ("jumping" in Italian). Strictly speaking it should mean *spiccato* bowing, but in actual practice it is often seen in connection with the *jeté*.

(6) Martelé (martellato):

Ex. 10. First Symphony

BRAHMS

This is a quick, hammerlike bowing in which the bow is stopped abruptly at the end of each stroke so that there is a clear-cut separation between the notes. The *martelé* is normally performed at the point of the bow but may also be done at the frog to produce a heavier effect. It is usually indicated by "arrowheads" over the notes, as in Example 10.

(7) Successive down-bows:

Ex. 11. *Capriccio Italien*

TCHAIKOVSKY

This marking is sometimes used when a very decided break between notes is in order. Since the bow must be lifted and returned to the string between each two notes, the separation comes about automatically. This type of bowing had better not be used for more than a few notes at a time, and it is not practical when the notes move along too quickly. The effect of successive down-bows is vigorous, almost savage—particularly on the lowest string of each instrument.

(8) *Staccato.* A word of warning is necessary here about the use of the term *staccato.* To the pianist and wind instrument player it means merely "short"; to the string player it generally means a specific type of bowing. True, notes played with *staccato* bowing will be more or less short, but not all passages involving short notes call for the use of *staccato* bowing. In fact, *spiccato* is used much more frequently than *staccato* for that effect, in string playing.

In a true string *staccato,* a rapid series of notes is taken on an up-bow with a separate "push" for each note. The stroke is so difficult that it is confined to virtuoso solo work and is impractical for orchestral writing. But there are two types of *staccato* bowing, often called "group *staccato*," that are quite usable in the orchestra:

Ex. 12. Eighth Symphony

This first type (the first three notes of Example 12) is an up-bow stroke and consists of two or three (rarely four) notes which are made to sound separately under the same bow.

Ex. 13

The second type (Example 13) can be performed on either an up-bow or a down-bow. It consists of two repeated notes with a separation between that is produced by a momentary stopping of the bow. Illogically, the notation usually involves a dot above or below the *second* of the two notes, although the first is actually the one that is shortened in performance. Versions (a), (b), (c), and (d) will all sound alike.

(9) *Louré:*

Ex. 14. Second Symphony

Copyright, 1903, by Breitkopf & Haertel. By permission of Associated Music Publishers.

Louré bowing is used chiefly in music of a slow, *espressivo* character. Two or more notes (seldom more than four) are taken on one bow, with a separate pressure on each note and a very slight separation between each two. This is a bowing which occurs rather infrequently, and the term *louré* itself is little used by players.

(10) Bowed tremolo:

(a) Unmeasured:

Ex. 15

In the unmeasured form of the bowed tremolo, the bow is moved back and forth over the string as rapidly as possible. Three bars through the stem are ordinarily interpreted to mean an unmeasured tremolo, though sometimes in very slow tempo four bars through the stem are used to insure that the notes are not played as measured thirty-seconds. It is best to write in the word *tremolo* (abbreviation, *trem.*) in doubtful cases. The expression "at point" or *punta d'arco* in tremolo passages signifies that the tremolo is to be made at the point of the bow, in order to achieve a delicate, wispy sound. In some passages the unmeasured tremolo gives an effect of energy and excitement; at other times (especially when used high and softly) it can produce a shimmering, ethereal effect.

EXAMPLES OF BOWED TREMOLO (UNMEASURED)

Ex. 16

(a) *Tristan and Isolda*

WAGNER

(b) Second Symphony   (c) *Prelude to The Afternoon of a Faun*

MAHLER   DEBUSSY

Example 16 (b) copyright assigned, 1942, to Hawkes & Son (London) Ltd. By permission of the copyright owner, Boosey & Hawkes, Inc. Example 16 (c) permission for reprint granted by Jean Jobert, Paris, France; Elkan-Vogel Co., Inc., Philadelphia, Penna., copyright owners.

(b) Measured:

Ex. 17

The measured tremolo, as its name implies, calls for a definite number of repeated notes, the number being determined by the notation. One line through a quarter-note or half-note stem means eighth notes; two lines, sixteenths. One line through an eighth-note stem means sixteenths; two lines, thirty-seconds; and so on. Triplets are indicated by a figure three above each note, or occasionally by three small dots placed next to the note head. Probably the safest way is to write out the actual notes involved in a measured tremolo for one measure at the beginning of the passage; after that, the simplified notation may be used. This method is shown in Example 18(a).

Tremolos (particularly the unmeasured variety) have been so over-exploited in romantic music and in music of the "horse-opera" variety that they have lost a good deal of their effectiveness and had better be used sparingly and with caution today.

EXAMPLES OF BOWED TREMOLO (MEASURED)

EXAMPLES OF BOWED TREMOLO (MEASURED)

Ex. 18

(a) Sixth Symphony   BEETHOVEN

(b) *Fantastic Symphony*   BERLIOZ

(c) Symphony in D minor   FRANCK

(d) Fifth Symphony   SIBELIUS

With special permission from Wilhelm Hansen, Copenhagen.

(11) Fingered tremolo (slurred tremolo):

Ex. 19

In the fingered tremolo, which is usually unmeasured and which ordinarily involves two notes on the same string, one finger remains fixed on the lower of the two notes while another finger alternately plays and releases the upper note very rapidly so that a kind of "trill" between the notes results. The bow moves over the string in the normal way rather than quickly back and forth as in the bowed tremolo. The two notes involved are most often a 3rd apart, though intervals up to the diminished 5th are possible on the violin. On the viola, the limit had better be a perfect 4th, and on the cello a major 3rd. In notating fingered tremolos each note is given twice the value it should have, mathematically speaking. Presumably the theory is that the two notes of each pair sound so nearly at once that each note can be given full value. Frequently, fingered tremolos are written this way:

Ex. 20

That is, the two notes of each pair are crossed with themselves. Forsyth comments that this is merely "a pretty arrangement for the eye of the score-reader" and that with a whole group of strings the same sound results whether the intervals are written upward or downward. It would appear, then, that a single-line part like the fingered tremolo in Example 19 is sufficient. The fingered tremolo gives a delicate rustling effect that is elusive and attractive. It is most often used as a background for solo passages played by woodwinds or horn. Fingered tremolos involving notes on two different strings are possible but not very satisfactory. They are better avoided.

EXAMPLES OF FINGERED TREMOLO

Ex. 21

(a) *Prelude to The Afternoon of a Faun*   (b) *Fingal's Cave* Overture

DEBUSSY   MENDELSSOHN

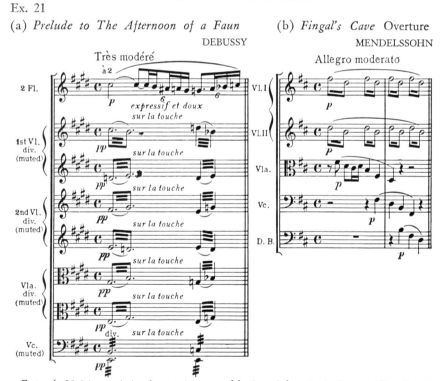

Example 21 (a) permission for reprint granted by Jean Jobert, Paris, France; Elkan-Vogel Co., Inc., Philadelphia, Penna., copyright owners.

SPECIAL EFFECTS

Several special effects are obtainable on stringed instruments:

The mute, a small clamp of wood, metal, rubber, leather, or plastic which fits onto the bridge, reduces the volume of tone and gives it a veiled, wistful quality. The Italian term for "with mute" is *con sordino* (or *sordina,* as it is spelled in modern Italian usage), often abbreviated to *con sord.* "Without mute" is *senza sordino.* At least two bars of moderate 4/4 time (preferably more) should be allowed for putting on mutes and at least one bar for taking them off.[3] It is usually wise to write, in the parts, "Put on mutes" in the rest preceding the muted passage and "Take off mutes" in the rest following it, so that the players will be prepared in plenty of time for the passage to follow. A little-used effect calls for the mutes to be put on or taken off one player at a time, or one desk at a time, over a given number of measures. ("Desk" or "stand" is used to describe each group of two players; that is, the two who sit side by side and read from the same music.) The double bass uses a mute less often than the other stringed instruments, since the unmuted bass tone can be reduced to a whisper and can be made to blend fairly well with the other strings muted.

Sul ponticello[4] means "on the bridge" and is used to describe the effect in which the bow is drawn across the strings at or near the bridge instead of at the normal place. The resulting sound is glassy and eerie in quality. The device is probably most effective when used with a bowed tremolo.

"On the fingerboard" is the direction used when the player is to bow over the fingerboard instead of at the usual place. The sound produced is softer and less vibrant than the normal tone. The Italian equivalent is *sul tasto* (or *sulla tastiera*); but as the device is most characteristic of French scoring, *sur la touche* is perhaps the most familiar form.

Scordatura involves an abnormal tuning of one or more strings. Sometimes it is used to extend the range of an instrument (Strauss, *Ein Heldenleben,* second violin, before figure 42), sometimes to allow a particular pitch to be played as an open note (Stravinsky, *The Rite of*

---

[3] The "Heifetz" mute is so constructed that it can be clamped to one of the strings in the unused area below the bridge, when not in use. It can therefore be put on and taken off more quickly than the ordinary mute.

[4] Examples of the *sul ponticello* effect can be found near the beginning of Bartók's Concerto for Orchestra and at figure 219.

Spring, last note in the cellos), sometimes to create a special color (Mahler, Fourth Symphony, second movement, solo violin).

Col legno [5] (literally, "with the wood," in Italian) means that the back of the bow is to be used in playing. This is a rarely used effect and one which is confined almost entirely to repeated-note rhythmic figures. The sound is rather brittle and dry, and little volume is possible.

The expression used for cancelling any of these special effects is *modo ordinario* ("in the ordinary way").

Two notes connected by a line are played in such a way that the notes in between sound as a *glissando.* That is, the finger slides along the string instead of stopping each note separately. The glissando effect may be made very pronounced or may be reduced to an almost imperceptible connection between the notes. In the more moderate form, it is sometimes known as a *portamento* and is quite often introduced by the player, even where no direction is present, in order to give an extremely legato effect.

If half a string group is wanted on a part, the indication is "$\frac{1}{2}$ Violins I" or "$\frac{1}{2}$ Double Basses," etc. In Italian scores, *la metà* (the half) is often used instead, while the German equivalent is *die Hälfte.*

When the effect of only a few strings on a part is desired, the passage may be marked "1st desk only" or "1st two desks only," etc.

Finally, there is the possibility of using stringed instruments in a solo capacity, when a more intimate, personal quality is wanted. The direction in such cases is "1 solo violin," or "2 solo violas" (if two parts are involved) or "4 solo cellos," as the case may be. Such solo parts are usually written on a separate staff, just above the string group to which the solo instrument belongs, though if the rest of the string group is not playing, a separate staff need not be used.

Natural Harmonics

Harmonics are simply overtones of the strings. They have a flutelike, silvery quality that can be highly effective as a special color. In orchestral writing they are apt to be used for isolated notes or for short melodic lines in a moderate tempo. Rapid successions of them are difficult to perform and should be avoided.

In the remarks at the end of Chapter III it was explained that strings, like other sounding bodies, vibrate not only as a whole but

---

[5] Excellent examples of *col legno* passages occur at the beginning of Holst's *The Planets* and in Bloch's *Schelomo* (figure 6).

in halves, thirds, fourths, and so on at the same time, thus producing overtones. These are normally heard as parts of the composite tone. But we can isolate them by touching the string lightly at certain points:

(1) In the middle (an octave above the pitch of the open string); the result is a harmonic an octave higher than the pitch of the open string.

(2) One third of the string length from either end (either a perfect 5th above the open pitch or at the point where the note would ordinarily be played); the result is a harmonic an octave and a 5th higher than the open pitch.

(3) One fourth of the string length from either end (either a perfect 4th above the open pitch or at the point where the note would ordinarily be played); the result is a harmonic two octaves higher than the open pitch.

(4) One fifth of the string length from either end (either a major 3rd above the open pitch or at the point where the note would ordinarily be played) or two fifths of the string length from either end (either a major 6th or a major 10th above the open pitch); the result is a harmonic two octaves and a major 3rd higher than the open pitch.

Other harmonics above this are possible but are seldom seen in orchestral writing. Even number 4 is used infrequently. Harmonics such as these, which are overtones of an open string, are called "natural" harmonics. Following is a chart showing the natural harmonics available on each of the violin's four strings, along with the notation involved. Notice that in some cases the same pitch occurs as a natural harmonic on two different strings.

NATURAL HARMONICS

Ex. 22

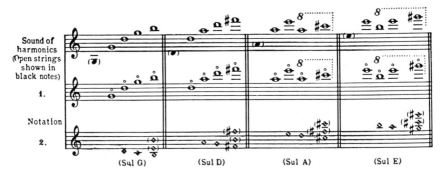

Sound of harmonics (Open strings shown in black notes)

1.

Notation

2.

(Sul G)   (Sul D)   (Sul A)   (Sul E)

The first natural harmonic on each string, the one an octave above the open note, is always notated at actual pitch with a small circle over it. The other natural harmonics may be notated in either of two ways, depending on how they are to be played. As explained earlier, they may be produced by touching the string lightly at either one of two points (more than two in the case of the fourth overtone). Notation 1 in Example 22 is used if the string is to be touched lightly at the point where the note would ordinarily be produced. Notation 2 shows, by means of a diamond-shaped note, another point on the string which can be touched lightly to produce the same harmonic. (The actual pitch of the harmonic usually does not appear in this case, although some composers prefer to include it as well.) With Notation 2 the string to be used is often indicated below the note—for example, "sul D" or "D string" or "III."

As a general rule, this second method is somewhat easier than the first in performance. On the other hand, the playing method called for by Notation 1 is preferable in cases where the hand is already high on the string and would have to make an awkward jump to the other end of the fingerboard in order to use the second method. Some writers on orchestration recommend using Notation 1 exclusively for natural harmonics, the player then choosing the easiest method of playing the note. However, Notation 2 appears frequently in scores, and the author consequently feels that students should understand it as well.

Although these points—and others in connection with harmonics—have a way of sounding complicated on paper, they can be made quite clear in a few minutes by means of an actual demonstration with a stringed instrument. The writer therefore hopes that such a demonstration can be arranged at the time this material is taken up.

Artificial Harmonics

In order to produce as harmonics notes that are not overtones of the open strings, a slightly different procedure is necessary. The string is pressed down firmly by the first finger at a point two octaves below the pitch of the desired harmonic; at the same time, the fourth finger touches the string lightly at a point a perfect 4th higher, which is equivalent to dividing the unstopped portion of the string into quarters. A harmonic two octaves above the firmly fingered pitch results. (This is like number 3 of the natural harmonics, except that a stopped pitch rather than an open one is used as fundamental.)

To illustrate: if we finger ♯o firmly, then touch the string

lightly at ♯o , the note ♯o will sound as a harmonic.

The usual notation for this would be ♯♯o with the lightly touched pitch indicated by a diamond-shaped note. As a rule, the actual sound is not even shown (though sometimes it is included as well, making three written notes for one sound!). A question that students invariably ask at this point is: Why not avoid all these complications by simply writing the passage at actual pitch and marking it "harmonics"? This is what Forsyth calls "the lazy way," and it is not recommended; it saddles the player with the problem of figuring out the most convenient method for producing each harmonic—a problem that is apt to waste time in rehearsal and one that should rightfully have been solved in advance by the arranger. The same objection applies to the practice of indicating all harmonics by circles over the notes.

Let us go back, now, and review the process of writing a note as a harmonic. The orchestrator should first see whether the note is playable as a natural harmonic. If it is, that way is usually easier and therefore preferable. If the note cannot be played as a natural harmonic, the following procedure can be adopted for writing it as an artificial harmonic: measure down two octaves from the actual pitch desired and write that note (with the proper time value), then write a diamond-shaped note a perfect 4th higher. (Notice that to make a *perfect* 4th, accidentals must often be added.) For example, if the following passage were to be played in harmonics,

Ex. 23

(a)

we would write:

(b)

Here the last note, A, could be played as a natural harmonic and would almost certainly be taken that way by the player even though it is written as an artificial harmonic. This substitution of the "artificial" for the "natural" notation when number 3 of the natural harmonics occurs in a series of artificial harmonics is a license that has come to be more or less accepted.

Artificial harmonics other than those involving the stretch of a 4th are possible but are seldom used. To give just one example: if the player touches the string lightly with his fourth finger a perfect *5th* above the stopped note, a harmonic a 12th higher than the stopped tone results.

It is obviously impossible to play more than one note at a time as an artificial harmonic—except for two artificial harmonics a perfect 5th apart, which can be played as a double stop by pressing two adjacent strings down firmly with the first finger and touching the two strings lightly a perfect 4th higher with the fourth finger.

What has been said about harmonics on the violin applies equally to the viola. Artificial harmonics are extremely difficult for the cello and out of the question for the double bass except in the higher positions; they should therefore be ruled out for these instruments except in virtuoso solo work. Natural harmonics are practical for both, in orchestral writing, however.

EXAMPLES OF NATURAL HARMONICS

Ex. 24

(a) *Capriccio Espagnol*

RIMSKY-KORSAKOFF

(b) Concerto for Orchestra

BARTÓK

Vl. I
div.

(c) *Pictures from an Exhibition*

MUSSORGSKY-RAVEL

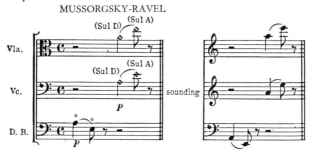

Vla.

Vc.

D. B.

(d) *The Rite of Spring*

STRAVINSKY

Vla.
(1 desk)

(These harmonics are performed by sliding the finger lightly over the C string between middle C and c³. The harmonics shown result automatically.)

EXAMPLES OF ARTIFICIAL HARMONICS

Ex. 25

(a) *Iberia*

DEBUSSY

Librement expressif

Vl. I
(1st half)

(b) *Capriccio Espagnol*

RIMSKY-KORSAKOFF

SUGGESTED ASSIGNMENTS

A. Know:

(1) The various types of bowing, the names commonly used for them, and the indication for each.

(2) Special effects obtainable on strings and the names for them.

(3) Principles involved in writing harmonics (natural and artificial) and the proper notation of each type.

B. Show on the staff how each of the following harmonics will actually sound, and indicate whether each is a natural or an artificial harmonic (the abbreviations "Nat." and "Art." may be used). The notation shown here need not be recopied; simply number each pitch.

Ex. 26

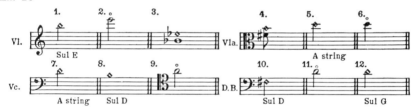

(Remember that the double bass sounds an octave lower than written, even in harmonics.)

C. Write the following concert pitches as harmonics for the instruments shown. In cases where a pitch can be produced as either a natural or an artificial harmonic, choose the natural harmonic. If there are two or more ways of notating the same natural harmonic, show these. If a note cannot be played as a harmonic, write "Impossible."

Ex. 27

D. The following are suitable as exercises in scoring for string orchestra. Include bowing indications (slurs and any other markings necessary).

(1) Schumann, *Träumerei* from *Scenes from Childhood.*

(2) Schumann, *Curious Story* from *Scenes from Childhood.*

(3) Tchaikovsky, *Morning Prayer* from *Album for the Young.*

(4) Beethoven, Sonata Op. 2, No. 2, 2nd movt. (*Largo Appassionato*) first 8 bars.

(5) Beethoven, Sonata Op. 2, No. 1, 2nd movt. (*Adagio*) first 8 or first 16 bars (melody may be doubled an octave lower beginning with ninth measure).

(6) Beethoven, Sonata Op. 10, No. 3, 3rd movt. (*Menuetto*) first 16 bars, or first 54 bars.

(7) Beethoven, Sonata Op. 10, No. 2, 3rd movt. (*Presto*) first 32 bars.

(8) Bach, Prelude in Bb minor, No. 22, Book I of *The Well Tempered Clavier*.

Suggested Listening

STRINGS

Vivaldi, Concerti.
Corelli, Concerti Grossi.
J. S. Bach, Suites for Strings; Brandenburg Concerti Nos. 3 and 6.
C. P. E. Bach, Symphony No. 3 in C major.
Handel, Concerti Grossi.
Mozart, *Eine Kleine Nachtmusik; Divertimenti.*
Tchaikovsky, *Serenade for Strings,* Op. 48.
Arensky, *Variations on a Theme of Tchaikovsky.*
Miaskovsky, Sinfonietta.
Sibelius, Canzonetta.
Schönberg, *Verklärte Nacht.*
Bloch, Concerto Grosso for string orchestra (with piano).
Bartók, *Music for String Instruments, Percussion and Celesta.*
Vaughn-Williams, *Fantasy on a Theme of Thomas Tallis.*
Stravinsky, *Apollon Musagète.*
Barber, *Adagio for Strings.*
William Schuman, *Symphony for Strings.*
Britten, *The Young Person's Guide to the Orchestra,* Theme D.

Chapter V

THE WOODWINDS

THE FLUTE

Italian: Flauto   French: Flûte   German: Flöte
        Flauti   Flûtes   Flöten

Ex. 1

* Some flutes have the low B.

Somehow it is always difficult for the orchestration student who does not play a wind instrument to understand the wide differences in power and quality between the various registers of each woodwind. To complicate matters still more, there is no general principle that applies to all the woodwinds in this respect; some are thick and heavy in their bottom register, thin and light at the top, while others reverse this relationship. In the case of the flute, the bottom octave is weak and somewhat breathy, but it has a velvety, sensuous charm that is shown off to good advantage in such scores as Debussy's *Prelude to The Afternoon of a Faun.* Since little volume is possible in this low register, accompaniment must be kept light if the flute is to come through. From ♪ the tone becomes progressively brighter and stronger. The notes above this have considerable strength and a haunting, silvery brilliance. However, from ♪ upward the tone tends to be shrill, and the notes are less easy to produce. This extreme upper register should not be used at softer dynamic levels. Most orchestration books list C as the top note possible on the flute; but since the C♯ and D above this can actually be played and are

71

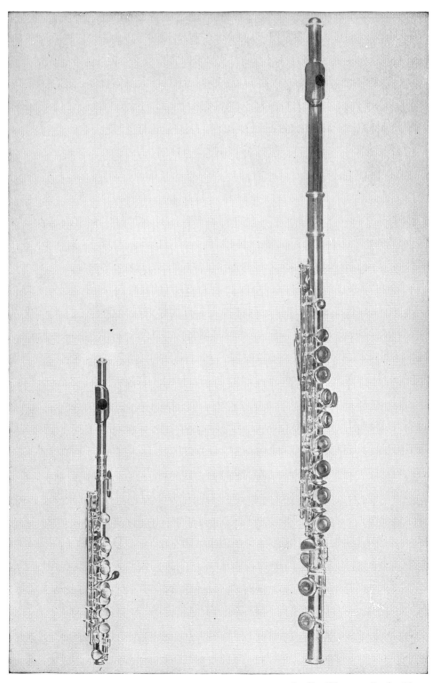

Piccolo   Flute

called for in certain scores (particularly those by Richard Strauss), it seems reasonable to include them in the "possible" range. On the other hand, their quality and intonation are apt to be inferior. Consequently they are not suitable for sustained tones but are useful chiefly for finishing out phrases that extend momentarily above the high C. Some flutes are built to include a B below the bottom C, and that note is occasionally called for in scores. Obviously, it is better avoided unless one is sure of having a flute with the low B extension on hand. An important point in favor of the extension is the fact that it makes the low C stronger and more easily playable.

The flute is equally at home in sustained melodies or in florid passages. Because of its lightness and grace, it is especially good at airy, scherzo-like parts and ornate "filigree" work. Rapid repeated notes, double-tonguing, triple-tonguing and flutter-tonguing (to be discussed later) are all practical and effective on the instrument, as are rapid scales and arpeggios. All trills are possible except those on or above [music] and the following: [music]. In fact, there is little the flute cannot do, from a technical standpoint, in either a legato or a staccato. Although its smaller counterpart, the piccolo, has the distinction of being the most agile of the woodwinds, the flute is a very close second.

An important point to remember is that the flute requires a great deal of breath in playing and that plenty of rests are therefore desirable. Of course it is possible for the player to take a breath very quickly (between phrases, for example), but too much of this sort of thing without a rest is tiring. Rests give the flutist—or *flautist,* to use the traditional name—a chance not only to breathe more comfortably but to relax his lips.

EXAMPLES

Ex. 2

(a) Third Symphony   BEETHOVEN

(b) *Dance of the Reed Flutes*

(c) First Symphony

(d) *Daphnis and Chloe* Suite No. 2

Permission for reprint granted by copyright owner, Durand et Cie, Paris, France; Elkan-Vogel Co., Inc., agents for the U.S.A.

(See also the flute parts in the excerpts from Debussy's *Prelude to The Afternoon of a Faun* given in Examples 16 [c] and 21 [a] in Chapter IV.)

THE OBOE

Italian: Oboe	French: Hautbois	German: Oboe
Oboi	Hautbois	Oboen
		Old spelling: Hoboe(n)

Ex. 3

The oboe, along with the English horn, bassoon, and contra bassoon, belongs to the double-reed branch of the woodwind family. Its spicy,

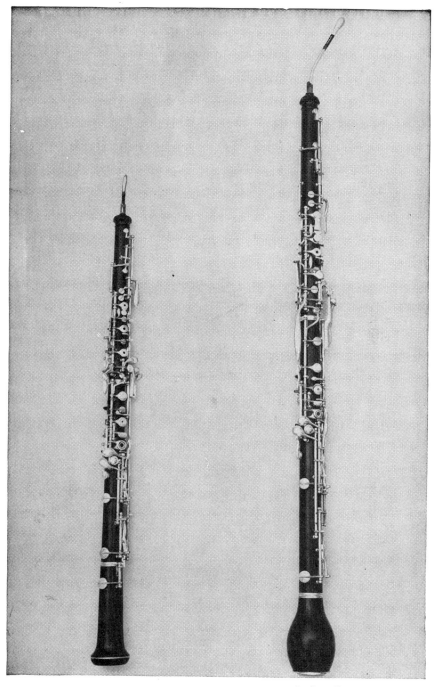

Oboe   English Horn

75

somewhat nasal tone is one of the most distinctive of orchestral colors—
one which has a way of cutting through other colors and of standing
out against any background. For this reason, the oboe is an ideal solo
instrument. It can be poignant or gay, and it is especially well suited
to melodies of a pastoral nature. Although not as agile as the flute
or the clarinet, it can perform with considerable speed and flexibility
if need be, either legato or staccato. This is not to imply that it is
valuable *only* in a solo role, for it is also useful in combination with
other instruments. However, one must be a little careful about giving
it a subordinate voice in a lightly scored passage, since its incisive tone
may come through too prominently for "background." Another point
to remember is that the highly colored oboe timbre becomes tiresome
to the ear if used for too long at a time.

Below about the oboe tends to sound a bit thick and
coarse—"honky," as oboe players sometimes put it. For that reason,
these bottom notes (particularly the low B♭) are better avoided in any
passage where the oboe is to be heard prominently. Parts that dip
down into this lowest register but quickly get away from it are not
objectionable; the main point is not to stress these very low notes in
solo work. Occasionally, however, they are used intentionally to
achieve a special effect—as in Stravinsky's *Symphony of Psalms,* where
they give an ultra-reedy, primitive flavor, and in Prokofieff's *Peter
and the Wolf,* where they serve admirably to personify the duck.

From is the oboe's most useful and characteristic
register. Above that the tone becomes thinner and less pungent,
though quite usable up to about . The notes above this
are generally impractical for orchestral use. On some French oboes
even the high A is possible, and the French school of woodwind playing allows for the writing of higher oboe parts than is practical in the
United States.

All trills are available except the half-step trill on the bottom B♭,
though trills involving the top F and G are better avoided.

Double-tonguing and triple-tonguing, being very difficult on the
oboe, are rarely used; but the instrument is capable of playing fairly

rapid repeated notes even with single-tonguing. As intimated earlier, it should not be asked to play extremely fast or intricate passages. Unlike the flute, it requires very little expenditure of breath in performance. But the player has a different problem, that of *holding in* the air until the next breathing point while using only a small amount of it in playing. Consequently, sufficient rests are as essential in oboe parts as in flute parts, if for a slightly different reason. In addition to being an uncommonly taxing instrument, the oboe is a sensitive and somewhat unpredictable one as well. Notes must be humored and cajoled; the reed is delicate and must be "just so"; temperature and atmospheric conditions can produce unexpected and disastrous results. In short, the oboe is something of a temperamental *prima donna,* but an indispensable one in the orchestra.

EXAMPLES

Ex. 4

(a) Third Symphony

(b) Seventh Symphony

(c) Second Symphony

(d) *Iberia*

Permission for reprint granted by copyright owner, Durand et Cie, Paris, France; Elkan-Vogel Co., Inc., agents for the U.S.A.

The Clarinet

Italian: Clarinetto	French: Clarinette	German: Klarinette
Clarinetti	Clarinettes	Klarinetten

Ex. 5

In the past clarinets pitched in various keys were used. Of these, the two chief survivors today are the clarinet in B♭ and the clarinet in A, the first being the more commonly used of the two. Both are transposing instruments—that is, they are not written at actual pitch In the case of the B♭ clarinet, the part must be written a major 2nd (a whole step) higher than the sounds desired, while the part for the A clarinet is written a minor 3rd higher than the sounds. For the benefit of students who have not had experience with transposing instruments, let us elaborate a bit on this system and give some examples to show how it works.

The B♭ clarinet is so labeled because B♭ is the sound that results when written C is played. That is, when the B♭ clarinet player sees [music] on the page, he uses the fingering which will produce the sound [music]. Consequently, if we want the B♭ clarinet to *sound* [music], we must write [music]. On the A clarinet, the note A is the sound that results when written C is played. Therefore, if the sound [music] is wanted on an A clarinet, we must write [music], a minor 3rd higher. In dealing with transposing instruments remember that the key of the instrument is the sound that results when written C is played.

Example 16 shows how a passage (given first at actual pitch) would be written for B♭ and A clarinets respectively.

Ex. 6

Notice the inclusion of key signatures. The chart below gives the key signature that would be used by each of the two instruments in each of the major keys. The term "concert key" means the actual or sounding key. The word "concert" is also applied to notes—for example, "concert G," meaning the actual sound G as opposed to the written G on a transposing instrument.

Ex. 7

It may be helpful to point out that in dealing with transposing instruments we encounter two types of transposition: (1) the "reading" type—that is, the kind that is involved when we are reading a score and have the problem of converting *transposed* pitches to *actual* (or "concert") pitches, and (2) the "writing" type, in which we must convert *actual* pitches to *transposed* pitches. (The difference between the two types is, of course, only one of direction.) If this distinction is understood at the outset and kept in mind, a good deal of confusion can be avoided.

Considering the complications which the transposition system involves for both orchestrator and score reader, a very natural question at this point is, "Why must it be used at all?" Although a complete answer to that question would entail excursions into technical points of acoustics and fingering, certain general reasons for the use of the system can be cited here: as far as resonance and good intonation are

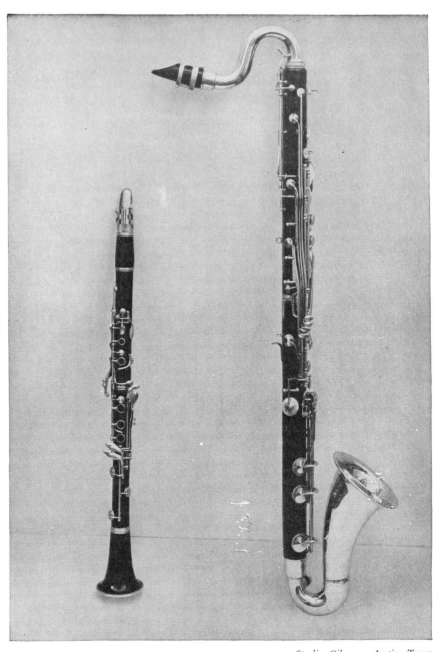

Clarinet   Bass Clarinet

concerned, the B♭ and A clarinets are superior to the now obsolete C clarinet. Since they started out as transposing instruments and have been treated as such ever since, a change to another method of notation now would be all but impossible. (Certain composers, notably Prokofieff, have taken to writing the parts for clarinets and other transposing instruments at actual pitch in the score; but even in such cases the individual parts for the players are written in transposed form.) An advantage of the transposition principle as applied to clarinets is this: it allows for a pattern of fingering common to clarinets of different sizes; the player need not learn a new fingering in order to perform on an alto or bass clarinet, for example. Instead it is the notation which changes in each case.

As a general rule, key signatures involving flats are easier for the instruments pitched in flat keys, while instruments such as the A clarinet find the sharp keys a bit more comfortable. However, the B♭ clarinet is frequently called on to play in keys up to three or four sharps, while the simpler flat keys are perfectly practical for the A clarinet. The advantage of having the two instruments available is that if a part would involve awkward fingering on one, it can nearly always be played with relative ease if assigned to the other. In general, the B♭ clarinet is first choice, the A clarinet being selected chiefly in cases where the B♭ instrument would have to play in a difficult key.

By way of illustration, let us suppose that we are to score a piece in the key of E♭ major, concert. If we use the B♭ clarinet, its part will be written in F major (an easy key for the instrument) while the A clarinet would be written in the key of G♭ major (difficult)—or, enharmonically, F♯ major (also difficult). Obviously, the B♭ instrument is the better choice here. But suppose that the music to be scored is in A major, concert. The B♭ clarinet would call for a signature of five sharps, while the A clarinet would be written in C major. In such a case, the A clarinet would be the better choice. Of course there are certain keys which are suitable to either instrument. For example, in music in G major, concert, the B♭ clarinet could play in A major about as easily as the A clarinet could play in B♭ major. However, the B♭ instrument would probably be chosen here, simply because it is the more commonly used and more generally available of the two.

Sometimes parts are best written enharmonically. For instance, if we are using B♭ clarinet and we come to a section in B major, a transposition of the part up a major 2nd would bring us out in the key of C♯ major (seven sharps) whereas the enharmonic equivalent, D♭ major (five flats), would be a great deal easier and should of course be chosen. Notice that such enharmonic respellings alter the interval used in the "transposition by interval" method.

Although changes from B♭ clarinet to A clarinet (or vice versa) in the midst of a work are possible and are occasionally called for, they are not recommended; the clarinet that has been lying unused will be cold and will consequently tend to be flat in pitch and sluggish in its general response until it has had time to warm up. There is, by the way, a slight difference in tone quality between the B♭ and the A instruments, but it is scarcely apparent to any but the most sensitive ear.

What has been said here about the use of the A clarinet does not apply in school orchestras. There the B♭ clarinet is used exclusively. The problem of difficult key signatures never arises because the concert keys are chosen with an eye to keeping the B♭ instruments in the easier keys.

The bottom octave or so of the clarinet is called the *chalumeau* register. It has a dark, strangely hollow quality, as if the instrument were being played in a barrel. Notice that although the written range of both B♭ and A clarinets is the same, the A clarinet can go a half step lower in sound that the B♭ instrument, since the low written E sounds D on the B♭ clarinet and C♯ (or D♭) on the

A clarinet.[1] The middle register, roughly from 🎼 to

🎼 , is rather "gray" in quality and not too strong, while

the octave above this (sometimes known as the *clarion* register) is

clear and bright. Above about 🎼 the tone is apt to be shrill

and the intonation doubtful. It is true that on paper the clarinet's "possible" range extends up to a high C above this. But these very high notes are simply not usable, for all practical purposes. Even in band work, where clarinets are often taken higher than in the or-

---

[1] Some B♭ clarinets include this low concert D♭ (written E♭), but since one can never be sure of having one of these instruments on hand, it is safer not to write that note in B♭ clarinet parts.

chestra, a written  is usually considered the practical up-

ward limit.   Occasionally the very shrillness of this top register is used
for humorous or grotesque effects, as in Stravinsky's *Petrouchka,*
where the high notes of the clarinet imitate the sounds of a peasant's
reed pipe as he plays while his bear dances.

Of all the woodwinds, the clarinet is the most sensitive in the matter
of dynamic range and control.   It can reduce its warm, round tone
to an incredibly soft whisper and can achieve the subtlest nuances of
color and phrasing.   These abilities make it an ideal solo instrument
for *espressivo* melodies.   In agility, it nearly equals the flute; it can
perform rapid runs and arpeggios, skips, trills, and legato or staccato
effects.   However, because it is a single-reed instrument, it is somewhat limited in its ability to play rapid repeated notes.

In treatises on the clarinet, much has been made of the "break," a
point on the instrument at which an awkward change of fingering is
involved,[2] and of the register associated with it, which includes some
notes of slightly inferior quality.   From the standpoint of the fingering problem, the actual break occurs between the written notes

.   Passages which pass through this area

in either direction cause no particular difficulty; it is only when a
part involves a continuous use of these notes that the part becomes unduly awkward.   As for tone quality, the three written notes

(particularly the B♭) are the weakest on the in-

strument and are better not stressed in solo passages.   Because of
modern improvements in clarinet construction, the break is now much
less of an obstacle than it once was.   In fact, clarinet players today
seem rather unconcerned about this difficulty that was apparently
something of a "thorn in the flesh" for players of an earlier day.

Likewise, certain trills that were once listed as "awkward" or

---

[2] In connection with this point at which the player begins to repeat his fingering pattern, it
might be mentioned that the clarinet, being cylindrical, "overblows" at the 12th, whereas the
oboe and bassoon, which are conical, overblow at the octave. (The flute, although cylindrical,
behaves like an open pipe and consequently overblows at the octave.)

"better avoided" in clarinet writing are now quite usable. In fact, all trills are now practical on the instrument.

Although it is not the intention here to go into the historical background of instruments, it is interesting to note that the clarinet did not begin to be accepted as a member of the orchestra until Mozart's day; only two of the Mozart symphonies contain clarinet parts.

EXAMPLES

(All examples are given as written in the score. Those for Bb clarinet will sound a major 2nd lower, those for A clarinet a minor 3rd lower.)

Ex. 8

(a) Sixth Symphony

(b) First Symphony

(c) Overture to *Tannhäuser*

(d) *Capriccio Espagnol*

THE BASSOON

Italian: Fagotto	French: Basson	German: Fagott
Fagotti	Bassons	Fagotte

Ex. 9

The Italian and German names come closer to giving an actual picture of the bassoon than the English or French equivalents do. It is easy enough to see how the instrument might suggest a "fagot," for it is rather like a long stick bent back upon itself.

Although the bassoon is, like the oboe, a double-reed instrument, its tone is much less nasal and less highly colored than that of the oboe. In fact, its characteristic quality is a relatively neutral one, so that it is apt to be largely absorbed by any other orchestral color it is doubled with. For example, if bassoon is doubled with cellos (as it very frequently is), the cello tone will predominate but will have more body and focus than it would alone.

In the bottom octave or so of the bassoon, the tone is dark and full, even a little "gruff" in the bottommost notes, which are difficult to produce *pianissimo*. The next octave is middle ground, neither notably dark nor light in color, but probably the most used register of the instrument. The notes in the top octave become progressively thinner, until above about "A 440" they take on a pinched, complaining quality. Stravinsky, with his penchant for exploiting extreme registers, uses these top notes in a wonderfully effective bassoon solo at the beginning of *The Rite of Spring*. But such passages are extremely difficult, and it is better to let A or Bb suffice as an upward limit, generally speaking. When the part goes too high to be comfortably written in the bass clef, the tenor clef may be used.

The bassoon is sometimes spoken of as "the clown of the orchestra." Bassoonists resent the title, and with good reason. For while certain passages (especially *staccato* passages) have a way of sounding comical on the instrument, it can perform many other types of music effectively, including sustained melodies of a serious nature.

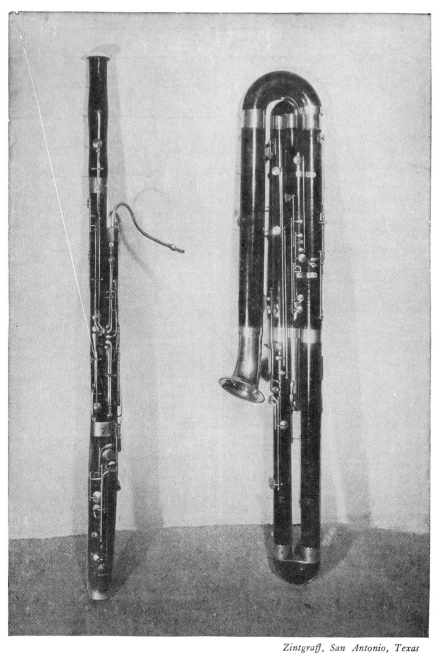

Bassoon   Contra Bassoon

Technically, it is quite agile and is capable of making wide and sudden leaps. Because it does not have a great deal of power and because its color is so readily absorbed by that of other instruments, it is easily covered by the rest of the orchestra and should not be pitted against too heavy a background in solos. Probably its most frequent function is that of reinforcing other instruments in the bass or tenor registers.

There are a few trills to be avoided: those on D♭, E♭, or G♭ in all octaves, on ╫ and below ╫ .

EXAMPLES

Ex. 10

(a) Fifth Symphony

BEETHOVEN

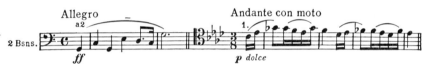

(b) Fourth Symphony

TCHAIKOVSKY

(c) *The Sorcerer's Apprentice*

DUKAS

Permission for reprint granted by copyright owner, Durand et Cie, Paris, France; Elkan-Vogel Co., Inc., agents for the U.S.A.

(d) Concerto for Orchestra

BARTÓK

Allegretto scherzando ♩=74

I
Bsns.
II

OTHER WOODWINDS

In addition to the woodwinds just discussed, there are others which are sometimes used: the piccolo, the English horn, the bass clarinet and the contra bassoon.[3] Except for the piccolo, which is generally found even in the medium-sized orchestra, they are "extras" used chiefly in works scored for large orchestra. Occasionally, one or more of them may be included in smaller groups for the sake of a particular tone color or special effect.

The Piccolo

Italian: Flauto Piccolo   French: Petite Flûte   German: Kleine Flöte
         (or) Ottavino

Ex. 11

Sounding an
8ve higher

Just as the double bass is written an octave higher than it sounds in order to keep the part more nearly within the staff, the piccolo is written an octave lower than the sounds desired in order to avoid too many leger lines above the staff. Even so, the player must often cope with three or four leger lines; but he becomes occustomed to reading these and seems to prefer them to an "*8va*" sign over the notes written an octave lower. Although there is a D♭ piccolo that is commonly used in bands, the instrument in C is the only one that figures in orchestral scores.

---

[3] The E♭ clarinet might also be included in this list, but since it appears somewhat less frequently than the other instruments mentioned here, discussion of it is reserved for Chapter XVII.

The piccolo is without doubt the most agile instrument of the orchestra, able to perform incredibly fast runs, skips, arpeggios, and elaborate figurations of all kinds. On the other hand, it is not often used for slow *cantabile* passages, though certain contemporary scores contain solos of a quiet, sustained nature that are surprisingly effective.

The bottom octave of the instrument is so weak and breathy as to be nearly useless in heavily scored passages. In fact, there is not much point in having the piccolo play at all in a *tutti* unless it is above a written or so, for it will not have enough strength or brilliance to make any difference. Notes below this are usable when the background is not too heavy. It should be noted that the written piccolo range does not include the low C possible on the flute. The second octave, from , is clear and bright, while notes above that are more piercing. The top A is apt to be too shrill for comfort, and the Bb above that difficult to produce (and to listen to!). Some orchestration books give a C above this as possible, and it is true that certain skilled players can coax the sound from their instruments, but on most piccolos (at least those in this country) the note is simply nonexistent.

Obviously the piccolo's most valuable talent is its ability to add a brilliant edge to a melodic line. It frequently doubles other woodwinds (or even strings) an octave higher. Now and then it is written so as to sound in unison with the flute to reinforce the flute's top tones. Like most brightly colored instruments, it cannot be used too continuously without losing in effectiveness; furthermore, if overused, it may give an unintentional "military band" feeling because of its long association with band music.

The fingering for piccolo is the same as that for flute, and the third flute player of an orchestra often doubles on piccolo. That is, he plays either a flute part or a piccolo part, as required; he may change from one instrument to the other several times in the course of a work, as directed by the composer or arranger. Of course such changes require at least two or three measures of rest, preferably more. This arrangement is often described in scores by the expression "Flute III interchangeable with piccolo." If only two flutes are used, the second

flute player may double on piccolo. Occasionally the piccolo part is
listed below the flutes in the score in cases where the player is to
change to flute III. But most often it is listed at the top of the page,
and in many scores a player is assigned exclusively to the piccolo part.
One hazard involved in changing from flute to piccolo (or *vice versa*)
is that whichever instrument has been laid aside temporarily will be
cold when it is picked up again; as a result, it will probably be flat
in pitch and a bit sluggish in general responsiveness. Players like to
have a few measures of rest in which to warm up the new instrument
before actually playing.

EXAMPLES

(Sounding an octave higher)

Ex. 12

(a) Fourth Symphony

TCHAIKOVSKY

(b) *Háry János* Suite (*Viennese Musical Clock*)

KODÁLY

*Copyright assigned to Hawkes & Son (London) Ltd., 1939. By permission of the copyright
owner, Boosey & Hawkes, Inc.*

(c) *Petit Poucet* (*Hop o' My Thumb*) from *Mother Goose* Suite

RAVEL

*Permission for reprint granted by copyright owner, Durand et Cie, Paris, France; Elkan-Vogel
Co., Inc., agents for the U.S.A.*

(d) Seventh Symphony

SHOSTAKOVITCH

The English Horn

Italian: Corno Inglese   French: Cor Anglais   German: Englisch Horn

Ex. 13

Sounding a
perfect 5th lower

Just how the English horn received its name and why it is not called "alto oboe" or some similar name are matters that have occupied writers on orchestration over the years. One theory that has been neither proved nor disproved is that because of the angle near the end of the instrument it was once called *"cor anglé"* in French, and that *"anglé"* became confused with *"anglais"* because of the similarity in pronunciation. That still leaves the term "horn" unexplained. Anyone who has ever read a program note on the English horn has been subjected to the inevitable comment that it is "neither English nor a horn."

The modern instrument, which is straight rather than "angled," differs from the oboe chiefly in being longer and having a bulbous distension at the end of the bell. The tone is akin to that of the oboe but more sonorous and melancholy. Possibly because of this serious quality, the English horn is seldom called on to play fast, technically complicated music, and it is not a particularly agile instrument by nature. The part for it is written a perfect 5th higher than the sounds desired.

Although the low B♭ is obtainable on the oboe, the lowest written note on the English horn is a B♮, sounding E below. Now and then one comes across an instrument that has the low B♭ (concert E♭) but not often enough to justify writing the note as a general practice. The bottom notes of the English horn are not only usable but highly effective; strangely enough, they do not seem to suffer from the coarseness that afflicts the lowest tones of the oboe. There is seldom any need to take the English horn above the written note , even though notes up to a 3rd higher are possible. Moreover, the instrument loses some of its characteristic color in its topmost register and is consequently less effective there.

EXAMPLES

(Sounding a perfect 5th lower)

Ex. 14

(a) Symphony in E minor (*New World*)

DVOŘÁK

(b) Symphony in D minor

FRANCK

(c) *La Mer*

DEBUSSY

Permission for reprint granted by copyright owner, Durant et Cie, Paris, France; Elkan-Vogel Co., Inc., agents for the U.S.A.

The Bass Clarinet

Italian: Clarinetto Basso   French: Clarinette Basse   German: Bassklarinette

Ex. 15

(a)

Sounding a
major 9th lower

(or)

(b)

Sounding a
major 2nd lower

* Some bass clarinets have the low E♭.

Physically, the bass clarinet differs from the clarinet in having a curve near the mouthpiece and an upturned bell, the whole shape being a little like that of a saxophone. Although at one time there was a bass clarinet in A, it is now extinct. Therefore, the player must use the B♭ instrument and transpose when he plays a part written for bass clarinet in A.

In approaching the notation of the bass clarinet, we come across a rather confusing convention: when written in the treble clef, the instrument sounds a major 9th lower than written; but it may also be written in the bass clef, in which case it sounds a major 2nd lower than written. To give an example of the two methods of notation, the concert pitch [music] would be written [music] in the treble clef, whereas the same sound written in the bass clef would be [music] .[4]

The first method is the more widely used of the two. (It is invariably used in band work, incidentally.) But skilled players seem to have no particular preference for one or the other. As a rule, it is best to write the part either all in the treble clef or all in the bass clef, though a change from one clef to the other in the same part is possible.

In its bottom octave the bass clarinet is extremely dark, almost sinister, in quality. The color becomes progressively less somber above that until, in the top octave, it is a bit strained and "white." There is little point in writing for the instrument in this top register, since other instruments can take these notes with better effect. But in its middle and lower registers the bass clarinet is valuable not only

---

[4] These two types of notation are sometimes known, respectively, as the "French system" (treble clef) and the "German system" (bass clef). However, these names must not be taken too literally, since there are instances of bass clef parts in French music and of treble clef parts in German music.

for doubling bass and tenor parts but in a solo capacity. Wagner is particularly fond of using it as a solo instrument to give a sense of gloom and impending tragedy. Other composers have exploited what Forsyth calls its "goblinesque" quality, a certain attractive grotesqueness. Although not quite so agile as the clarinet, it can get around with considerable speed. And it shares the clarinet's phenomenal control of volume and dynamic nuance.

In some scores, the bass clarinet is interchangeable with the second or third clarinet; that is, the two parts are played by the same person. This is obviously a sensible arrangement where both instruments are not needed at once, and particularly where there is only a small part for the bass clarinet, or for the second or third clarinet.

EXAMPLES

(The example for bass clarinet in A [bass clef] will sound a minor 3rd lower. The examples for bass clarinet in Bb will sound a major 9th lower when written in the treble clef, a major 2nd lower when written in the bass clef.)

Ex. 16

(a) *Tristan and Isolda*   WAGNER

(b) Symphony in D minor   FRANCK

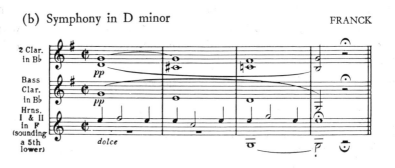

(c) *The Rite of Spring*   STRAVINSKY

The Contra Bassoon or Double Bassoon

Italian: Contrafagotto   French: Contre-basson   German: Kontrafagott

Ex. 17

Sounding an 8ve lower[5]

* The low A is included only on certain recent models.

As might be expected, the contra bassoon is one of the more ponderous instruments of the orchestra, in both appearance and sound. In fact, because of its great size it must stand on the floor in performance. Its tone is somewhat rough and thick; very soft effects are difficult to achieve, especially in the lower register. As a result, the instrument is chiefly valuable for adding volume and incisiveness to the bass parts in loud, heavily scored passages. Occasionally, it is used in other ways; for example, to add a sombre tinge to low melodic lines, or as a solo instrument to produce a rather grotesque effect. There is seldom reason to use it in its upper register, since bassoons or bass clarinet are better equipped to play these notes. Like the double bass, it is written an octave higher than it is to sound.[5]

As has been intimated, many scores contain no part for contra bassoon. That is as it should be, for unless the instrument is actually needed for purposes of volume or special color, it is better omitted. Budding orchestrators sometimes discover to their dismay that contrabassoon parts which looked harmless on paper give the effect of the proverbial "bull in the china shop" in performance.

It might also be pointed out that most school orchestras and even

---

[5] In a few scores (Wagner's *Parsifal* and Debussy's *Iberia* and *La Mer*, for instance) the contra-bassoon part is written at actual pitch.

many semi-professional orchestras do not own a contra bassoon, or, if they own one, do not have a competent player on hand. Consequently, it is always something of a gamble as to whether the part will really be played, unless one is sure of getting a major orchestra to perform the score.

Although Beethoven and Brahms wrote contra-bassoon parts that went as high as (written) ⸫, notes above ⸫ are difficult, and many orchestration books give that Eb as the highest note possible on the instrument. Heckel now makes a contra bassoon that is capable of playing the low A, one half step below the Bb usually given as the bottom note. (Incidentally, this A is the lowest note on the piano.)

Rapid, intricate parts are not well suited to the technique of the contra bassoon. Its part should be fairly simple and should contain plenty of rests.

EXAMPLES

(Contra-bassoon parts sounding an octave lower)

Ex. 18

(a) *The Sorcerer's Apprentice*   DUKAS

Permission for reprint granted by copyright owner, Durand et Cie, Paris, France; Elkan-Vogel Co., Inc., agents for the U.S.A.

(b) *Beauty and the Beast* (from *Mother Goose* Suite)   RAVEL

Permission for reprint granted by copyright owner, Durand et Cie, Paris, France; Elkan-Vogel Co., Inc., agents for the U.S.A.

(c) *Through the Looking Glass* (*Jabberwocky*)   TAYLOR

By permission of the copyright owner, J. Fischer & Bro., New York, N. Y.

(Written notes)

Ex. 19

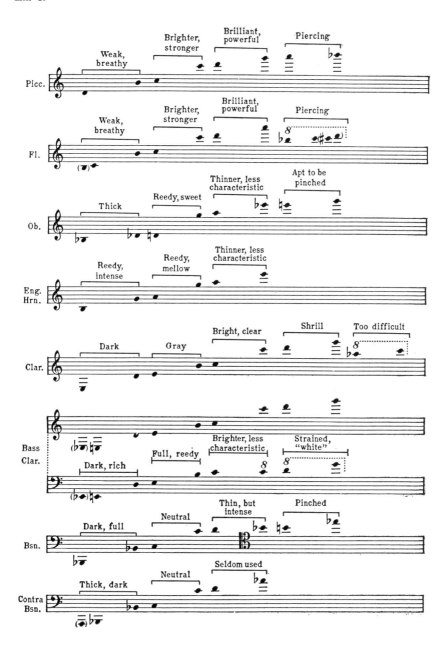

97

SUGGESTED ASSIGNMENTS

A. Know:

  (1) Ranges (possible and practical) of flute, oboe, clarinet, and bassoon.
  (2) Ranges (possible and practical) of piccolo, English horn, bass clarinet, and contra bassoon.
  (3) Transpositions where involved.
  (4) Colors and relative strengths of the various registers of each woodwind.
  (5) Particular abilities and limitations of each woodwind.

B. Transpose the following melody for: (1) Bb clarinet; (2) clarinet in A; (3) English horn. Then assume that the melody is to be played an octave lower (in sound) by the bass clarinet and write the transposed part; first in treble clef, then in bass clef. Include the proper key signature in all cases.

Ex. 20

SUGGESTED LISTENING

PICCOLO

Tchaikovsky, Fourth Symphony, 3rd movt., measure 194.
Pierné, *Entrance of the Little Fauns* from *Cydalise.*
Debussy, *Iberia,* Part I (*Par les rues et par les chemins*) many passages.
Ravel, *Mother Goose* Suite: II. *Petit Poucet,* figure 7; III. *Laideronette, Impératrice des Pagodes,* figure 1; *Daphnis and Chloe* Suite No. 2, figure 183.
Kodály, *Háry János* Suite, Part II (*Viennese Musical Clock*) and Part IV (*The Battle and Defeat of Napoleon*).
Shostakovitch, Seventh Symphony, 1st movt., figure 14.
Britten, *The Young Person's Guide to the Orchestra,* Variation A.
Instruments of the Orchestra (Victor, 20522 B).

FLUTE

Bach, Suite in B minor for flute and strings; Brandenburg Concertos Nos. 2, 4, 5.
Beethoven, Third Symphony, last movt., measure 190, also measure 292.
Mendelssohn, Fourth Symphony (*Italian*), last movt., measure 6.
Brahms, First Symphony, last movt., measure 38.
Tchaikovsky, Piano Concerto in B-flat minor, beginning of 2nd movt. (*Andantino*).
Dvořák, Fifth Symphony (*New World*), 1st movt., figures 5 and 12.
Bizet, *Carmen,* Entr'acte between Acts II and III.
Debussy, *Prelude to The Afternoon of a Faun,* beginning and many other passages.
Ravel, *Daphnis and Chloe* Suite No. 2, 3 bars after figure 176.
Kennan, *Night Soliloquy* for flute, strings, and piano.
Britten, *The Young Person's Guide to the Orchestra,* Variation A.
Instruments of the Orchestra (Victor, 20522 B).

OBOE

Bach, Brandenburg Concertos Nos. 1, 2.

Beethoven, Third Symphony, 2nd movt. (*Marcia Funebre*) measure 8; Sixth Symphony, 3rd movt. (*Scherzo*) measure 91; Seventh Symphony, 1st movt., measure 300.

Schumann, Second Symphony, 3rd movt. (*Adagio espressivo*) measure 8.

Brahms, Violin Concerto, beginning of 2nd movt.

Mahler, *Das Lied von der Erde,* beginning of 2nd movt.

Debussy, *Iberia,* Part II (*Les parfums de la nuit*) beginning, also 4 bars before figure 40.

Ravel, *Le Tombeau de Couperin,* Trio of the *Rigaudon; La Valse,* figure 18.

Strauss, *Death and Transfiguration,* measure 30; *Don Quixote,* 8 measures before figure 3.

Shostakovitch, First Symphony, beginning of 3rd movt.

Britten, *The Young Person's Guide to the Orchestra,* Variation B.

Instruments of the Orchestra (Victor, 20522 B).

ENGLISH HORN

Berlioz, *Fantastic Symphony,* beginning of 3rd movt. (*Scène aux champs*).

Wagner, *Tristan and Isolda,* beginning of Act III.

Franck, Symphony in D minor, 2nd movt., near beginning.

Dvořák, Fifth Symphony (*New World*), 2nd movt., near beginning.

Debussy, *Nocturnes:* I. *Nuages,* measure 5; *La Mer,* figure 16.

Sibelius, *The Swan of Tuonela.*

Stravinsky, *The Rite of Spring,* section entitled *Ritual of the Ancestors,* figure 129; *Petrouchka,* 9 bars after figure 72.

Instruments of the Orchestra (Victor, 20522 B).

CLARINET

Beethoven, Fourth Symphony, 2nd movt., measure 26; Sixth Symphony, 2nd movt., letter D.

Weber, Overture to *Oberon,* measure 64.

Schubert, Symphony in B minor (*Unfinished*), 2nd movt., measure 66.

Tchaikovsky, Fifth Symphony, beginning; 2nd movt., measure 66; 3rd movt., measure 28; Sixth Symphony, 1st movt., measure 163, also measure 326.

Debussy, *Iberia,* measure 8.

Rachmaninoff, Second Piano Concerto, 2nd movt., near beginning.

Stravinsky, *Petrouchka,* figure 100.

Prokofieff, *Peter and the Wolf,* figure 11 ("The Cat").

Britten, *The Young Person's Guide to the Orchestra,* Variation C.

Instruments of the Orchestra (Victor, 20522 B).

BASS CLARINET

Wagner, *Tristan and Isolda,* Act. II, "King Mark's Song."

Tchaikovsky, *Nutcracker* Suite: *Dance of the Sugar Plum Fairy.*

Strauss, *Don Quixote.* Variation III.

Stravinsky, *Petrouchka,* figure 65 (The Moor dances).
Instruments of the Orchestra (Victor, 20522 B).

BASSOON

Beethoven, Fifth Symphony, 2nd movt., measure 205.
Tchaikovsky, Fourth Symphony, 2nd movt., measure 77; Sixth Symphony, beginning; last movt., measure 30.
Rimsky-Korsakoff, *Scheherazade,* 2nd movt., measure 5.
Mussorgsky-Ravel, *Pictures from an Exhibition,* beginning of Part II (*The Old Castle*).
Dukas, *The Sorcerer's Apprentice,* figure 7.
Stravinsky, *The Rite of Spring,* beginning; *Petrouchka,* 4 bars after figure 68 (end of Moor scene).
Bartók, Concerto for Orchestra, beginning of Part II (*Giuoco delle Coppie*).
Britten, *The Young Person's Guide to the Orchestra,* Variation D.
Instruments of the Orchestra (Victor, 20522 B).

CONTRA BASSOON

Mahler, Ninth Symphony, last movt., measure 28.
Ravel, *Mother Goose* Suite: IV. *Les Entretiens de la Belle et de la Bête,* figure 2.
Dukas, *The Sorcerer's Apprentice,* figure 42.
Taylor, *Through the Looking Glass,* Part II (*Jabberwocky*) figure 13.
Stravinsky, *Petrouchka,* 9 bars after figure 72.
Instruments of the Orchestra (Victor, 20522 B).

Chapter VI

THE WOODWIND SECTION

THE PROPORTIONS of woodwind sections of various sizes were listed in Chapter I, and it might be well to look over that material once again before going on with this chapter. The average woodwind section consists of two flutes, two oboes, two clarinets, and two bassoons ("woodwinds in pairs"), plus piccolo if desired. Although major orchestras also include English horn, bass clarinet, and contra bassoon, most school orchestras and some nonprofessional orchestras do not. Consequently, unless one is sure of getting a performance by an orchestra that does have these "extra" woodwinds, it is safer to write for woodwinds in pairs. In scoring for groups of limited size, it is a good idea to remember the possibility of letting the second flute player double on piccolo, the second oboist on English horn, and so on.

As has been mentioned earlier, the orchestra of the classical period did not regularly include clarinets. For example, the woodwind section used in the early Haydn symphonies consists of one or two flutes, usually two oboes, and one or two bassoons. But by Beethoven's time, woodwinds in pairs (including clarinets) had become the accepted arrangement.

The table on page 4 shows the standard order in which instruments are listed on the page. This consistency of arrangement is obviously a great help to the eye of the conductor or the scorereader. The only possible variation in order is the placing of the piccolo part below that of flutes I and II in cases where the piccolo is interchangeable with flute III.

As a rule, each pair of woodwinds is written on the same staff. When the two instruments are playing different parts, the upper notes are normally taken by the first of the pair, the lower notes by the second. As with *divisi* string parts on one staff, a single stem for both

notes may be used as long as the time values in both parts are the
same, but separate stems must be used if the time values are different:
Ex. 1

If the parts cross briefly, both can still be written on the same staff,
the abnormal arrangement of the parts being shown by the direction
of the stems. But if they involve continuous crossing or are so
independent as to be awkward on one staff, it is better to use separate
staves.

We now come to a point that should be noted very carefully, for it
seems to be one that students have a hard time remembering. Whenever two wind instruments are written on the same staff and a single
melodic line is involved, indications must be included to show whether
the passage is to be played by the first instrument of the pair, by the
second, or by both. Otherwise the part is simply ambiguous. If the
first is to play, either of the following systems may be used:
Ex. 2

(a)   (b)

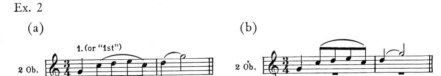

(The first arrangement here is the easier and more commonly used
of the two.) Similarly, if the second instrument[1] is to play, the part
could be written in either of these ways:
Ex. 3

(a)   (b)

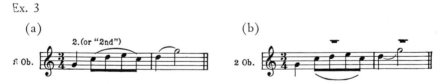

In case the passage is a solo, the word "solo" should be written in
at the beginning of it. Solos are usually, but not necessarily always,

---

[1] Sometimes "1º" and "2º" are used to designate the first and second of each pair. These
are abbreviations of the Italian words "primo" and "secondo," corresponding to our "1st"
and "2nd."

given to the first of each pair. Sometimes the solo indication is used even when the passage in question is not the chief melodic idea but must be played in such a way as to give it a certain prominent or important quality. If both instruments of a pair are to take a melodic line in unison, the passage can be written in either of the following ways:

Ex. 4

(a)   (b)

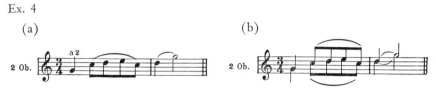

(Literally, "a 2" means "to two" in Italian.)   Here, again, the first way is the usual one; the "double-stem" system used in the second version is normally reserved for passages where both instruments play in unison for just a few notes, as in the following:

Ex. 5

If a melodic line to be played by both instruments in unison is of solo quality, the word "soli" may be written in at the beginning of it. The direction "a 2," by the way, is never used for passages in which the two instruments play *different* parts; in such cases no indication is needed, since it is quite obvious that both instruments are playing.

For the benefit of students who have played in bands, it might be well to point out that although the expressions *divisi* and *unisono* are appropriate in band music where a whole section of clarinets is to divide or unite, these terms are used only for strings—never for winds— in an orchestra.

When one instrument of a pair is already playing and the other enters, it is customary to label the entering voice as being 1. or 2. and to show at what dynamic level it should enter.   All dynamic markings must be shown beneath each staff, of course, just as with strings.

TONGUING AND SLURRING

In performing on a wind instrument it is possible to articulate each note with a separate "ta" [2]—in which case the note is said to be "tongued"—or to slur it with the note that precedes or follows. Where no slur mark is present, the note is to be tongued. For instance, in the following passage the first two notes are slurred together, the next two are slurred, the next four are slurred, the next note is tongued separately, and so on.

Ex. 6. Third Symphony

BRAHMS

But there is no break in sound between the last note of each slurred group and the note that follows; the general effect is *legato*. For an even smoother, more *legato* effect, the whole passage could have been slurred together. Or it might have been written entirely without slurs (each note tongued separately) if a sharply *marcato* effect had been wanted. And there are possibilities other than the one shown that involve alternate slurring and tonguing. When repeated notes occur, they must be tongued (though not necessarily sharply) in order to sound with a fresh attack. For example:

Ex. 7

(a)   (b)

However, slurs plus dots or slurs plus a line next to each note are sometimes used to indicate a "soft tonguing," even with repeated notes:

Ex. 8

(a)   (b)

---

[2] Or variations of this syllable, depending on the instrument and register involved.

The second type of notation here would imply a kind of pressure on each note, with less separation between notes than in the case of the dots.

In some scores, phrasing rather than slurring is shown in the wood-wind parts. But since phrasing and slurring are indicated in exactly the same way, players are frequently in doubt as to which is which, and the whole question becomes hopelessly confused. One possible solution is the use of dotted lines for phrasing, solid lines for slurring (or *vice versa,* as long as one way is used consistently). There has been some successful experimentation with this plan already. But until some such system comes into general use, it seems best to indicate slurring rather than phrasing in woodwind parts. If necessary, breathing points between phrases may be indicated by the same symbol used in vocal music: ’.

A question that often arises is this: when strings and woodwinds play the same melodic line, what is the relationship between bowing in the strings and slurring in the winds? There is no hard and fast rule to follow here. In some cases the slur marks in the woodwinds will correspond with the bowing slurs in the strings, and certain composers use this approach more or less consistently. Certainly a general unity of effect is desirable; for example, a sharply *marcato* passage would undoubtedly call for separate bows in the strings along with separate tonguings in the woodwinds. But there are many cases in which the actual slurrings in the two sections will not necessarily be the same. Sometimes, for instance, several measures of a wind part will be slurred together, whereas the strings will need to change bow a good many times within the course of these measures.

In double-tonguing the player interrupts the air stream by rapidly alternating the letters T and K with his tongue:

Ex. 9

In triple-tonguing the pattern is TKTTKT, etc. (or TTKTTK), which is suited to music involving triplet figures. Both types of tonguing are useful in articulating passages which are so fast that single-tonguing would be impractical. Both are easy and effective on the flute but impractical on the clarinet and bassoon. Although most orchestration books speak of them as being out of the question for the oboe as well, some skilled oboists are able to achieve them.

Flutter-tonguing (German: *Flatterzunge*) comes rather under the heading of special effects. To produce it the player executes a rapid roll with his tongue. The result is a kind of eerie whir which may be applied either to sustained tones or to melodic lines. Strauss and Stravinsky, in particular, are fond of using it for very rapid scale passages. The indication is usually the same as that for unmeasured tremolos in the strings—three lines through the stem—plus the word "flutter-tongue" written in. Sometimes, especially in very fast passages, the indication "flutter-tongue" alone suffices. The effect is well suited to the flute and piccolo, possible (though less easily produced and rarely used) on the clarinet, and impossible on the oboe.

There are two matters involving attack and release in wind instruments that need to be mentioned. The first is the *fp* or *sf p* effect, in which the tone is started with a strong attack and then reduced in volume immediately. After that, it may be sustained at a constant dynamic level or allowed to diminish even more (*fp, diminuendo*) or made to increase in volume (*fp, crescendo*). In any case, the *fp* marking indicates an effect rather than a particular degree of volume and may be used at any dynamic level, from very soft to very loud. This device is of course not the exclusive property of the woodwind and brass sections, for the strings and the percussion make frequent use of it.

The other matter is a point of notation which arises constantly in orchestral scoring. Whereas in piano and vocal music sustained tones followed by a rest are usually written ♩ ▬ or ♩. ❳ or ○ | ▬ , etc., a more usual plan in the orchestra is to write ♩ ♪❼ ❳ or ♩. ♪❼ or ○ ⏐♪❼❳ ▬ , the sustained tone being tied into the beginning of the next beat. The reason is this: if the first notation is used, players tend to differ as to the exact point at which they release the note (since it is difficult to cut off the sound on the last fraction of a beat), and a "ragged" effect is likely to result when a group is involved. The second notation gives an easier and more definite cut-off point and consequently leads to a cleaner, more unified release. Of course there are cases where, for harmonic or other reasons, it would be inappropriate to tie the notes into the next beat; but for the most part this system is preferable, not only in woodwind writing but in the strings, brass, and percussion as well.

Muting possibilities in the woodwinds are few and seldom used. As has long since been pointed out, it would be difficult to devise a flute mute that would not strangle the player. The clarinet can reduce its tone to the merest whisper anyway and consequently has no need for a mute. With the oboe it is possible to achieve a muted

effect (chiefly on the notes ⬚) by inserting a chamois or cloth into the bell. However, this system has a tendency to throw certain notes out of tune. An example of muted oboes can be found in the closing measures of Stravinsky's *Petrouchka*. Muting of the bassoon can be accomplished in the same fashion or with an actual mute, and although this effect is never called for specifically in scores, some bassoonists employ a mute in very soft passages to reduce the volume of tone in the lower register of the instrument, especially

between ⬚ and ⬚ . One disadvantage of this arrangement is that it makes the bottom B♭ unplayable.

Scoring for Woodwinds in Pairs

The same chorale excerpt used earlier for examples of string scoring has been selected for purposes of illustration here:

Ex. 10. *Jesu, meine Freude*

BACH

We are going to confine ourselves, at first, to a woodwind section consisting of two flutes, two oboes, two clarinets, and two bassoons. First of all, let us examine the ranges of the voices and see what instruments could take them (ruling out for the moment the possibility of transposing the excerpt). The bass could be taken only by the bassoon, since that voice goes too low for any of the other instruments.

The tenor could be taken by the bassoon or the clarinet (the latter in its dark *chalumeau* register).   The alto, with its B at the end, is too low for most flutes, and even if we were sure of having a flute with the low B on it, that register of the instrument is so weak that good balance would be very hard to achieve.   Although the alto is within the range of the oboe, the oboe's low B tends to be a bit coarse in quality; consequently the clarinet would be a better choice for that voice.   The soprano could be taken by flute, oboe, or clarinet, though it would be relatively weak on flute and rather "gray" on clarinet. Here are some possible scorings, then:

Ex. 11

Versions (a) and (b) would sound exactly alike.   In (b) clarinets in A have been used instead of B♭ clarinets, and the bassoons have been written in the tenor clef.

Versions (c) and (d) differ from the preceding ones in that the top voice, in the oboe, will stand out sharply from the other voices below. Any separate color on a part will tend to produce that result, but the distinctive oboe tone has a particular way of asserting itself.

In version (e) two flutes are used on the melody to give more body in the weak lower register of the instrument and to bring about better balance.

Version (f) has been included as an example of what *not* to do. The oboe would outweigh the flute in that register and would be too prominent in character for an inner voice. The doubtful quality of the low B has already been mentioned.

Various slurrings have been used here for purposes of illustration.

Assuming that there is no reason why we must stick to the original key, transposition will give us a good many new possibilities. By placing certain of the instruments higher in their range, we can arrive at better resonance and blend:

Ex. 12

One undesirable feature of (a) and some of the other versions in Example 12 is the fact that the oboes play the interval of a 4th in a sustained chord (at the end). This is not a good plan, as a rule, because the incisive oboe color accentuates the "bareness" of the 4th.

Sixths or 3rds sound much better. But if we are to give the two top voices to the oboes here, there seems to be no way of avoiding the 4th—except by changing the original voice-leading in the cadence and having the second oboe go from F♯ up to G (instead of down to D), thus omitting the 5th of the chord.

The objections that applied to version (f) in Example 11 do not apply to (c) in Example 12 because the oboe is in a sweeter, thinner register and because the flute is better able to assert itself in this higher version. Even so, the flute has been marked one degree louder than the other instruments to make doubly sure that it comes out clearly on the melody.

Version (d) in Example 12 involves the use of mixed colors (flute plus oboe) on the two top parts, whereas we have used mostly pure colors previously. Notice that 2 clarinets and 2 bassoons are indicated here, for the sake of proper balance. It would have been possible to mix clarinet and bassoon colors on the tenor and bass parts, also.

So far we have used only the original four-voice structure, with no octave doublings. Doublings of the soprano—or of all three upper voices—an octave higher will allow the flutes and clarinets to play in a much brighter, more telling register:

Ex. 13

(c)

In Example 13 (a) the melody is doubled an octave higher in the flutes, while the first oboe doubles the melody in unison with the first clarinet. In (b) the alto and tenor are both doubled an octave higher (in the clarinets) in addition to the melody an octave higher in the flutes. In (c) the melody, alto, and tenor are all doubled an octave higher, and the melody is doubled an octave lower in the bassoon. Remember that not all pieces of music lend themselves to a doubling of the melody an octave below the original pitch. In some cases the result would be too muddy.

Notice that the clarinets frequently play above the oboes, in terms of pitch, even though they are listed below them on the page. Actually, the strongest register of the oboe is roughly ⟨♪⟩ , while the clarinet's brightest and most solid octave is ⟨♪⟩ .

Therefore, when brilliance and power are called for, it is far better to place the clarinets higher than the oboes.

SCORING FOR A LARGE WOODWIND SECTION

Following are three possible ways of scoring the same chorale excerpt for a woodwind section that includes piccolo, English horn, bass clarinet, and contra bassoon in addition to woodwinds in pairs. Three different gradations of coloring have been aimed at: brilliant, medium, and dark. In Chapter X, more will be said about color possibilities as well as about woodwind doublings and various "voicings" in chords scored for wind instruments.

Ex. 14

Notice that in Example 14 (b) clarinets in A have been chosen in order to avoid a key signature of six sharps (or six flats) for the B♭ clarinet. Inasmuch as the only bass clarinet in current use is one pitched in B♭, we are forced to write its part in either six sharps or the enharmonic equivalent of six flats. The latter key has been chosen here as being a bit less awkward for a B♭ instrument.

In the dark version (c) the piccolo has been given rests. Obviously the brilliance of its upper register is not wanted here, and it is so weak and breathy in its bottom octave that in this case there is no point in writing for it there.

Having learned in harmony courses that parallel 5ths are generally unacceptable in Bach style, students may wonder about the 5ths that occur in Ex. 14(c) on the second and third beats of the clarinet part. (They also occur in certain preceding versions but are not as easily seen there.) Actually, these are not parallel 5ths of the *verboten* variety at all; they are merely an inversion of the parallel 4ths in the original, brought about by the doubling of the melody an octave below the original pitch. Since they are not a part of the basic four-voice harmonization, there is not the slightest objection to them.

Suggested Assignments

A. Know:
   (1) Instruments involved in the "average" woodwind section and in the "large" woodwind section.
   (2) Arrangement of the woodwinds on the page—order and grouping.
   (3) Indications for showing whether the first or second of each pair is to play or whether both are to play.
   (4) Indications for slurring, tonguing, and phrasing.
   (5) Principles of balance in the woodwind section.
   (6) Ways of achieving brilliant or darker coloring in woodwind scoring.

B. The following are suitable as exercises in scoring for woodwinds:
   (1) Bach, any of the chorales. Select a short phrase from one of these and score it: (a) in three different ways for woodwinds in pairs, using no octave doublings; (b) in two different ways for large woodwind section, using octave doublings.
   (2) Beethoven, Sonata Op. 2, No. 1, 3rd movt. (*Menuetto*). Omit trio.
   (3) Beethoven, Sonata Op. 2, No. 2 (*Scherzo*). Omit trio.
   (4) Beethoven, Sonata Op. 7, 3rd movt. (*Allegro*). Omit trio.
   (5) Beethoven, Sonata in B♭, Op. 106, 2nd movt. (*Scherzo*) to key change.
   (6) Chopin, Prelude in A major (No. 7 of 24 Preludes).
   (7) MacDowell, *From Uncle Remus* (from *Woodland Sketches*).

(8) Mussorgsky, *Tuileries—Children Quarreling at Play* from *Pictures from an Exhibition*.

(9) Mussorgsky, *Promenade* (version preceding *Ballet of the Chickens in their Shells*) from *Pictures from an Exhibition*.

(10) Debussy, *The Little Shepherd* (No. 5 from *The Children's Corner*).

(11) Mendelssohn, *Song without Words* No. 41 (A major) (for large woodwind section).

SUGGESTED LISTENING

WOODWINDS

Mozart, Divertimenti and Serenades for woodwinds.

Beethoven, Violin Concerto, 1st 9 measures.

Mendelssohn, *Scherzo* from *Midsummer Night's Dream* music, beginning and other portions.

Tchaikovsky, Fourth Symphony, 3rd movt., *Meno mosso* section (middle).

Rimsky-Korsakoff, *Russian Easter,* opening measures (rare unison doubling of all woodwinds).

Wagner, Overture to *Die Meistersinger,* measures 122–134 (Eb major, *Im mässigen Hauptzeitmass*).

Strauss, *Don Quixote,* Variation I (imitation of rural band).

Mussorgsky-Ravel, *Pictures from an Exhibition, Promenade* preceding Part II (*The Old Castle*); Part III (*Tuileries*); *Promenade* preceding Part V; Part V (*Ballet of the Chickens in their Shells*).

Stravinsky, *Symphony of Psalms,* Fugue, beginning; *The Rite of Spring,* beginning; *Petrouchka,* number 13 (page 22 in Kalmus edition) and following.

Bartók, Concerto for Orchestra, Part V (*Finale*) measures 148–175 (*fughetta* beginning with bassoon solo).

Britten, *The Young Person's Guide to the Orchestra,* Theme B, also fugue (at end) up to E.

Chapter VII

THE HORN

Italian: Corno	French: Cor	German: Horn
Corni	Cors	Hörner

Ex. 1

The name "French horn" is seldom used by musicians. The instrument is referred to simply as "the horn," and that name is sufficient even in scores. Occasionally in French scores one finds the term *cor à pistons,* meaning "valve horn" as opposed to the old natural horn without valves; but that direction is unnecessary nowadays, since all horns in current use are valve horns.

In order to understand the workings of the horn, we must know something about the basic principles on which brass instruments operate. Whereas most of the woodwinds make use of a reed, brass instruments do not, but instead involve a mouthpiece and an air column vibrating sympathetically with the player's lips. Fractional vibrations of the air column produce overtones, and a certain number of these may be made to sound by proper use of the breath and lips. The fundamental or generating tone itself is either very difficult or unobtainable on most brass instruments. If the length of tubing is altered by means of valves (or a slide, in the case of the trombone), a new set of overtones results. For purposes of initial tuning, each brass instrument is equipped with a "tuning slide" which enables the player to vary the basic tube-length of the instrument somewhat.

Although in construction and technique of performance the horn is clearly a brass instrument, its tone is capable of blending almost

---

[1] For an explanation of the transposition in the case of horns in other keys, and for comments on the old system of notation in the bass clef, see text.

Studio Gilmore, Austin, Texas

French Horn

equally well with either woodwind or brass, and it is very often used as if it were a member of the woodwind family. Its bore, incidentally, is predominantly conical in shape.

Being essentially hunting horns and valveless, the horns of Haydn's and Mozart's day could play only the notes of one harmonic series at a time, plus a few rather uncertain intermediary tones made possible by the insertion of the hand in the bell of the horn and/or by "lipping." Parts for the instrument were therefore extremely limited from a melodic standpoint, and chromatic passages were out of the question altogether. To cope with the problem of music in different keys, a system of "crooks" was in use, a crook being a piece of tubing which could be inserted into the tubing of the horn to alter the pitch of its fundamental tone and thus create a new harmonic series. The crook to be chosen was indicated by a direction at the beginning of the work or movement: "Horn in E♭" or "Horn in A," etc., as the case might be, and the part was invariably written in the key of C. The (written) notes of the harmonic series usable on the horn were:

Ex. 2

(difficult)

"Out of tune" notes (according to our system of tuning) are shown in black. The F, for example, was really something between an F and an F♯ and could be humored so as to produce either note. Of course the actual sound of the horn's notes depended on the crook being used. Following is a table to show how the instrument sounded when crooked in various keys:

Horn in	Sounding
B♭-alto	a major 2nd lower than written
A	a minor 3rd lower than written
G	a perfect 4th lower than written
F	a perfect 5th lower than written
E	a minor 6th lower than written
E♭	a major 6th lower than written
D	a minor 7th lower than written
C	an octave lower than written
B♭-basso	a major 9th lower than written

("Alto" and "basso" are used here to mean "high" and "low" respectively.)

According to Forsyth, horns in C-alto, A♭-alto, D♭, B-basso, and A-basso "existed as workshop curiosities only." However, the fact that parts for certain of these horns appear in orchestral literature would seem to indicate that they were actually used, although it is possible that the parts were played on horns crooked in other keys, the player transposing the part. Apparently Horn in F♯ was used only once, by Haydn in his *Farewell* Symphony.

Here is an excerpt from a horn part of the classical period:

Ex. 3. Sixth Symphony

(a)

HAYDN

which will sound:

(b)

Another characteristic passage for natural horn is shown next:

Ex. 4. Overture to *Der Freischütz*

C. M. VON WEBER

During the classical period one pair of horns was generally used when the music was in major. But if the music was in minor, the practice was to use two pairs of horns, one pair pitched in the "home" key, the other pair in the key of the relative major. By means of this arrangement, the second pair of horns took care of certain important notes that were not available as members of the harmonic series in the home key. Later on, the device of using two pairs of horns pitched in different keys was sometimes employed even in major keys to provide richer possibilities in writing for the horns and to allow for modulations.

We are told that in the day of the natural horn the player kept an assortment of crooks hanging on his arm in order to be prepared for necessary changes! Fortunately for player, composer, and audience, the introduction of valves revolutionized the technique of horn playing and the type of part that could be written for the instrument. Instead of having only one harmonic series at a time to work with, the horn now boasted seven different series (the results of various combinations of the three valves), and a complete chromatic scale was available for the first time. As a result, the horn achieved the status of a real melodic instrument. Although the invention of valves occurred in 1813, the valve horn did not come into general use until about the middle of the century, and even then the natural horn continued to be used with it for many years.

Horn in F seems to have proven the most satisfactory of the many possibilities once used, and it has survived as the one horn in general use today. (In band music, Eb horn is still used much of the time, but arrangers for symphonic band seem more and more disposed to write for F horn, and players often use the F horn even when the part is written for Eb horn.) Parts written originally for the natural horn are played today on the valve horn in F. This means that the player must transpose as he goes—unless, of course, the original part was for horn crooked in F.

It should be pointed out that many of our finest symphony players use the so-called "double horn," which has two sets of tubing, one in F and one in (high) Bb; a lever enables the player to switch instantaneously from one to the other. Because of its shorter tubing, the Bb horn (that is, the Bb part of the double horn) allows for greater facility. But its use is entirely optional with the player, and the transposition problems involved in switching to Bb horn are his concern; the part is always written as if for F horn—a perfect 5th higher than the sounds desired. Although the Bb horn is capable of producing certain very low pedal tones not available on the F horn, these have little practical value.

Traditionally, the horns are written without key signature, sharps and flats being written in wherever necessary. However, it is possible nowadays to use a key signature, and that plan would seem to be a sensible one in scoring music of a diatonic nature. Enharmonic notation (for example, Bb instead of A♯) is not uncommon in horn parts

There is a curious tradition that formerly applied to the writing of horns in bass clef: when notated in bass clef, horn in F was written a perfect 4th lower than the sound desired instead of a 5th higher.[2] Fortunately, this apparently pointless custom seems to be dying a natural death, and the newer practice today is to write horn in F a 5th higher than the sounds even when it is notated in bass clef. Examples of the two systems of notation follow:

Ex. 5

| Actual sound desired | Old notation | New notation |

Because players have become used to the old system, it is wise to include a note in scores and parts, whenever the new system is used, to the effect that notes in bass clef are intended to sound a 5th lower. If all this seems illogical and confusing (and it is both), there may be some consolation in the fact that bass clef need seldom be used for horns. Their parts should be written in treble clef wherever possible, even if several leger lines below the staff are involved; bass clef is really needed only for extremely low tones.

In its bottom register, say up to the written note [♪] the horn is inclined to be a bit "fuzzy" in tone, somewhat lacking in focus, and often doubtful in intonation. This register is useful chiefly for sustained tones; melodic passages at this level are generally awkward and ineffective. From [♪] up to about [♪] (written), the tone is considerably brighter. This is the middle and most characteristic register, in which the horn does the greatest part of its playing. From [♪] to the top [♪] the notes become progressively more brilliant. Just as the high notes of a tenor voice sound much higher than they would if sung at the same pitch by a soprano, the top notes of the horn give the impression of being extremely high

---

[2] The same principle governed the bass-clef notation of horns in keys other than F. Horn in E♭ was written a minor 3rd lower than the sounds instead of a major 6th higher; horn in D was written a major 2nd lower instead of a minor 7th higher; and so on. In each case, the interval involved in the transposition in bass clef was the inversion of the interval that figured in the normal transposition in treble clef.

because the player must strain somewhat to get them. Notes above

written  are difficult to produce, and they should be "led

up to;" that is, the player should not be asked to attack them without preparation. Also, they are almost impossible to play softly. Consequently it is better not to write for the horn in this register unless it is meant to be heard prominently.

There is a certain "division of labor" among the four horns which are commonly used in the orchestra today. In order to understand this point we must first become acquainted with the traditional arrangement of the horns in harmonic passages. Horns I and II are normally written on one staff, horns III and IV on the staff below, and one might naturally suppose that in writing a four-note chord for horns, the two highest notes would be given to horns I and II and the two bottom notes to horns III and IV. But this is where tradition steps in and dictates a different procedure: the horns are written so as to interlock on paper; that is, horns I and III take the high notes, horns II and IV the low notes. For example, if we were to score an F major

triad  for four F horns, it would look like this:

Ex. 6

Even when only the first three horns are playing, horn III is generally placed between horns I and II (in a chord).

Because the first-horn and third-horn players are accustomed to taking the higher notes, they have become specialists in this upper register; likewise, the second-horn and fourth-horn players are especially adept at taking lower pitches. Consequently, we might divide the general range given at the beginning of this chapter into two "usual" ranges, one for each pair of horns:

Ex. 7

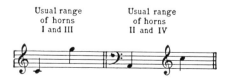

The chief point here is that a tight, tense "lip" is required for high pitches, while lower notes call for a much looser embouchure; there is therefore a definite advantage in being able to concentrate on one general type of embouchure instead of having to switch constantly from one kind to another. Of course there is a "middle ground" (roughly from written) in which all the horns can play equally comfortably. And it must not be inferred from this talk of specialization that each pair of horns is never asked to exceed its own "usual" range. Particularly in passages where all four horns play in unison, the second and fourth are often taken quite high along with the first and third, and it is possible, though rare, for the first or third horn to play even in the very low register.

The horn is not by nature a particularly agile instrument. Very fast running passages and quick leaps are simply not in its province (except, with limitations, in virtuoso solo work). And because the player must "hear" each note in his mind's ear before playing it, the melodic lines written for the instrument should be as smooth as possible and should avoid awkward leaps. Also, there should be sufficient rests. Since the horn is undoubtedly one of the most demanding and difficult of all orchestral instruments, scoring for it must be approached with special care and understanding.

Horns may be employed in various ways in the orchestra. The most important of these are:

(1) *On harmony parts.*

In its middle register, the horn tone is ideal for background, because it can be made unobtrusive without losing in warmth or body. Usually these harmony parts are sustained, although sometimes they consist of repeated notes or short figures repeated. Incidentally, repeated notes on the horn do not sound as sharply articulated as do repeated notes on some other instruments. The effect is more that of a "pulsation" on the pitch involved. A typical example of the horns in a harmonic role is given here. (The melodic line in the violins has been included in order to show how the harmony parts fit into the general musical scheme. Of course there are many other instruments playing.)

Ex. 8. Symphony in D minor

FRANCK

Simply because the horns can handle this sort of part so successfully, there is a temptation to use them constantly in this way, with a resulting monotony of color and general effect. It is largely this constant use of the horns on middle register harmony parts that gives orchestral music of the romantic period its characteristic plushy richness.

(2) *In a solo capacity.*

The horn is excellent as a solo instrument. It can be tender or heroic, as the music demands, and it possesses a wonderful nobility and breadth of tone all its own.

Ex. 9

(a) Third Symphony

BRAHMS

(b) Fifth Symphony

TCHAIKOVSKY

(c) *Siegfried*

WAGNER

(d) *Till Eulenspiegel*

1st Hrn.
in F

(3) *Two or more horns in unison on a melodic line.*

Horns are frequently doubled on a part, sometimes for purposes of volume or balance, occasionally to give a greater degree of security in difficult passages. All four horns playing in unison, *f* or *ff*, give an especially robust, heroic sound.

Ex. 10

(a) Symphony in E minor (*New World*)

DVOŘÁK

Hrns.
III & IV
in C

(b) *Don Juan*

STRAUSS

4 Hrns.
in F

(c) First Symphony

HANSON

4 Hrns.
in F

Copyright, 1929, by Howard Hanson.

In cases where horns I and III play one melodic line and horns II and IV another for considerable length of time, it may be easier to write I and III on the upper staff and II and IV on the lower, with an "a 2" indication on each staff. That way, only two melodic lines instead of four need be written for the horns.

The chamber orchestra usually includes one horn; the "small" orchestra, one or two. While four is the standard number written for today, it is possible, of course, to use only three if that number seems

best fitted to the demands of the music in question. In most symphony orchestras one can see five horn players on the stage. This
does not mean that there are five separate horn parts. The extra player
is an "assistant first horn" player; that is, he sits beside the first horn
player and doubles the first horn part at times, for added security or
volume; or he may play some of the part by himself, allowing the
first-horn player to "save himself" for important solo passages to
follow. Certain works are actually scored for more than the standard
four horns. Stravinsky writes for eight horns in *The Rite of Spring,*
where the proportions of all sections are unusually large; and the
orchestra used by Wagner in the *Ring* includes eight horns (four of
these alternating with Wagner tubas).

It might be well to include a word about Wagner's horn notation,
for it is likely to be confusing—and understandably so. The horn
parts are intended to be played on valve horns, yet they are written as
if for a succession of natural horns pitched in different keys. For example, we may have a passage for horn in Eb, then a few measures
for horn in G, then a passage marked "Horn in F," and so on. It is
difficult to follow the logic of this strange system.

In most of the examples quoted above, the horn took the "theme"
or most important musical idea. But it can be equally effective on
subordinate countermelodies. Several horns in unison may even be
allotted to such a part if considerable volume and a broad, virile effect
are in order.

SPECIAL EFFECTS

The tone quality of the horn is controlled chiefly by the position
of the player's hand in the bell of the instrument. Normally, the hand
is inserted only part way into the bell and cupped. But there are
special effects which demand a slightly different technique. Muting,
for example, may be achieved by inserting the hand a little farther
into the bell. Or an actual mute made of metal, wood, or cardboard
may be used. Players seem to differ in their preference for one or
the other of these methods; some employ both at different times—the
hand method for short muted passages, a mute for longer passages.
The choice depends partly on the instrument being used. In any
case, this question need not be settled by the orchestrator. All he
needs to do is to include the direction *"con sordino"* or "mute" at the

appropriate spot, and the player will produce the muted effect in whichever way he prefers. As with the strings, at least a measure or two in moderate time should be allowed for putting on or taking off mutes. (Of course with the hand-muting method the change from open to muted sound or *vice versa* can be made instantaneously.) The muted effect is indicated in French by *"sourdine"* and in German by *"mit Dämpfer"* or *"gedämpft."* When a return to the unmuted tone is wanted, the direction is *"senza sordino"* or "open" (*"ouvert"* in French, *"offen"* in German). An "O" above the note is sometimes used as a symbol for "open."

Even if it were possible to describe tone color accurately in words, it would be difficult to give a description of the muted horn that would apply to all players and all instruments. The basic tone quality of the individual instrument, the style and technique of playing used, and the player's conception of how a muted tone should sound all enter in. But as a general comment it can be said that muting cuts down the volume of sound and veils the tone slightly. Below a certain point,

say a written 🎼 , muted notes are difficult, although a skilled

player can mute as low as 🎼 .

An excellent example of muted horns can be found in the closing measures of Debussy's *Prelude to The Afternoon of a Faun.*

"Stopped" notes on the horn are produced by inserting the hand (or a mute) so far into the bell that the opening in it is almost completely blocked, the tones being "forced" out. The resulting sound is curiously nasal and metallic, with a sharp edge to it. It is especially effective for single notes, played *"fp."* In both muting and stopping, the volume is reduced and (unless a non-transposing mute is used) the pitch is altered to such an extent that the player must employ fingerings which differ from those used for the corresponding open tones. But he will make this adjustment automatically, and it need not concern the arranger; stopped tones are notated in the same way as open tones, as far as pitch is concerned. There are two methods for indicating the stopped effect, either or both of which may be used: (1) The French word *bouché* (or simply "stopped" in English) is written in. The German equivalent is *gestopft;* the Italian, *chiuso.* (2) A small cross is placed above each note to be played stopped. In the following example, both indications are present.

Ex. 11. *Capriccio Espagnol*

RIMSKY-KORSAKOFF

Another much-used direction in horn writing is the French word *cuivré,* meaning "brassy." The brassy quality is attained chiefly by increased tension of the lips and is possible in connection with open, muted, or stopped notes. *Bouché-cuivré,* a composite term often encountered, calls for a tone that is both stopped and brassy. Where only a suggestion of brassiness is wanted, Debussy marks the passage *"cuivrez légèrement"* (literally translated, "brass lightly").

"Bells in the air" (*pavillons en l'air* in French; *Schalltrichter auf* in German) is a rarely used effect for which the horn is turned with the bell pointing upward, so that the sound is projected outward toward the audience more directly than in the normal playing position. Inasmuch as the hand cannot be used in the bell here, the tone is completely open and lacking in any subtlety of coloring. "Bells in the air" is therefore appropriate only for loud, hearty passages in which refinement of tone is not called for.

The horn has an uncanny ability to sound as if it were being played a great distance away. When that effect is wanted, the part should be marked *pp* or even *ppp,* and the word *lontano* ("distant" in Italian) may be added. To achieve this effect, some players employ a partly muted tone; others mute completely; while still others play "open" but extremely softly.

One of the most successful sounds available on the horn is the *fp* effect mentioned earlier. Used with a stopped tone it has a biting, almost snarling quality, while in open horn it is dramatic and arresting.

Ex. 12

(a) Fifth Symphony

BEETHOVEN

(b) Symphony in B minor (*Unfinished*)

For the sake of completeness, it might be well to mention the horn's ability to play glissandos involving certain notes. But since this is a rather grotesque and extremely rare device, a detailed account of it is not included here. One example may help to give some idea of the effect and the notation for it:

Ex. 13. *The Rite of Spring*

SUGGESTED ASSIGNMENTS

A. Know:
   (1) The extreme possible range of the horn and the usual ranges of horns I and III and horns II and IV.
   (2) Transposition (including the old system of notation in the bass clef).
   (3) Differences between the old "natural horn" and the modern valve horn, both as to their operation and the type of part written.
   (4) The color and weight of the horn in various registers.
   (5) The particular abilities and limitations of the horn.
   (6) Special effects on the horn and foreign names for them.

B. Find five examples of parts for horns in keys other than F and rewrite them for F horn (a few measures will suffice for each example). Write the original version above and the rewritten version on a staff below it.

C. Notate the melody on page 98 for: (1) horn in F; (2) horn in Eb; (3) horn in C; (4) horn in E; (5) horn in D; (6) horn in Bb basso. Omit the trill on the next to the last note.

SUGGESTED LISTENING

HORNS [3]

Mozart, Symphony No. 40 (K. 550), 3rd movt., Trio.
Beethoven, Third Symphony, 3rd movt. (*Scherzo*), Trio.
Mendelssohn, Nocturne from *Midsummer Night's Dream* music, beginning.
Brahms, Bb major Piano Concerto, beginning; First Symphony, last movt., beginning of *Più Andante* section; Third Symphony, 3rd movt., measures

---

[3] Examples of the horns in conjunction with the rest of the brass section are included in the *Suggested Listening* at the end of Chapter IX.

40–52 and 98–110; Fourth Symphony, 2nd movt., beginning and many other passages.

Tchaikovsky, Fifth Symphony, 2nd movt., beginning.

Rimsky-Korsakoff, *Capriccio Espagnol*, section II (*Variazioni*), beginning.

Dvořák, Fifth Symphony (*New World*), 1st movt., beginning of *Allegro molto* following introduction; last movt., 11 bars after figure 6, also numerous other passages.

Strauss, *Don Juan*, measure 311; *Till Eulenspiegel*, measure 6; Waltzes from *Der Rosenkavalier*, especially beginning.

Ravel, *Pavane pour une Infante Défunte*, beginning.

Shostakovitch, Fifth Symphony, 2nd movt., at figures 54, 56, 70, and 72.

Hanson, First Symphony, 2nd and 3rd movts. in particular.

Britten, *Serenade for Tenor, Horn and Strings*, Op. 31; *The Young Person's Guide to the Orchestra*, Variation J.

Instruments of the Orchestra (Victor, 20523 A).

Chapter VIII

THE TRUMPET, TROMBONE, AND TUBA

THE TRUMPET

Italian: Tromba   French: Trompette   German: Trompete
      Trombe   Trompettes   Trompeten

Ex. 1

In B♭, sounding
a major 2nd lower
In C, sounding
as written[1]

The history of the trumpet parallels that of the horn in a good many respects. For a long time trumpets, like horns, were valveless and could play only the notes of one harmonic series at a time. Parts for them were written as if in C, and crooks of varying lengths were used to make them sound in the desired key. An indication at the beginning of the score ("Trumpets in E♭" or "Trumpets in F," etc.) told the player which crook to use. The introduction of valves performed the same service for trumpets as it did for horns; that is, gave them a complete chromatic compass and enabled them to play a very different and much more interesting sort of part.

But the transition from the old natural trumpet to the valve trumpet was not simply a matter of the addition of valves. Changes in the length and bore of the instrument took place, with the result that the modern trumpet is a great deal smaller than its ancestor, has a brighter and lighter tone quality, and is more flexible. As Forsyth puts it, "It is not merely that the instrument has become chromatic. It has also become, except in name, a different instrument."

Like the natural horn, the natural trumpet had a usable harmonic series of these (written) notes:

---

[1] Transpositions for trumpets in other keys are discussed in the text.

130

Ex. 2

*Found occasionally in scores of the classical period but not practical on the modern trumpet.

But, unlike the natural horn, it could not fill in certain intermediate tones by the use of the hand in the bell and was therefore even more limited than the natural horn in the type of part it could play. In Beethoven's day the following "crookings" were possible:

	Trumpet in	Sounding
Sounding higher than written	F	a perfect 4th higher than written
	E	a major 3rd higher than written
	Eb	a minor 3rd higher than written
	D	a major 2nd higher than written
	C	as written
Sounding lower than written	Bb	a major 2nd lower than written
	A	a minor 3rd lower than written

Today, parts are written either for trumpet in Bb or trumpet in C. It should also be mentioned that the slide on the Bb trumpet can be adjusted so as to pitch the instrument in A. However, that adjustment brings about serious intonation problems; consequently, parts for A trumpet are seldom employed nowadays. Although not so widely used as the Bb trumpet, the C trumpet seems to find favor with the contemporary composers, many of whom write for it entirely. It is a bit more brilliant and facile than the Bb instrument; but, on the debit side, its tone is generally not quite so rich. Another disadvantage is that many players own only a Bb trumpet and must therefore transpose in order to play C parts. In school orchestras, the Bb instrument is invariably used.

The modern trumpet, in its open form, has a harmonic series an octave higher than that shown for the natural trumpet in Example 2. The other series available by means of valve combinations have as their bottom playable notes the six semi-tones below middle C, respectively. In each series, the seventh partial (sixth overtone) is flat and is normally avoided.

Studio Gilmore, Austin, Texas

Cornet

Trumpet

From about (♪ to ♫) is the trumpet's most-used register.
Notes below the C tend to be a little less penetrating, while those above
the F are more difficult to produce softly and are best "led up to."
Although high C is given as the top note possible, symphonic trumpet
parts do go as high as D or E on rare occasions; but the part never
stays that high. Even so, such passages are apt to be a bit uncom-
fortable for everyone concerned.

At this point, readers who have had some experience with trumpet
playing in the dance orchestra are sure to object that the upper limit
given here for the trumpet is much too conservative. It is perfectly
true that some dance band trumpeters go up to (♪♯♫) or even
higher. But they usually achieve these very high notes only at the
expense of tone quality; the "squealy" shrillness that goes with this
pitch level would hardly be appropriate in the symphony orchestra.
Furthermore, a good many of these players use small shallow-cup
mouthpieces to produce their fantastically high trumpet work, a
method not acceptable to symphonic players.

In Bach's day, trumpet parts commonly lay in the extreme upper
register of the instrument (a large trumpet in D). Such parts are
unreasonably high for the modern Bb and C trumpets and are usually
played today on a small trumpet, most often the one in D.

Obviously the trumpet is a much more agile and quick-speaking
instrument than the horn. It can manage runs and arpeggios and
skips as long as they are not extremely fast, but such passages should
not be too extended or too frequent. Its use in fanfares is such a
familiar and natural one as scarcely to require comment. (See the
Beethoven and Strauss excerpts in Example 3.) Rapid repeated notes
and double-tonguing and triple-tonguing are particularly well suited
to the character of the instrument; even flutter-tonguing is possible.
Along with the trombone, the trumpet is capable of tremendous volume
and has extraordinary powers of crescendo.

As to tone color, the trumpet lacks the noble warmth of the horn
but has, instead, a bright, incisive quality that is especially effective
in crisp, assertive passages. While it can also play more lyrical melodies, there is a certain danger involved: if the melody is strongly

romantic in feeling, the trumpet may sound a little "over-ripe," a little too reminiscent of the "Hearts and Flowers" type of cornet solo.

Incidentally, the trumpet and cornet must not be thought of as being one and the same instrument. The cornet, which is seldom employed in symphonic music today, is shorter and of slightly different shape (roughly two thirds conical and one third cylindrical, whereas these proportions are approximately reversed on the trumpet). Also, the cornet tone is a bit mellower and more romantically colored than the trumpet tone. Some French scores contain parts for cornets, but these parts are often played on trumpets. Cornets, like trumpets, may be pitched in B♭ or (rarely) C; the B♭ instrument is standard in band work. Everything possible on the trumpet is possible on the cornet, and the two instruments have the same range.

Muting is a frequent and effective device in orchestral trumpet writing—effective as long as it is not used too often or for too long at a time. All that was said about muting in connection with the horn applies here, except, of course, that the trumpet cannot be muted with the hand as the horn can, but must use an actual mute. To the symphony trumpet player, "mute" means straight mute unless another special kind is indicated; so far the many other types used in the dance orchestra have been little exploited in serious symphonic music,[2] though the Harmon mute is occasionally called for. The straight mute produces a cutting, nasal quality and reduces the volume of tone somewhat. The trumpet has no actual equivalents of the horn's *bouché* and *cuivré* effects.

EXAMPLES

Ex. 3

(a) *Leonore* Overture No. 3

BEETHOVEN

---

[2] Among these other types are the cup mute, the "wah-wah" version of the Harmon mute, and the Solotone mute. Straight mutes may be made of wood or fiber, each type producing a somewhat different sound. There is also the possibility, usable with either open or muted trumpet, of pointing the bell of the instrument into a hat or some similarly shaped object to achieve a more subdued tone. The direction is simply "hat." Still another device is the use of a "plunger," which greatly reduces the volume of tone.

(b) *Scheherazade*

RIMSKY-KORSAKOFF

(c) *Ein Heldenleben*

STRAUSS

(d) Fifth Symphony

SIBELIUS

(e) *Schelomo*

BLOCH

THE TENOR TROMBONE

Italian: Trombone   French: Trombone   German: Posaune
        Tromboni   Trombones   Posaunen

Ex. 4

As a rule, instruments pitched in keys other than C are transposing instruments. Not so with the tenor trombone; although built basically around the harmonic series of Bb, it sounds as written. It may be notated in either bass or tenor clef, the latter being commonly chosen for higher passages so as to avoid the use of too many leger lines. (In music for school orchestra, however, the bass clef is used exclusively for the trombone parts.) The alto clef, found in some older scores, is almost never employed for the trombone nowadays. It is a hang-over from the days when there was an actual "alto trombone."

The mechanism of the instrument differs radically from those of the horn and trumpet in that it includes no valves.[3] Instead, the length of tubing is varied by means of the *slide*. Seven different positions of the slide are possible, each one producing a different harmonic series. The seven fundamentals or generating tones of these series are the following:

Ex. 5

Although the first three of these "pedal tones" are just playable, their quality is so poor that they are almost never used. The Bb comes the closest to being acceptable. For all practical purposes, the range starts with the first overtone of the lowest fundamental—that is, with . Adding to this the other playable overtones in that same series, we get the following complete list of notes available in this bottom position (known as seventh position):

---

[3] Valve trombones have been built and have had a considerable vogue abroad, notably in Italy; but they have never had any wide acceptance in the United States.

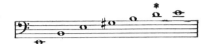

In sixth position the notes playable are:

And so on, up to first position, where additional overtones may be used to stretch the upper range a bit higher:

Ex. 8

By adding a B♮ and C♯ at the top of the second position, we get a complete chromatic scale up to the second F above middle C as a possible range. But the top E♭, E, and F are more difficult and are almost never used. The note is a safer upward limit for the practical range, and in actual practice trombone parts in the orchestra only rarely go that high.

In music for the trombone, it is not so much distance between notes as distance between positions that determines the technical difficulty of the part. A little reflection on the "position" principle will make it clear that certain notes can be taken in one of two or more different positions. For example, ⬛ can be taken in the first position (series on B♭) or the fourth position (series on G) or the seventh position (series on E), and the player can choose whichever position is easiest. With three choices, one of them is bound to be close to the position he is already playing in, and such cases should cause no difficulty. But certain notes, such as those shown next, can be taken in only one position:

Ex. 9

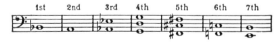

---

* The seventh partial (sixth overtone) in each position is slightly flat. However, it can be brought into tune by an adjustment of the slide, in all positions except the first. There the slide is already drawn up as far as it will go, and a raising of the flat pitch is therefore impossible

For the seventh position the slide is extended its full length; for first position it is drawn up as far as possible in the other direction. Therefore, very rapid or repeated changes from first position to seventh position (or *vice versa*) are awkward and are better avoided. Occasional changes of this sort, when not too fast, are acceptable. Although changes involving other distant positions—such as the second and sixth—are less difficult, frequent use of them in a rapid tempo naturally does not make for grateful trombone writing.

In order to illustrate what *not* to write for the trombone, we have devised the diabolically awkward passage shown next. (The numbers above the notes refer to the positions involved.) An actual performance of this by a trombonist will show, very graphically, why such changes as these are best avoided.

Ex. 10

It should be remembered that because the notes of the harmonic series lie closer together in the trombone's upper register, the whole problem of position becomes less acute there and the instrument therefore has a greater degree of agility in this register than it does in the lower portions of its compass.

The trombone's lowest register is dark and full. The low E tends to be slightly inferior in quality and is perhaps better avoided in any prominent passage. Other than that, the entire range up to an octave or so above middle C is solid and effective, the notes becoming progressively more brilliant toward the top.

A basic problem in trombone playing is the difficulty of achieving a completely legato effect when a change of slide is involved. If the player were to keep the air column vibrating continuously, he would produce not only the actual notes intended but a glissando between each two of them as the slide moved from one position to another. Consequently, he must stop the air column momentarily between notes. To give the effect of a legato connection under these circumstances would seem to be impossible, yet experienced trombonists succeed in doing it surprisingly well, especially at softer dynamic levels. The gap between notes is so slight as to be scarcely apparent to the ear. (Of course two notes in the same harmonic series, such as ♩ and ♩, require no change in the position of the slide and can therefore be played *legatissimo* by means of a "lip slur".) Granted that trombonists are adept at overcoming this difficulty, it is still doubtful whether the trombones would be chosen over other instruments to play a flowing melody in the orchestra. At least they are better suited to other types of parts.

In its most familiar role, the trombone is an instrument that excels at loud, heroic passages. But it can also play softly, either on the chief musical idea or as background; this side of its nature is too often forgotten. Rapid running passages and light, fanciful parts that skip around a great deal are obviously not well suited either to trombone technique or to trombone quality. However, the instrument can play rapid repeated notes or *short* figures that move quickly.

Muting on the trombone works just as it does on the trumpet, and the effect is relatively the same. Even though the mute cuts down the volume somewhat (in addition to altering the quality), the muted trombone can still hold its own in a *tutti*.

The glissando effect mentioned earlier is normally avoided; but there are times when it is used purposely for comic or bizarre passages. The usual indication in the part is a line between the notes to be connected and the abbreviation *gliss*. This is a device which has long since lost its novelty; when used in serious music today, it has a tendency to sound merely vulgar and dated.

As a point of historical interest, it might be mentioned that although the trombone was written for as early as 1600 or so by Gabrielli and was later used by Mozart, Gluck, and others in opera, its first appearance in an actual symphony occurred in Beethoven's Fifth Symphony.

At one time there was a complete "family" of trombones: alto, tenor, bass, and double-bass. The alto and double-bass trombones have long since fallen into disuse, and it appears that the bass trombone in F (or G) is in the process of following suit. For their third trombone, most orchestras in this country now use, instead, a B♭ trombone equipped with an "F attachment," a mechanism that makes the notes down to low C possible. Often the instrument is made with a very large bore

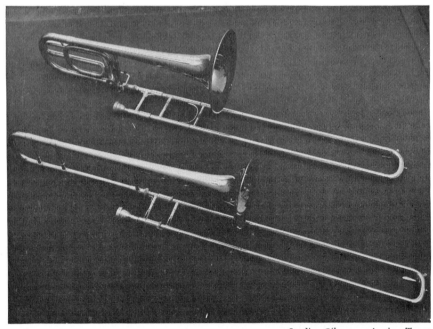

Studio Gilmore, Austin, Texas

Bass Trombone

Tenor Trombone

and bell, and in this form is generally called a bass trombone. Since the older bass trombone in F is still encountered occasionally, a brief commentary on it is included next.

Nowadays even the first and second (tenor) trombones in many orchestras are equipped with the F attachment, chiefly because it simplifies the technical problem by eliminating certain awkward changes of position. For example, the passage on page 138 would be a great deal easier on a trombone with the F attachment. Some bass trombones are built with an E attachment as well and are able to play down to the low B.

THE BASS TROMBONE (IN F)

Italian: Trombone basso   French: Trombone basse   German: Bassposaune

Ex. 11

Here, again, we are dealing not with a transposing instrument but with one that happens to be built with a note other than C as its fundamental. Like the tenor trombone, it sounds as written. There is also a bass trombone in G (likewise nontransposing) which is sometimes used and which is preferred in some other countries, notably England. In any case, bass-trombone parts are always written in the bass clef, never the tenor.

The instrument is slightly larger all around than the tenor trombone, and its tone is a little heavier in quality. Sometimes it plays the bass, either alone or in unison or octaves with the tuba; at other times it plays the tenor voice, leaving the bass to the tuba.

EXAMPLES

Ex. 12

(a) First Symphony   BRAHMS

(b) Overture to *Tannhäuser*   WAGNER

(c) *Petrouchka*   STRAVINSKY

(d) *Mathis der Maler*   HINDEMITH

Reproduced by permission of Schott & Co., Ltd., London.

(In [a] the complete scoring [except for timpani] is included to show how the bassoons, contra bassoons, and horns are combined with the trombones to complete the harmony.)

THE TUBA

Italian: Tuba   French: Tuba   German: Basstuba

Ex. 13

Tubas in C, BB♭, E♭, and F are employed in the orchestra today, the choice of instrument resting with the player and being determined by the range of the part, fingering problems, and personal preference, among other things. All the tubas mentioned are nontransposing (that is, sound as written) and all are four-valve instruments. While they differ slightly as to range, it seems unnecessary to catalog the individual ranges here, since in writing a tuba part we can be governed by the composite range given above, and since all these tubas are capable of playing within the "practical" range shown.

The tuba seldom has occasion to go very high, inasmuch as the notes in the upper part of its register are as a rule better given to trombone or horn.[5] On the other hand, it need not be kept "grumbling in its boots." Incidentally, the extremely low notes, those below the low F, tend to be weak and rather flabby in quality and are consequently better avoided. The instrument seems to be most effective when used neither very low nor very high but in its middle register.

For such a large instrument it is perhaps more agile than might be expected, though of course there are definite limits to the speed and complexity of the parts it can play. Since it calls for the expenditure of a great deal of breath in performance, parts for it should not be too continuous and should include sufficient rests.

The tone quality of the instrument has been alternately praised and maligned in orchestration books. The writer's experience indicates that with a good instrument and a good player the tuba tone can be unusually velvety and pleasant in soft passages, robust and exciting in a *forte* or a *fortissimo*. It is a tone which differs somewhat from that of the trumpet and trombone in being "rounder" and less cutting.

---

[5] An exception is the amusing passage from Stravinsky's *Petrouchka,* quoted at the end of this section, where the tuba in its extreme upper register gives exactly the right "lumbering" effect for a dance by a trained bear. But this sort of thing comes under the heading of special effects and is not recommended for everyday use.

Tuba

This difference results partly from the fact that the tuba is, like the horn, essentially conical in bore, whereas the trumpet and trombone are predominantly cylindrical. Also, the tuba bore is relatively larger than that of the other brass instruments (the horn included).

Muting of the tuba is a device which is employed only rarely. An example may be seen in the introduction of Strauss's *Don Quixote*.

The most frequent use of the tuba in the orchestra is as a bass for the brass section; but it may also be used to strengthen the double basses or lower woodwinds. On rare ocasions, it may take the bass alone or play a solo part.

Because it is so often combined in unison with the double bass and the contra bassoon, both of which sound an octave lower than written, students have a way of insisting that the tuba should use the same transposition. At the risk of sounding repetitious, we might include a final reminder to write the tuba part at its actual pitch.

SUGGESTED ASSIGNMENT

Know:
(1) Ranges of the trumpet, trombone, and tuba.
(2) Transpositions where involved.
(3) Principles involved in the positions on the trombone and in the various harmonic series available on the other brass instruments by means of different valve combinations.
(4) Colors and relative weights in different registers.
(5) Abilities and limitations.
(6) Possibilities for muting and special effects.

EXAMPLES

Ex. 14

(a) Prelude to *Die Meistersinger*

WAGNER

(b) *Siegfried*

WAGNER

(The tuba is used here to personify Fafner, the dragon.)

(c) *Don Juan*

STRAUSS

(d) *Petrouchka*

STRAVINSKY

Suggested Listening

TRUMPET

Beethoven, *Leonore* Overture No. 3, measure 272.

Wagner, Prelude to *Parsifal,* measure 9; *Siegfried,* scenes of Mime; *Die Meistersinger,* scenes of Beckmesser (latter two are examples of *muted* trumpet).

Scriabin, *The Poem of Ecstasy,* 4 bars after figure 32; many other passages.

Mussorgsky-Ravel, *Pictures from an Exhibition,* opening *Promenade;* also Part 6 (*Samuel Goldenberg and Schmuyle*), figure 58 (muted trumpet).

Strauss, *Ein Heldenleben,* fanfare section, figure 42; *Don Quixote,* figure 3 (muted trumpets).

Debussy, *Nocturnes:* II. *Fêtes,* 9 bars after figure 10 (3 muted trumpets).

Ravel, *Daphnis and Chloe* Suite No. 2, 2 bars before figure 204.

Stravinsky, *The Rite of Spring,* 4 bars before figure 84 (muted).

Bloch, *Schelomo,* figure 5.

Copland, Third Symphony, fanfare section near beginning of 4th movt. (figure 85).

Britten, *The Young Person's Guide to the Orchestra,* Variation K.

Instruments of the Orchestra (Victor, 20523 A).

TROMBONE

Mozart, Requiem, *Tuba Mirum.*

Berlioz, *Roman Carnival* Overture.

Wagner, Overture to *Tannhäuser,* letter A; *The Ride of the Valkyries.*

Rimsky-Korsakoff, *Russian Easter* Overture, letter M.

Tchaikovsky, Fourth Symphony, last movt., measure 84; Sixth Symphony, last movt., letter L.

Strauss, *Salome,* closing scene (muted trombone).

Mahler, Third Symphony, 1st movt., figure 33.

Sibelius, Seventh Symphony, 1st movt., letter L.

Stravinsky, *Pulcinella,* Minuet movt.; *Petrouchka,* figure 112.

Britten, *The Young Person's Guide to the Orchestra,* Variation L.

Instruments of the Orchestra (Victor, 20523 A).

TUBA

Wagner, *Siegfried,* beginning of Act II.

Mussorgsky-Ravel, *Pictures from an Exhibition,* beginning of Part 4 *(Bydlo).*

Strauss, *Don Quixote,* figure 3 (muted tubas), figure 9, etc. (This work illustrates the use of both tenor and bass tubas.)

Stravinsky, *Petrouchka,* 2 bars after figure 100.

Shostakovitch, First Symphony, 3rd movt., before figures 7 and 20.

Britten, *The Young Person's Guide to the Orchestra,* Variation L.

Instruments of the Orchestra (Victor, 20523 A).

Chapter IX

THE BRASS SECTION

THE BRASS section to be used here for purposes of illustration is the average one: four horns, two or three trumpets, three trombones, and tuba.

An accepted axiom in scoring for brass is this: if the dynamic marking is *mf* or louder, two horns are needed to balance one trumpet or one trombone; below that dynamic level, one horn will give satisfactory balance. Consequently we must know just how loud a passage is to be before we can score it properly for brass. In the examples that follow, various dynamic markings have been assumed.

The horns have been written in some cases without key signature (the traditional way) and in others with key signature (which seems the more sensible way here). As in the examples for woodwinds, different possibilities in slurring have been shown.

Once again we have elected to use the chorale excerpt that has served for illustration in earlier chapters:

Ex. 1. *Jesu, meine Freude*

BACH

Following are some of the many ways in which the passage could be scored for brass instruments.

Ex. 2

Version (c) shows how the instruments would normally be arranged in scoring for a brass quartet.

Although the arrangement of the horns in (f) might appear to be a
natural and workable one, it is actually not too satisfactory. The
range in most four-voice music is such that the first horn is apt to be
taken uncomfortably high, while the fourth horn is so low that it may
become "fuzzy" and unsolid. With good players, this sort of arrangement is possible in certain pieces; with school groups or less experienced performers, it had better be avoided.

Unlike the versions above, those that follow use keys other than
the original, and all but (a) include octave doublings.

Ex. 3

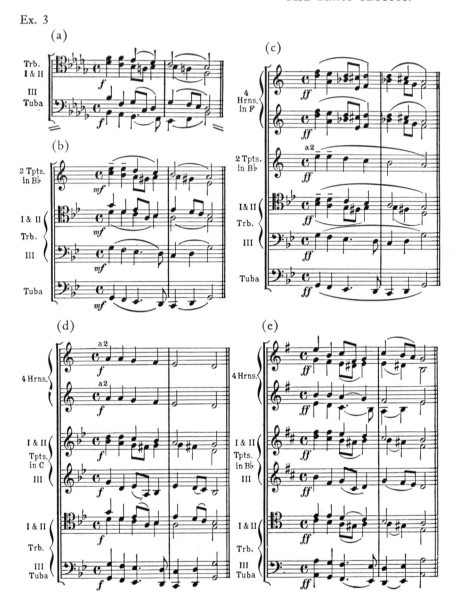

In Example 3 (c) the upper octave of the chorale melody has been given to two trumpets in order to bring it out more strongly than the other voices, while in (d) the bottom octave of the melody has been "weighted" a great deal more heavily than normal balance would require (four horns in unison plus a trombone).

In (d) and (e) three trumpets rather than two are included. Since third trumpet parts are apt to get down into the lower, less penetrating register, it is often a wise idea to reinforce them with a trombone or a horn (or even two horns). That has been done here, in (d) with a trombone, in (e) with a horn. Of course if the third trumpet part lies fairly high, no such reinforcement is necessary.

In general, trumpets and horns sound better in close spacing (close position) than they do in open. Trombones may also be arranged in close spacing in their middle and upper registers. (If placed quite high, they give an effect of great brilliance.) But since they must often play the lower notes of the harmony—where close spacing would be too muddy—they are seen about as frequently in open spacing. Such arrangements as  in three trombones give a fine solid resonance.

Beginning orchestrators often make the mistake of expecting the brass instruments to enter on an extremely high note. Such entrances are risky. Although they may be successful "on good days when the wind is right," they are more often disastrous. And even when successful, they are apt to sound unpleasantly strained and tense. The following concert pitches might be set as safe upward limits for entrances, in trumpet, horn, and trombone, respectively:

Ex. 4

Horn   Trumpet   Trombone

Of course higher pitches are practical when the player has a chance to "lead up" to them instead of having to hit them without preparation.

The excerpt that follows is a good example of effective scoring for brass choir alone. The complete scoring is shown here except for two chords for full orchestra which occur at the two holds. The second of these chords (the one in the last measure) is given, in condensed form at concert pitch, on page 168.

Ex. 5. *Mathis der Maler*

HINDEMITH

Reproduced by permission of Schott & Co., Ltd., London.

SUGGESTED ASSIGNMENTS

A. Know:
  (1) Make-up of the average brass section.
  (2) Arrangement of instruments on page—order and grouping.
  (3) Principles of balance as applied to the brass section.
  (4) Commonly used "voicings" (in brass scoring).
B. The following are suitable as exercises in scoring for brass:

(1) Bach, a short excerpt from any of the chorales, to be scored for: (a) two Bb trumpets and two trombones; (b) two C trumpets, one F horn, and one trombone; (c) full brass section, including three trumpets if desired. In this last version use octave doublings.

(2) Bach, *Wachet Auf* (chorale).

(3) Schumann, *Important Event* from *Scenes from Childhood*.

(4) Schumann, *Norse Song* from *Album for the Young*.

(5) Mussorgsky, *Promenade,* beginning of *Pictures from an Exhibition*.

(6) Grieg, *Sailor's Song*.

(7) Chopin, Prelude in C minor.

(8) *America* (the original key of F need not be retained here).

Suggested Listening

BRASS

Dvořák, Fifth Symphony (*New World*), last movt.

Brahms, First Symphony, last movt., "chorale" section.

Franck, Symphony in D minor, last movt., "chorale" section.

Wagner, Prelude to *Parsifal;* Funeral Music from *Götterdämmerung;* Overture to *Tannhäuser*.

Tchaikovsky, Fourth Symphony, 3rd movt., Tempo I following the *Meno mosso* section; last movt., many passages.

Rimsky-Korsakoff, *Capriccio Espagnol,* beginning of section IV (*Scena e Canto Gitano*).

Mussorksgy-Ravel, *Pictures from an Exhibition,* opening *Promenade;* Part 8 (*Catacombe*); Part 10 (*The Great Gate of Kiev*).

Kodály, *Háry János* Suite, Part IV (*The Battle and Defeat of Napoleon*).

Bartók, Concerto for Orchestra, Part I (*Introduzione*), measure 342 (about the middle); Part II (*Giuoco delle Coppie*), measures 123 (middle portion); Part V (*Finale*), measure 556.

Hindemith, *Mathis der Maler,* "Alleluia" at end (brass parts shown on page 152); also many other portions, especially 1st movt.

Stravinsky, *Fire Bird* Suite, *Finale*.

Britten, *The Young Person's Guide to the Orchestra,* Theme C.

Respighi, *Pines of Rome,* last section (*Pines of the Appian Way*); *Roman Festivals*.

Chapter X

SCORING OF CHORDS FOR EACH SECTION AND FOR ORCHESTRA

Woodwind Chords

There are four ways in which instruments of different kinds may be combined in a chord. These are demonstrated here, using wood-winds in pairs. (All notes shown are actual sounds.)

Ex. 1

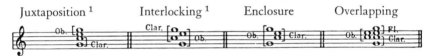

Juxtaposition is used very frequently. Pairs of instruments are simply put side by side, usually in the normal order of register.

Interlocking has the slight advantage of mixing the colors in such a way that a more homogeneous blend results. However, there are cases in which interlocking does not work well. For instance, in the following chord the second flute would be relatively weak:

Ex. 2

And a similar lack of balance would result if interlocking forced the oboe, for example, to play in an abnormally high register where it would be too thin.

Enclosure is likely to be less successful than the first two methods in arranging woodwinds, at least when one *pair* encloses another.

---

[1] In Rimsky-Korsakoff's *Principles of Orchestration* the translator has used the term "over-laying" rather than "juxtaposition" and "crossing" rather than "interlocking." Certain other orchestration books refer to interlocking as "dovetailing." The terms chosen here are those which seem to offer the least chance for ambiguity or confusion.

The difficulty is that when two instruments of a kind are spread an octave or more apart, they are likely to be playing in different registers and therefore to differ considerably from each other in strength and color; consequently, balance and blend may suffer. Consider the difference in sound between the first and second flutes in this chord, for example:

Ex. 3

(The second flute is obviously too weak here.)   On the other hand, if a pair is enclosed by two *different* instruments, the effect may be perfectly good:

Ex. 4

The overlapping method, though much in vogue during the classical period, is seen less often today.   Its weakness is the fact that the outer notes (especially the bottom one) are not as strong as the others.

Whereas overlapping involves only a partial duplication of notes, there is another more complete and balanced form of duplication that is much used, as in arrangements such as these:

Ex. 5

The obvious question at this point is: how does the arranger decide on the best method to use?   There is no general answer that can be given to that question; range, voice-leading, instruments involved, the coloring desired, and other factors will all enter into the choice.   Juxtaposition and interlocking are chosen much more frequently than the other methods, however.   And of course in actual practice two or more methods are often used in the same chord—when the chord consists of more than four notes.   In any case, the difference in sound between a chord that uses juxtaposition, let us say, and one that uses interlocking is not really a very startling one. The important thing is to plan for proper balance and blend, whichever system is chosen.

It should be understood that this material on voicing is illustrated by isolated chords only for the sake of convenience and that it applies to the part-writing of harmonic successions as well.

Except in small orchestras which include only one of each wood-wind, chords are rarely arranged with a different color on each note:

Ex. 6

Because of the several different timbres involved in such an arrange-ment, a good blend is difficult to achieve. If the chord were a widely spaced one in a higher register, the resulting sound would be some-what better:

Ex. 7

However, this sort of spacing is almost never used today in writing for wind instruments in the orchestra. Although at one time wood-wind chords were often arranged with gaps between the upper chord members, the current practice (which is certainly preferable) is to write the upper woodwinds in close spacing. Of course the occasional gaps that occur as a result of special voice-leading or doubling are not objec-tionable (Example 8 [a] and [b]) nor is the octave gap that is caused by a doubling of the top voice an octave higher (8[c]):

Ex. 8

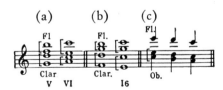

Before going on to the examples of chords scored for woodwinds, the reader would do well to review the hints on spacing and doubling given at the end of Chapter III. One small point might be added here, even though it does not figure in the scoring of isolated chords: when a progression involves both stationary and moving voices, it is better to give the stationary voices to one color, the moving voices to another:

Ex. 9

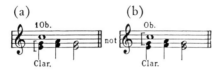

In the examples that follow, some of the chords are scored for wood-winds in pairs plus two horns (the latter included because they are so often combined with woodwinds). Another section of the illus-trations makes use of a large woodwind section: piccolo, two flutes, two oboes, English horn, two clarinets, bass clarinet, two bassoons, and contra bassoon. And there are a few examples for woodwinds in threes, a less frequently used combination. With both the large woodwind section and woodwinds in threes, juxtaposition works far better than any of the other systems. Interlocking is especially un-successful in the case of woodwinds in threes because it pushes instru-ments of a kind too far apart:

Ex. 10

Complete duplication, with three of each woodwind, allows for a uniformly mixed color in three-note chords:

Ex. 11

In scoring for a large woodwind section, the piccolo may double the flute an octave higher or may take the top chord tone immediately above the flutes. The English horn may be placed just below the oboes to form a three-note chord in close spacing (the most usual arrangement) or it may play lower down, with other instruments between it and the oboes. The bass clarinet, on the other hand, is much less often placed immediately below the clarinets to form a three-note chord; it is far more apt to take the bass, since it is most effective in its lower and middle registers. It is, in fact, better than the bassoon for the bass of a woodwind chord; it has enough body to give a solid foundation to the chord, whereas two bassoons would often be required to achieve the equivalent sense of solidity. The role of the contra bassoon as the rock bottom of the chord is an obvious one. It normally doubles the bass an octave lower.

Most of the chords in the following examples are scored in such a way as to be fairly brilliant in coloring, but in two of them, (g) and (m), the instruments have been placed relatively low in their respective registers to produce a darker coloring. The clarinets in their bottom octave are particularly good at adding a sombre tinge. Obviously, there is no point in including the piccolo in such cases, and even the flutes have been omitted in (m). In fact, any instrument may be omitted at any time for the sake of color or volume—or possibly to keep it fresh for an entrance that is to follow.

Ex. 12

(For woodwinds in pairs and two horns)

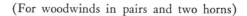

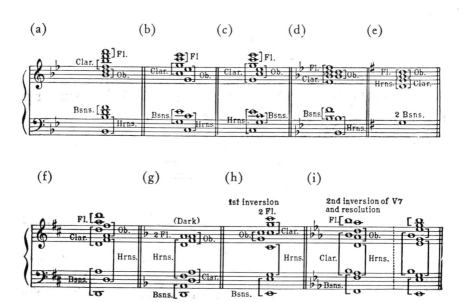

(For large woodwind section)

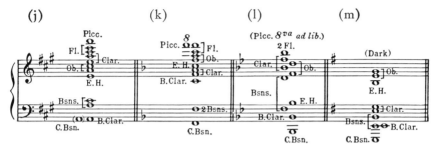

(For woodwinds in threes)

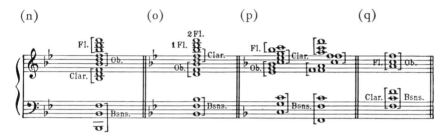

In general, the same dynamic marking can be given to all the instruments in each one of the arrangements just shown. One possible exception concerns the horns. Since they are capable of a more robust *forte* than any of the woodwinds, it would be safer to mark them *mf* when the woodwinds are marked *f,* and *f* when the woodwinds are marked *ff.*

BRASS CHORDS

Juxtaposition, interlocking, and enclosure are all used frequently in scoring chords for brass. Overlapping as a method is rarely seen, though a low trumpet note is sometimes overlapped by the top trombone or by a horn for the sake of better balance.

If our brass section consists of four horns, two trumpets, three trombones, and tuba, we have ten instruments. As long as the dynamic marking is softer than *mf,* these instruments can actually play ten notes. But in a *mezzo-forte* or louder, the horns will normally be used two to a note, and the section can then cover only eight notes at the most. When chords of more than eight notes are to be scored *forte* or louder for the brass section we have just described, the two-horns-to-a-note principle must obviously be abandoned; the horns are given four different pitches and (when possible) marked one degree louder than the rest of the brass. This type of arrangement is shown in Example 13 (i). Of course if the chord to be scored has fewer than eight notes, instruments may simply be omitted, or certain ones may be doubled on a pitch so as to bring out a particular voice if that is appropriate.

Some of the following examples have been scored for two trumpets, some for three, since brass sections vary in that respect. Three would seem to be the more satisfactory number, because it allows for a complete three-note harmony in the trumpet color.

As before, the chords have merely been sketched on two staves at concert pitch. It should perhaps be stressed that the examples here and elsewhere in this chapter make no pretense of exhausting all the possibilities; they simply show some of the more usual arrangements.

CHORDS FOR BRASS

Ex. 13

(With two trumpets)

(With three trumpets)

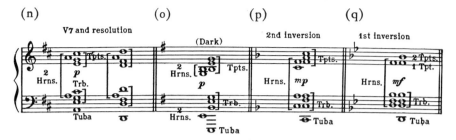

STRING CHORDS

Having wended his way through the maze of possibilities in scoring woodwind and brass chords, the reader may be relieved to be told that the problem of scoring chords for strings is a bit less involved. In the first place, the difference in color between one string group and another is not nearly so decided as the difference in color between, say, a flute and an oboe. Consequently the strings present fewer problems of blend. And they do not vary in strength from register to register as much as the woodwinds do. This means that balance is more easily calculated.

On the other hand, strings involve two possibilities that wind instruments do not: (1) double, triple, and quadruple stops; (2) the use of an entire section that can be divided into any number of parts. As pointed out earlier, double stops may be used even in sustained chords, whereas triple and quadruple stops are valuable principally for short, sharply punctuated chords. In this latter type of chord, the main objectives are usually maximum resonance, fullness, and volume, and it is unnecessary to worry much about exact balance or correct voice-leading because the chord is not heard long enough for these features to be very apparent to the ear. The open strings so often involved in chords of this sort not only give added resonance but simplify the technical problem of the player.

As for *divisi* writing, remember that the fewer the players the riskier it is to divide a section. This is particularly true of division into more than two parts. Ideally, of course, we are scoring for an orchestra of the proportions of the Boston Symphony, in which case a *divisi a 4* passage for the violas is quite practical. But the sad reality of the matter is that we are much more likely to be working with a college orchestra that is able to muster only three viola players, fugitives from the violin section, who have had only a limited amount of experience in playing the viola. Under such circumstances, division into four or more parts is obviously an impossibility; and division into three parts, though possible, is hardly advisable if the parts involve any technical difficulties, for each player is left alone and unsupported on a part. Furthermore, when such small string groups are divided, the result is a solo quality rather than a group quality on each voice. (It takes at least three violins or violas on a part to give the effect of a group of strings.) While the other string groups tend to be somewhat better staffed than the viola section, they can still suffer from overdivision if the orchestra is not full-sized or if the players are inexperienced.

Juxtaposition (illustrated in the first three of the chords in Example 14) is by far the most usual method used in arranging strings. On rare occasions, interlocking is employed to achieve a more complete blend (d). Overlapping of one string group with another (also rare) produces a richer, more "lush" quality (e). Enclosure seldom figures in string scoring. As mentioned earlier, open harmony is more successful in strings than in woodwinds or brass. Examples (f) through (j), which are shown in actual score form, are string chords taken from orchestral literature. Each illustrates a particular effect or device. Notice the interlocking of the notes in the triple stops in (f), a frequent arrangement in multiple-stop chords. Interlocking also figures in (g) and (h).

Ex. 14

(Condensed at actual pitch)

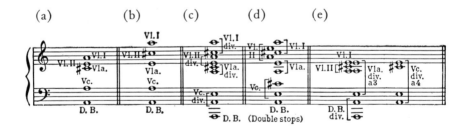

(In score form)

(f) Beethoven, Seventh Symphony (last movt., letter **A**)
(g) Hindemith, *Mathis der Maler* (second bar)
(h) Strauss, *Don Juan* (eight bars after G)
(i) Bartók, Concerto for Orchestra (fifth bar of Finale)
(j) Wagner, *Lohengrin,* Prelude to Act I (beginning)

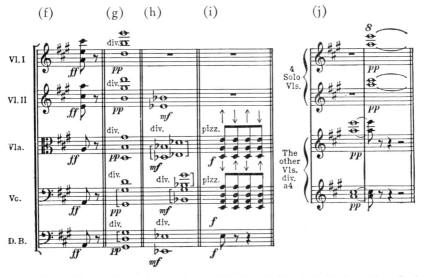

Example 14 (g) reproduced by permission of Schott & Co., Ltd., London; Example 14 (i) copyright, 1946, by Hawkes & Son (London) Ltd. By permission of the copyright owner, Boosey & Hawkes, Inc.

Chords for Orchestra

In considering the scoring of chords for orchestra, we must remember, first of all, that there is a vast difference in the weight of the three sections (woodwind, brass, and strings). That is, if each section is marked *ff,* the brass will be much louder than the woodwinds or strings. This is still true in a *forte,* although somewhat less so at softer dynamic levels. The first thing to do, then, is to arrange the brass section so that it will sound well in itself. There is never any question of attempting to fill in a gap in the brass harmony with a note in the woodwinds or strings; that will not work. The brass must be balanced as a unit.

If we carry this process over into the woodwinds and strings and arrange the chord in such a way that each section would sound com-

plete and balanced if played by itself, the composite sound of the three
sections playing at the same time is bound to be good. This is, in fact,
a fool-proof method and one that is often used. It is demonstrated in
Example 15 (a), (e), and others that follow here. But it is not the
only way, nor is it necessarily the most effective, because it sometimes
involves putting the upper woodwinds in the same register as the
trumpets, in which case the woodwinds are all but drowned out and
actually add little. If the flutes and clarinets, especially, are placed
well above the trumpets, they are better able to make themselves heard,
first because they are not covered by the trumpets in the same octave,
and second because they are much more powerful and brilliant in the
higher register. (We are assuming here that a loud, brilliant effect
is wanted.) With this sort of arrangement, there is often a gap in the
middle of the woodwind chord, but that is not objectionable. Although the woodwind section would not sound entirely satisfactory if
played by itself, it will be effective when combined with the brass and
strings.

The same general principle applies to the role of the strings in a
chord for orchestra. That is, they may either play the complete chord
or merely reinforce certain notes of it. But, unlike the woodwind
section, they are frequently arranged in open spacing; sometimes, in
fact, they are spread out even more widely, with gaps of an octave
or more between certain notes. At other times they are simply arranged in straightforward four-part fashion, using close spacing.
Octave doublings may be added or not, depending on whether a full,
rich effect is wanted. Some of the more likely possibilities can be seen
in the examples that follow, all of which are condensed at actual pitch.

Chords (a), (b), (c), and (d) in Example 15 use woodwinds in
pairs, (e) and (f) a large woodwind section. In (d) a dark coloring
has been aimed at. In (e) and (f) are shown two different scorings of
the same chord, the first very brilliant, the second about "medium"
color. Chords taken from well-known scores are given in (g) to (n).
The Beethoven chord is one of the short, "hammered-out" kind so
characteristic of his music.

CHORDS FOR ORCHESTRA

Ex. 15

(Condensed at actual pitch)

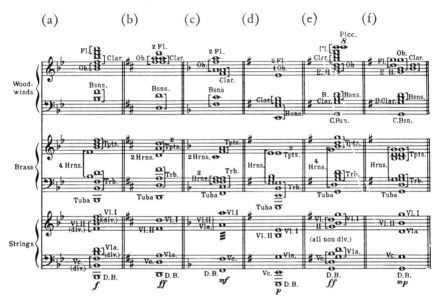

(The dynamic marking below each chord applies to all the instruments.)

(g) Beethoven, Fifth Symphony (bar 316)
(h) Franck, Symphony in D minor (last chord)
(i) Strauss, *Till Eulenspiegel* (five bars before figure 37)
(j) Wagner, *Götterdämmerung* (*Trauermusik,* bar 16)
(k) Wagner, *Tristan and Isolda* (last chord)

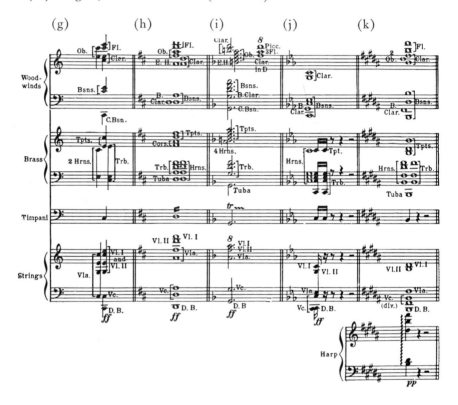

(1) Prokofieff, Fifth Symphony (last chord in first movt.)
(m) Strauss, *Sinfonia Domestica* (last chord)

(Four ad libitum saxophone
parts are not shown here.)

(n) Hindemith, *Mathis der Maler* (last chord)

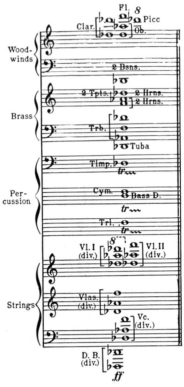

Example 15 (m) copyright, 1904, by Ed Bote and G. Bock, Berlin. By permission of Associated Music Publishers; Example 15 (n) reproduced by permission of Schott & Co., Ltd., London.

It should not be inferred from the comments and examples given here that in a chord for orchestra all the sections must have the same dynamic marking. There is no law, for instance, against marking the strings and woodwinds *ff*, the brass *f* or *mp* or even *pp*, if that will produce the particular sound that is wanted.[2] (It is important, by the way, to remember that the brass—particularly the trombones and horns—can provide an extremely quiet but rich background for the other instruments if need be.) Similarly, it would be perfectly possible to mark the strings louder than the woodwinds or *vice versa,* in order to bring out a certain timbre or register. However, there would seldom be any point in marking the brass much *louder* than the strings or

---

[2] The best examples of this approach to dynamic markings can be found in the scores of Mahler.

woodwinds, since the latter tend to be overshadowed by the brass even when the dynamic markings are equal. It should perhaps be mentioned that certain scores (particularly pre-twentieth-century scores) use "block" dynamics—all the instruments invariably marked the same in a *tutti;* but in such cases the conductor is obviously expected to adjust the dynamic proportions wherever that becomes necessary.

Dissonances are more prominent and acute when given to instruments of the same kind, milder when allotted to different instruments.

For instance,  accentuates the dissonance much more than .

It would be impractical to attempt to catalog all the doublings possible between woodwinds, brass, and strings. Some of the possibilities in woodwind and string doubling are discussed in Chapter XII, and a few of the combinations involving woodwinds and brass might be mentioned here. In general, the doubling of woodwinds in unison with brass makes the brass tone somewhat less transparent and brilliant in timbre; clarinets and flutes "soften the edges" of the trumpet tone, while oboes tend to accentuate the nasal quality of it. Clarinets in their *chalumeau* register add a rich, dark touch to the brass. Bassoons doubled in unison with horns or trombones make those instruments a little grayer and more opaque in quality; the bassoon color is largely absorbed by the brass color.

Leaving the matter of actual doublings, it might be helpful to pass on a small point which Rimsky-Korsakoff and others have mentioned: there is a certain resemblance between the tone of the oboe (or English horn) and that of stopped horn or muted trumpet; consequently, these instruments can be combined in a chord (on different notes) with surprisingly good results. Even the unmuted trumpet tone is close enough to the oboe tone for the two instruments to give a fairly unified sound when placed side by side. One hears chiefly the trumpet quality; in fact, such combinations may even give the illusion of being played entirely by trumpets. A similar affinity of tone quality exists (rather surprisingly) between the low notes of the flute and soft trumpet tones in that register.

SUGGESTED ASSIGNMENTS

Score the following chords as directed. The chords are to have the root in the bass unless an inversion is indicated. Either they may be written with a key signature (assuming that each is the tonic chord) or the key signature may be omitted and accidentals inserted where necessary. Include dynamics in every case. (Supply your own where none are given.) Use the principles discussed in the text to produce the type of coloring called for. You will achieve better results and save time in the long run if you sketch the layout of each chord at actual pitch before writing out the scored version.

   A. For two flutes, two oboes, two clarinets, two bassoons, and two horns:
    (1) F major, F in the soprano, brilliant.
    (2) C major, G in the soprano, medium color.
    (3) Eb major, 1st inversion, Eb in the soprano, brilliant.

   B. For piccolo, two flutes, two oboes, English horn, two clarinets, bass clarinet, two bassoons, and contra bassoon:
    (1) E major, G# in the soprano, very brilliant.
    (2) B major, B in the soprano, medium color.
    (3) D minor, A in the soprano, dark (omit piccolo).

   C. For four horns, two or three trumpets (Bb or C), three trombones, and tuba:
    (1) Db major, F in the soprano, brilliant, *forte*.
    (2) F minor, C in the soprano, medium color, *mezzo-piano*.
    (3) F major, F in the soprano, rather dark, *pianissimo*.

   D. For string orchestra:
The chord of G major, G in the soprano, arranged in four different ways to illustrate: (1) close spacing; (2) open spacing; (3) octave doublings (use either *divisi* writing or double stops or both here); (4) triple and quadruple stops (this chord is to be the short, vigorous type).

   E. For orchestra consisting of two flutes, two oboes, two clarinets, two bassoons, four horns, two trumpets, three trombones, tuba, and strings:
    (1) B minor, F# in the soprano, brilliant, *fortissimo*.
    (2) F major, A in the soprano, medium color, *pianissimo*.

   F. For orchestra consisting of piccolo, two flutes, two oboes, English horn, two clarinets, bass clarinet, two bassoons, contra bassoon, four horns, three trumpets, three trombones, tuba and strings:
    (1) Ab major, 2nd inversion, Ab in the soprano, very brilliant, *fortissimo*.
    (2) C minor, G in the soprano, medium color, *piano*.
    (3) E minor, G in the soprano, very dark, *mezzo-forte*.

Chapter XI

SPECIAL PROBLEMS IN TRANSCRIBING PIANO MUSIC

IN SCORING piano music for orchestra, the arranger often comes across certain features that are essentially pianistic rather than orchestral. In such cases, a literal transcription of the notes is apt to be awkward technically or ineffective or both; a better solution is to translate the effect wanted into orchestral terms.

In order to save space and to illustrate the points in question as simply as possible, the problem has been limited, in this chapter, to arrangements for string orchestra. However, except for devices and patterns peculiar to string writing, the material can be applied just as well to scoring for other instruments.

First of all, if the original music is in a remote key—say more than four sharps or flats—it is often a wise idea to choose a more comfortable and resonant key for the orchestral version (probably a half step higher if the piece is brilliant, a half step lower if it is not). This is particularly true in the case of school orchestras. The writer can already hear protests from the readers who have perfect pitch, for those people will be painfully aware of a transposition from the original key in music they know. And one does not have to have perfect pitch to object that altering the key of a work can destroy its characteristic color and flavor. Admittedly, the business of tampering with the composer's choice of key is questionable from an aesthetic standpoint. But the advantages to be gained from playing in a more grateful key are usually impressive enough to justify transposition. In choosing a key, it is well to remember that sharp keys are better than flat keys for the strings. Because of the tuning of stringed instruments the resonance is much greater in sharp keys, and the fingering is easier. This is only a general principle and does not mean that in string writing flat keys must be avoided like the plague.

Then there is the matter of the damper pedal, which figures almost constantly in piano music (this is the pedal on the right, which, when depressed, allows the tones to ring). Obviously, it must be changed— that is, raised and lowered again—at each new harmony if a blur is not to result. In some piano music these changes are indicated by a small "Ped." beneath the staff, with an asterisk for a release. But in a great deal of music, no directions for pedalling are shown; in such cases, the arranger must ask himself whether pedal would be used, and if so, what the effect would be. (Usually when no pedal is to be used in a given passage, *senza pedale* is written in.)

Here is the beginning of a Chopin *Nocturne:*

Ex. 1. Nocturne, Op. 9, No. 1

CHOPIN

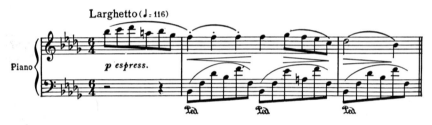

Because of the sustaining effect of the pedal, the music will actually sound more or less like this:

Ex. 2

Therefore, certain notes must be written with longer values in the orchestral arrangement than in the original piano version. Not all notes sustained in the piano version need be sustained in the arrangement; it is simply a matter of aiming at the general effect of the original. Very often it is possible to divide up the figuration among the various string groups. That has been done in Example 3 (which has been transposed to a better key for the strings).

Ex. 3

Or it may be possible to have some instruments taking the harmony in block-chord fashion while others take the figuration:

Ex. 4

In both versions, the background has been marked a degree softer than the melody so that the latter will be sure to stand out.

Incidentally, it is impossible to transfer music from one medium to another intelligently without understanding its harmonic structure. For instance, unless we are aware that the second harmony in this Chopin excerpt involves a tonic pedal-point beneath the dominant 7th, we may very well make the mistake of using the tonic note among the upper harmonies as if it were an actual chord tone (with very bad results) or of putting some other note in the bass, thereby destroying the pedal-point effect. If the harmonic skeleton of the original piece is not perfectly clear at the outset, be sure to analyze before going further.

In transcribing, it is sometimes best to change the pattern of the pianistic figuration altogether (not the harmony, of course, and usually not the *rhythm* of the figuration). Let us suppose that this bit from the last movement of the Beethoven *"Moonlight"* Sonata is to be scored for strings:

Ex. 5. Sonata, Op. 27, No. 2

BEETHOVEN

Although the "Alberti bass" figure in the left hand is *possible* for the cellos, it is not well suited to string technique, and the effect would be thin and a little ludicrous that way. Also, the spacing is poor for orchestral purposes; the third of the chord is too low, the small intervals are at the bottom, and there is a wide gap between the left-hand part and the melody in the right. It would be better to rearrange the chord and distribute the notes among the string groups, possibly like this:

Ex. 6

Example 7 shows another pianistic figure that is better rearranged.

Ex. 7

Here, again, the solution is to lift and respace. Of course there are other patterns of figuration that might profit from the same treatment.

Widely spread out arpeggio passages, such as the left-hand part in the next example, offer several problems in scoring.

Ex. 8. *The White Peacock*

In the first place, they cover so much ground that they can seldom be handled comfortably by any one orchestral instrument except the harp. Because of this fact and because the harp is so eminently suited to arpeggios, it is often the best choice for such passages (usually with sustained harmony elsewhere in the orchestra). But not all orchestras include a harp, and the instrument would not be appropriate in all types of music. Therefore, we had better be prepared to provide another solution if need be. In some cases it is possible to reduce the "spread" of the arpeggios to a point where they can be taken by one instrument (by one group in the case of the strings). Actual rearrangement of the figures will also be necessary here as a rule. Sometimes it is best to divide the figuration between two or more instruments, again with whatever rearrangement will make for grateful parts and effective sonorities. Example 9 shows one way in which the left-hand part of Example 8 could be transcribed for strings. (We are assuming here that the violins are engaged in playing the upper parts of the original version and therefore cannot be called on to help out with the figured background.)

Ex. 9

Occasionally, passages of the sort we have just been discussing can be carried over fairly literally into the orchestral version by simply dividing them among the strings. In such cases it is wise to let each string group end its figure *on* a beat instead of "up in the air" and to overlap the last note played by each group with the first note of the group that follows it. These points are illustrated in Example 10, which shows first the left-hand part of a piano piece and then a possible arrangement of it for strings.

Ex. 10

(a)

(b)

Sustained harmony in other instruments usually accompanies this sort of arrangement.

In piano music, melody and accompaniment are often assigned to the same hand, and it is important to distinguish one from the other in scoring. Example 11 illustrates this point.

Ex. 11

Here it is obvious that the right-hand part actually includes two distinct musical ideas—a melody on top (the first, third, and fifth eighth-notes in each measure) and a repeated-note figure below. This in spite of the fact that the notation gives the appearance of a single melodic line. In scoring the example, then, we would break up this line into its component parts and allot these to separate instruments. One possible version is given here:

Ex. 12

Chords like the following can be dramatic and effective on the piano:

Ex. 13

The same thing in the orchestra would sound poor; the bottom notes are much too thickly spaced for that low register, and the gap in the middle needs to be filled in. Something like the following might be a satisfactory solution in the strings:

Ex. 14

Triple and quadruple stops are used here for greater fullness and volume. Notice the use of open strings and of the interlocking principle.

It sometimes happens that piano music contains three-note chords which must be divided, in the orchestral arrangement, between second violins and violas. The best solution in that case is to give two notes to the second violins and one to the violas (which are fewer in number). The two notes in the second violins can be taken *divisi* or, if convenient, as a double stop; but this latter method should not be called for with inexperienced players or in a quick succession of chords where double stops would be awkward. Four-note chords can be taken by double stops in both second violins and violas or by *divisi* parts in each.

Broken octaves are especially characteristic of piano music of the Beethoven period:

Ex. 15. Sonata, Op. 22

BEETHOVEN

These are best rendered, in the strings, by this sort of arrangement:

Ex. 16

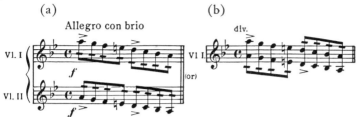

The same would apply to broken 6ths and other intervals (although broken 3rds are practical on most orchestral instruments).

In piano music of the Romantic period (especially in song accompaniments) this sort of tremolo sometimes appears:

Ex. 17

The obvious solution in the orchestra is a string tremolo:

Ex. 18

Although a bowed tremolo has been used here and is ordinarily preferable for such passages, a fingered tremolo might be employed if a softer, more placid effect were called for.

In piano music, chords are sometimes written with a wavy line at the left to indicate that they are to be arpeggiated or broken slightly, or the arpeggiation may be written out in small notes. At other times, the chord is broken into two parts, the lower part being played as a "grace-note" to the upper. Such devices may be introduced for the sake of artistic effect or (more often) out of sheer pianistic necessity, if the chords involve stretches that are too wide to be played at once. In any case, the arpeggiated or broken effect is best omitted altogether in transcribing such passages for orchestra. Following are three examples to illustrate this point. On the top staff are the chords as originally written; the bottom staff shows how they should be considered for purposes of orchestration.

Ex. 19

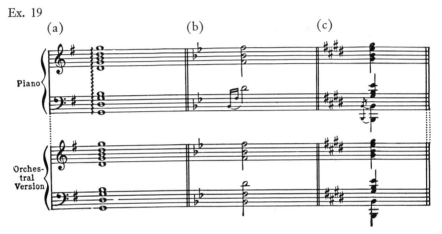

If the rolled chord effect is felt to be such an integral part of the music that it should not be changed, it may of course be given to the harp, which can perform it very naturally and comfortably.

Staccato notes in the piano version may be given to strings playing *pizzicato* or *spiccato* or even *détaché,* depending on the degree of shortness required and on the dynamics and tempo. Remember, however, that *pizzicato* is not practical in very fast passages and that *spiccato* is incapable of producing much more than a *mezzo-forte.*

Una corda, meaning literally "one string" in Italian, is the standard direction, in piano music, for using the soft pedal (the one on the left). In the orchestra, muted strings are often an effective parallel for the *una corda* sound on the piano. But there are other times when the muted effect would seem out of place, and in such cases very soft dynamic markings in the orchestral parts must suffice.

The author does not want to convey the impression that every piece of piano music can be successfully transcribed for strings—

or for orchestra. A good many works are so purely pianistic in conception that it would be absurd to attempt an orchestral version of them. Nevertheless, the problems discussed here are bound to come up from time to time, if only because so much of the work in orchestration courses consists (necessarily) in arranging piano music.

Suggested Assignments

The following are suitable as exercises in transcribing pianistic music for strings (or for other combinations). Bowing should be included in all cases. Respacing, filling of gaps, rearrangement of figuration, etc., are to be introduced where necessary.

(1) Beethoven, Sonata Op. 22, 1st movt., first 20 bars.
(2) Beethoven, Sonata Op. 10, No. 2, 1st movt., first 30 bars.
(3) Beethoven, Sonata Op. 2, No. 3, 1st movt., first 16 bars.
(4) Chopin, Nocturne Op. 9, No. 2 (Eb major) first 4 bars.
(5) Chopin, Nocturne Op. 27, No. 2 (Db major) first 5 bars.
(6) Kuhlau, Sonatina, Op. 20, No. 1, 3rd movt. (Rondo), bars 9–16 (or first 16).
(7) Grieg, Sonata in E minor (excerpts).
(8) Any of the works in the "Suggested Listening" list that follows. Much can be learned by making an orchestral arrangement of one of these from the piano score and comparing it with the published orchestral arrangement. In that case, the student should of course not listen to a recording of the published arrangement until he has completed his own scoring. Since most of these works suggest the use of the complete orchestra, projects in scoring them should preferably be delayed until Chapters XII through XVI have been covered.

Suggested Listening

The following are works which were written originally for piano and which have been arranged for orchestra, either by their composers or by other skilled orchestrators:

Bach, many works transcribed by Sir Edward Elgar, Sir Henry Wood, Leopold Stokowski, Alexandre Tansman, Schönberg, etc.
Brahms, *Variations on a Theme by Haydn* (issued first in a version for two pianos).
Grieg, *Aus Holbergs Zeit.*
Dvořák, *Slavonic Dances.*
Mussorgsky, *Pictures from an Exhibition* (orchestrated by Ravel and Sir Henry Wood among others).
Debussy, *Petite Suite.*
Ravel, *Pavane pour une Infante Défunte; Alborado del Gracioso; Mother Goose Suite; Le Tombeau de Couperin.*
Albéniz, *Iberia; Catalonia.*
Griffes, *The White Peacock.*

Chapter XII

SCORING FOR STRINGS, WOODWINDS, AND HORNS

IN AN EARLIER chapter we took up the arranging of chords for the various sections and for orchestra. There we made a practice of using all the instruments of a section in each chord, in order to learn how to calculate balance and blend in a complete group. In this chapter, a different problem is involved, one requiring much more taste and imagination and one that represents the usual situation in practical orchestration: we are given some music to score for an orchestra of a particular size, and we must choose the instruments that seem appropriate to the musical ideas. When an instrument is not actually needed in the scoring, it will simply be given a rest; even whole sections will rest from time to time. (In the full orchestra the brass section is apt to rest a good deal of the time; woodwinds, both individually and as a section, normally rest a bit more than strings.)

As we look over the music to be scored with an eye to the possible ways in which it could be orchestrated, there are certain questions that naturally suggest themselves:

What is the character of the passage in question—lyric and *espressivo,* or airy and fanciful, or sharply rhythmic, or dirgelike, or any one of the many other possibilities?

Does the passage suggest a relatively light or heavy scoring? Does it call for a simple texture or should it be expanded by means of octave doublings?

What coloring seems appropriate—brilliant or somber, warm or cool?

How does the passage relate to what has gone before and what is to come after it? (In other words, we must consider the form of the piece as a whole.)

What instruments are best fitted to play the respective parts from the standpoint of: (1) range; (2) technical abilities?

182

What *style* of scoring is appropriate, considering the period and composer involved?

Is the music chordal, or homophonic, or polyphonic, or a combination?

As for the last question, we have already had some experience in scoring a chordal texture, and comments on the arranging of polyphonic music are being saved for Chapter XVI. But this is a good point at which to consider the orchestration of homophonic music; that is, music that consists of a prominent melodic line against a subordinate harmonic background.

Suppose, for instance, that we wished to transcribe this excerpt from a Brahms piano piece for strings, woodwinds in pairs, and four horns:

Ex. 1. Intermezzo, Op. 119, No. 2 (middle section)

BRAHMS

Inasmuch as we cannot score this or any other music well without understanding its structure, we had better take time to do a little analyzing before going on to the actual business of orchestration. The harmony in the first measure proves to be tonic (E major) with a nonharmonic C♯ on the first beat in the right hand. (The important thing here is that the C♯ must not be included in the harmony parts. The "added 6th" effect would hardly be appropriate in Brahms!) Because of the sustaining effect of the pedal, the notes in the left hand which are written as eighths actually sound through the measure. The second measure involves a V⁷ sound above a tonic pedal point. (The

E in the bass has the effect of a pedal point since it is held through the bar by the pedal.) We are not going to pursue the harmonic analysis any further here, since the examples that follow involve only the first two bars and bars 9 and 10, which have the same harmonic pattern as the first two. Looking at the music from the standpoint of form, we discover that the eight-measure melody is repeated in octaves beginning with the up-beat to the ninth bar (not all of this repetition is shown here).

Now to make use of some of these observations in planning our scoring. First of all, we must find some way of approximating the sustained effect of the piano version in the orchestra. A good solution here is to add a B and G♯ on the first beat of the first measure (below the E in the treble staff) which will hold through the measure and then continue on harmony notes in the measures that follow. This has the added advantage of filling in the large gap that occurs at the beginning of each measure. Also, we shall want to hold the E in the bass, and it would even be possible to hold the B above it as well. The eighth-note arpeggios could be given entirely to cellos or divided between cellos and violas as in Example 2(b)—or even given to bassoons as in Example 3(d), although that plan seems a little less desirable. If a harp were included, it might take these arpeggio figures.

In music of this sort it seems appropriate to let the melody stand out clearly from the background, and we can best achieve that effect by giving the melody to one color, the background to another. In this case, the simplicity and delicacy of the first eight bars suggest a relatively light scoring—possibly a solo woodwind against soft strings. Flute, though weak in this register, would come through all right if the background were kept light, and it would have a certain quiet charm. Oboe (in its most characteristic register) would be more pungent and penetrating. Clarinet would also be possible—a bit more warm and romantic in quality than the other woodwinds. Incidentally, clarinet in A is preferable to B♭ clarinet here, since the latter would have to be written with a key signature of six sharps (or, enharmonically, six flats) while clarinet in A involves a signature of one sharp. Violins on the melody would be expressive and effective; the harmonic background in that case might be given to horns rather than strings, in order to let the melody stand out more sharply; or it could still be allotted to strings. (Muting of the string background would produce a slightly different color from the melody.) By taking the melody down an octave we could give it to the cellos or to one solo cello in a particularly expressive register of the instrument. If that is done, some rearrangement of the harmony parts is necessary. This last scoring is used in version 2(d).

As for the second eight measures, they seem to demand a fresh color on the melody as well as a little more weight. If a solo woodwind has been used in the first version, the melody might well be given to strings in octaves here, or to strings and woodwinds doubled in octaves. If strings took the melody in the first eight bars, an octave doubling of woodwinds would give the greatest contrast in the second eight; or here, again, the combination of strings and woodwinds in octaves would be effective. Even two-octave doublings could be used, as in versions (b), (c), and (d) of Example 3. There are additional harmony parts in the second eight bars.

Examples 2 and 3 that follow show some of the possibilities in scoring the first eight bars and the second eight bars, respectively. For reasons of space, only the first measure or two of each version is given here.

SOME POSSIBILITIES IN SCORING THE FIRST EIGHT MEASURES
OF THE BRAHMS EXAMPLE

Ex. 2

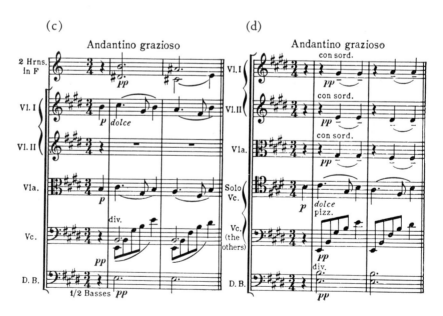

SOME POSSIBILITIES IN SCORING THE SECOND EIGHT MEASURES
OF THE BRAHMS EXAMPLE

Ex. 3

* Horn in bass clef to sound a 5th lower.

DOUBLINGS IN THE WOODWINDS

It is very common, in arranging, to give a melodic line to two or more different woodwinds in unison. We did not happen to make use of that device in the first eight measures of the Brahms example, but some woodwind doublings (both unison and octave) were involved in the scorings of the second eight measures. The list that follows shows some of the more usual combinations.

Unison Doublings in the Woodwinds	*Comments*
Flute and Oboe	Oboe predominates but is "softened" (in quality) by flute
Flute and Clarinet	Warm, round tone; not strong in the octave above middle C
Oboe and Clarinet	Mixes oboe's tang with clarinet's mellowness
Clarinet and Bassoon	Rich; somber if clarinet is low
Flute, Oboe, Clarinet	Thoroughly mixed color

Octave Doublings in the Woodwinds	*Comments*
{ Flute (upper 8ve) { Oboe (lower 8ve)	Good; frequent
{ Flute { Clarinet	Good; frequent
{ Oboe { Clarinet	Good; frequent
{ Clarinet { Oboe (or English Horn)	Infrequent with oboe; English horn usually better because its range extends lower
{ Clarinet { Bassoon	Very dark if instruments are in their lower register
{ Flute and Oboe { Clarinet and Bassoon	May take bassoon uncomfortably high; English horn may substitute for bassoon
{ 2 Fl., 2 Ob., 1 Clar. { 1 Clar., 2 Bns. (and/or { Eng. Horn)	Strong; good composite color; better balance with English horn included

Two-Octave Doublings in the Woodwinds	*Comments*
{ Flute { Oboe { Clarinet	Effective
{ Flute { Oboe { Bassoon	Fairly frequent in scores of the classical period (also with violins in the middle)
{ Flute { Clarinet { Bassoon	Effective
{ Flute { ----- (2 8ves { Bassoon apart)	Good. Omission of the middle octave makes for a particular effect
{ Flute { ----- (2 8ves { Clarinet apart)	Rare; unusual coloring; uses bright register of flute with dark register of clarinet

Three-octave doublings are possible with the addition of piccolo at the top, or bass clarinet or contra bassoon at the bottom; even four-octave doublings are occasionally seen.

There is not room here for detailed comment on the more rarely used doublings, such as flute and bassoon in unison, flutes an octave below oboes, low flutes with piccolo two octaves higher, clarinets two octaves apart, and so on. These combinations produce unusual and intriguing colors, but one must have a very intimate knowledge of the orchestra to use them successfully.

Doublings between Woodwinds and Strings

In unison doublings of woodwinds and strings, the woodwind tone tends to be overshadowed by that of the strings. Flute chiefly adds body—although not much. Oboe makes the string tone a bit more nasal and may even give it a pinched quality if the number of strings is small. English horn, on the other hand, can be combined with violas to produce an unusually poignant and attractive tone. (Remember, for example, the "love theme" in Tchaikovsky's *Romeo and Juliet*.) Clarinet lends a certain warmth and "roundness" to string timbre, plus a dark richness in its lower register. Bassoons are constantly associated with cellos or violas for the sake of added body. It might be mentioned, too, that the unison combination of horn and cello in the tenor register gives an expressive, noble sound that is well suited to slower, *cantabile* melodies.

Certain doublings in which a woodwind (or pair of woodwinds) plays one octave and strings another are effective and allow the woodwind tone to be heard more clearly than it is in unison doublings. Flute above violins is good; clarinet or oboe above violins less satisfactory. But clarinets can play an octave *below* violins with good effect, as can bassoons. The combination of woodwinds in octaves plus strings in octaves is a powerful and useful one.

In closing these remarks on doubling, it might be well to issue a small word of warning: remember that too constant use of mixed or composite colors becomes uninteresting and tends to make a score sound opaque and nondescript. Pure colors are needed for sparkle and transparency.

THE USE OF CONTRASTING SECTIONS

In order to deal with another aspect of scoring, let us turn to this small excerpt from the second movement of Beethoven's *"Moonlight"* Sonata:

Ex. 4. Sonata, Op. 27, No. 2 (second movement)

BEETHOVEN

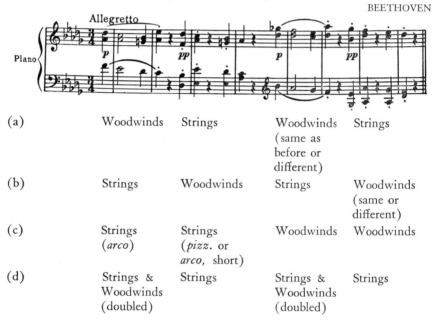

(a)	Woodwinds	Strings	Woodwinds (same as before or different)	Strings
(b)	Strings	Woodwinds	Strings	Woodwinds (same or different)
(c)	Strings (*arco*)	Strings (*pizz.* or *arco,* short)	Woodwinds	Woodwinds
(d)	Strings & Woodwinds (doubled)	Strings	Strings & Woodwinds (doubled)	Strings

Beneath the music are four possible "layouts," the sections being listed below the measures they would play. This passage involves two four-measure phrases, each one consisting of two segments. We can accentuate the strong antiphonal feeling between the segments of each phrase by using contrasting colors every two measures, as in (a), (b), and (d); or we can use one color on the first four measures, another on the second four—stressing, in that way, the antiphonal feeling between the two phrases, as in (c). Of course this excerpt is an extreme case; few pieces of music would lend themselves to so many contrasts of color within a few measures. It is quite possible to overuse the device of contrasted sections, with a resulting "patchy" quality in the scoring. This is, in fact, one of the most common failings of beginning orchestrators; they tend to think in terms of separate sections and to avoid the possibilities for combining instruments of different sections.

In the light of what was said earlier about avoiding remote keys, transposition to D major or C major might seem to be in order in this Beethoven excerpt.   However, the original key has been retained here, for several reasons: the music demands no great resonance and presents no technical problems; and most important of all, transposition to another key would completely destroy the striking parallel relationship between the somber C♯ minor of the famous first movement and the bright D♭ major of the second (it is assumed that both movements are being scored and that the original key is being retained in the first).

Of course the layouts shown beneath the excerpt do not exhaust the ways in which it could be scored.   They are merely a few possibilities that demonstrate the technique of contrasted sections.

This is the way version 4(a) might look, written out in actual score:

Ex. 5

SUGGESTED ASSIGNMENTS

A. Be able to comment on:

(1) Considerations in scoring music that involves a prominent melodic line against a subordinate background.

(2) Possibilities in contrasting one section of the orchestra with another.

(3) The effect of doubling various woodwinds with each other or with strings, either in unison or at the octave.

B. Score the first two bars of Mendelssohn's *Song without Words* No. 14 (C minor) in six different ways, for an orchestra consisting of strings, woodwinds, and horns. Use octave doublings of the melody in at least three versions.

C. Same assignment as B, but use the first four bars of Mendelssohn's *Song without Words* No. 20 instead.

D. The following are suitable as exercises in scoring for strings, woodwinds, and horns:

(1) Beethoven, Sonata Op. 10, No. 3, 1st movt.

(2) Beethoven, Sonata Op. 10, No. 3, 2nd movt. (*Largo e mesto*). Measures 30 to about 43 may be used as a separate assignment.

(3) Beethoven, Sonata Op. 27, No. 2, 2nd movt. (*Allegretto*), first 36 measures (a portion of this is used as an example in this chapter).

(4) Beethoven, Sonata Op. 90, 1st movt., first 24 bars (a good chance for the use of contrasting sections).

(5) Beethoven, Op. 14, No. 1, 2nd movt. (*Allegretto*), first 32 bars.

(6) Schumann, *Soldiers' March* from *Album for the Young*.

(7) Schumann, *Little Romance* from *Album for the Young*.

(8) Schumann, *Echoes from the Theater* from *Album for the Young*.

(9) Chopin, Prelude in A major.

(10) Tchaikovsky, *At Church* from *Album for the Young*.

(11) Tchaikovsky, *The Lark's Song* from *Album for the Young*.

(12) Tchaikovsky, *Polka* from *Album for the Young*. Score for small orchestra consisting of one flute, one oboe, one clarinet, one bassoon, one horn if desired, and strings.

(13) Grieg, Nocturne in C major.

(14) Scriabin, Etude in C♯ minor, Op. 2, No. 1.

(15) Debussy, *The Girl with the Flaxen Hair* (No. 8 in first book of Preludes).

E. The following require (or suggest) the use of a harp in addition to strings, woodwinds, and horns. It is therefore suggested that they not be assigned until after Chapter XIV has been studied.

(1) Fauré, *Pavane*.

(2) Debussy, *Clair de Lune* from *Suite Bergamasque*.

(3) Palmgren, *May Night*.

(4) Ravel, Minuet from Sonatine.

(5) Ravel, *Pavane pour une Infante Défunte*. (A good exercise in this case is to score the piece for two flutes, one oboe, two clarinets, two bassoons, two horns, harp, and strings, which is the instrumentation used by Ravel in his own scoring of the work; when you have completed your own version, compare it with Ravel's.)

Suggested Listening
SCORING FOR STRINGS, WOODWINDS, AND HORNS

Haydn, Symphonies.[1]

Mozart Symphonies [1]; Divertimenti; Overture to *The Marriage of Figaro*.[1]

Beethoven, Symphonies [1] (the Fifth, Sixth, and Ninth also include trombones).

Mendelssohn, *Midsummer Night's Dream* music (particularly the *Intermezzo* and *Nocturne*); Symphonies No. 3 and 4 [1]; *Fingal's Cave* Overture.[1]

Schumann, Second Symphony, 3rd movt.[1] (good example of different scorings of the same theme).

Brahms, Serenades; *Variations on a Theme of Haydn*.[1]

Schubert, Fifth Symphony.

Wagner, *Siegfried Idyll*.[1]

Debussy, *Prelude to The Afternoon of a Faun; Nocturnes:* I. *Nuages; Rondes de Printemps*.

Ravel, *Mother Goose* Suite; *Pavane pour une Infante Défunte; Le Tombeau de Couperin*.[1]

Prokofieff, *Classical Symphony*.

Delius, *On Hearing the First Cuckoo in Spring; Summer Night on the River*.

---

[1] These scores (or some of them, in the case of the Haydn and Mozart Symphonies) also include parts for trumpets. However, since in these cases the trumpets play only a small portion of the time, the works serve for the most part as examples of scoring for strings, woodwinds, and horns. The same is true, to a lesser extent, even of works scored for a larger instrumentation. That is, even when a full brass section is included, it will not play constantly by any means, and there will therefore be abundant instances of scoring that involves only woodwinds, horns, and strings.

Chapter XIII

THE PERCUSSION: INSTRUMENTS
OF DEFINITE PITCH

THE TIMPANI (OR KETTLEDRUMS)

Italian: Timpani   French: Timbales   German: Pauken

Ex. 1

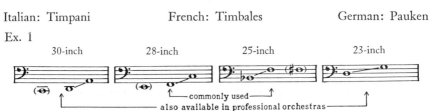

The spelling "tympani" (the plural of the Latin *tympanum*) is also widely used; but "timpani" (the plural of the Italian *timpano*) is preferred, inasmuch as Italian rather than Latin forms are used for most of the other instruments. Another point to note is that fact that "timpani" is already plural. The not uncommon error "timpanis" is just as absurd as "kettledrumses" would be in English.

There are two types of timpani to be considered: (1) the old hand-tuned type; and (2) the modern "pedal" or "chromatic" timpani, which did not come into general use until relatively recently. Although for all practical purposes the two have the same ranges and tone quality, they differ in their respective methods of tuning. In the case of the hand-tuned timpani, changes in pitch are made by tightening or relaxing screws around the edge of the "head," the piece of calfskin which is stretched across the top of the drum. Several measures (say at least six or eight in moderate 4/4 time) are required for each change, and the new pitch must be tested softly to make sure that it is just right. On chromatic timpani the pitch is controlled by a pedal and can be altered almost instantaneously. Players are fairly adept at adjusting the pedal to the right note by "feel," but they should be allowed a moment in which to check the accuracy of the new pitch.

Pedal Timpani

The great advantage of the pedal timpani is obvious. In addition to simplifying the life of the player tremendously, they make possible timpani notes at points where the old hand-tuned drums could not possibly have been ready in time. On rare occasions they may even play short melodic passages that move slowly enough to allow for pedal adjustments.

During the classical period, it was customary to write for two timpani (of the hand-tuned variety, of course). These were generally tuned in advance to the tonic and dominant notes in the "home key" of the composition and were not altered in the course of the work, although changes between movements of symphonies were sometimes called for. Later on, composers began to require changes in the midst of a composition or movement and to use three timpani instead of two.

Today most orchestras have at least three timpani on hand, and the larger professional orchestras include a complete set of four (of the sizes shown at the beginning of this chapter). Of these, at least two are usually pedal timpani, and in many cases all are of the pedal variety. When three timpani are used, they may consist of two 28-inch drums and one 25-inch, or two 25-inch drums and one 28-inch; or (less often) they may include a 30-inch or a 23-inch timpano, if these are available and the pitches required suggest their use. Unless one is sure of getting his score performed by a major orchestra, it is safest to plan the timpani part in such a way that it will be playable on not more than three timpani and will not go below 𝄢 or above 𝄢 .

As for school orchestras, few include more than two timpani, but these are of the pedal variety in many cases.

Normally there is one player for all the timpani, no matter what their number. If, as happens very infrequently, the part is designed to be performed by more than one player, that must be specially indicated. (See, for example, the *Fantastic Symphony* of Berlioz or Stravinsky's *The Rite of Spring*.)

Timpani are notated in the bass clef at actual pitch. Berlioz has pointed out that the sound we hear (that is, the notated sound) is actually the first overtone rather than the fundamental. The tuning of the timpani is indicated at the beginning of the composition, in either of the ways illustrated in Example 2.

Ex. 2

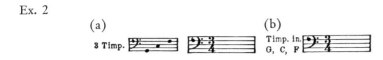

Ordinarily, the part is written without key signature, accidentals being added wherever necessary. In older scores even the accidentals are sometimes omitted, once the tuning of each drum has been shown. Another obsolete custom which is occasionally found in older scores is that of using the notes C and G to indicate the tonic and dominant notes, respectively, in keys other than C. In that case the actual tuning of the drums was of course shown at the beginning of the part.

As a general rule, timpani should be used only on notes that fit in as members of the harmony. The chord member most frequently allotted to them is the bass, but they may also take any other harmony note with perfectly good effect. For example, let us suppose that we have started a piece with three timpani tuned to G, C, and F as in the illustration above. At a certain point in the music we have a C major triad and want to include a timpani note or roll. C would be the most natural choice; but G would also fit in. In an F major triad either F or C could be used, with the tuning at hand, whereas G would be the only possibility in a G major triad. If a diminished 7th sound on G♯ (G♯, B, D, F) were involved, we would probably use the F already "set" on the top drum rather than tune the bottom drum up to G♯.

Let us imagine, now, that we have come to a G♭ major triad at a point where timpani are needed. With the present tunings, no one of the three drums is able to supply a tone that fits into the harmony. Assuming that there is time for a change before this passage, any one of five different retunings would give us a chord tone: (1) G down to G♭; (2) C up to D♭; (3) C down to B♭; (4) F down to D♭; or (5) F up to G♭. Any such change must be indicated in the part, preferably at the first rest where the player could make the change, so that he will have as much time as possible for the retuning operation. If the first of the five possible changes were chosen, we would write in the part "Change G to G♭." Scores using Italian terms throughout would say "G muta in G♭," the French version would be "Changez Sol en Sol♭," and in German the same direction would be "G nach Ges umstimmen." More than one change may be called for, provided there is sufficient time. It should now be obvious that in writing for timpani one cannot simply put down any notes desired and let the player worry about how to get them. It is necessary to score with a specific number of timpani in mind and to plan each note for a particular timpano; problems of retuning must be kept in mind constantly.

Occasionally it is possible to "get by" with timpani notes foreign to the harmony. These cases usually involve a chord of such short duration that the ear scarcely has time to be aware of the foreign timpani note before the next chord is heard. In a passage where the harmony is sustained, any deviation from a chord tone would be painfully apparent. In cases where it is impossible to prepare the required note on the timpani in time and a foreign note is unacceptable, one solution is to use the bass drum instead, since its pitch is indeterminate. The effect, of course, is not quite the same.

Single notes, rhythmic figures, and rolls are all effective on timpani. The roll may be written in either of these ways:

Ex. 3

(As with bowed tremolos in string writing, three lines through a stem ordinarily signify an unmeasured roll, whereas two mean measured sixteenths and one means eighths.) However, the trill sign is preferable for an unmeasured roll, because the other type of notation may be confused with an actual measured thirty-second note roll (particularly in slow tempos). Where several measures of roll are involved, it is safest to connect the notes with a tie to avoid any possibility that the player may think a fresh attack is wanted on each note:

Ex. 4

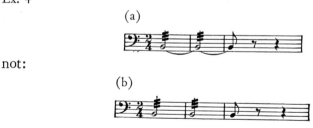

Or, if the trill sign is used, write as in Example 5(a).

Ex. 5

not:

With the last notation shown, the player would almost certainly make a new attack on each note. Notice that in these illustrations the roll is carried over so as to end on the beat. This is a frequent practice in percussion writing, the reason being that it is difficult to end a roll neatly "up in the air"; that is, on the last fraction of a beat. However, there are cases in which it would be inappropriate to carry the roll over into the next beat, and skilled players are able to cope with such spots. If a separately articulated stroke is wanted at the end of a roll, then the tie into the last note is omitted and the wavy line is stopped short of the last note:

Ex. 6

(Although rare in timpani writing, this effect is seen frequently in snare drum parts.)

Rolls (measured or unmeasured) on two different timpani are also a possibility:

Ex. 7

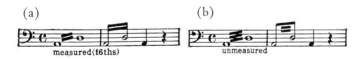

The importance of careful and detailed dynamic markings in percussion writing cannot be overstressed. It is not enough to write:

Ex. 8

The height of the crescendo here might be anything from *p* to *fff*, as far as the player can tell from the part. To give complete directions we would have to write:

Ex. 9

In long rolls it is not too much to indicate dynamics along the way:

Ex. 10

Probably the most frequent and obvious use of the timpani is that of "backing up" the rest of the orchestra in rhythmic figures.[1] At other times they may play a separate rhythm of their own. They are also excellent for reinforcing crescendos and for providing excitement or support in climaxes by means of rolls. They are seldom given extended solos, though isolated notes and groups of two or three notes played solo are frequent and highly effective. Good examples of solo writing for timpani can be found in the following works: Hanson, Third Symphony; Harris, Third Symphony (in the fugue); Strauss, *Burleska* for piano and orchestra; Shostakovitch, First Symphony (last movement). It is a mistake to think of the timpani as being valuable only for loud passages. Although they can supply a tremendous volume of sound, they are equally telling and dramatic in soft passages; in fact, their tone can be reduced to a barely audible pulsation. One word of warning might be added: because their tone quality is very different from that of other instruments, they must not be expected to "fill in" a chord tone by themselves—except that they can effectively play pedal points which are not doubled elsewhere in the orchestra.

Several special effects are possible on the timpani. One involves the use of wooden sticks, in place of the usual soft felt-headed sticks, to produce a harder, more sharply percussive quality (Italian: *bacchette di legno;* French: *baguettes en bois;* German: *mit Holzschlägeln*).

---

[1] It was conventional, in the classical period, to give the timpani and the trumpets the same rhythmic figure.

The indication for soft sticks is not normally included unless the player has previously been using hard sticks (Italian: *bacchette di spugna;* French: *baguettes d'éponge* or *baguettes molles;* German: *mit Schwammschlägeln*). Still different types of tone result from using sticks with Spanish felt heads or sticks with large or small heads. Another device calls for the use of both sticks at once on a drum; it is indicated by double stems. The result is thicker and weightier than the normal sound.

Ex. 11. Fourth Symphony

MAHLER

Revised edition copyright 1943. By permission of the copyright owner, Boosey & Hawkes, Inc.

It is also possible to play on two different timpani at the same time, as in this example:

Ex. 12. *Till Eulenspiegel*

STRAUSS

Berlioz even wrote three-note and four-note chords for timpani in the *Fantastic Symphony,* but of course these require two players. A particular tone quality can be achieved by striking the drum in the center instead of near the edge. (See Gershwin's *An American in Paris.*) And timpani may be muffled (or "muted") by placing a cloth about two inches square on the head of the drum near the edge. The Italian direction is *timpani coperti.* A special effect which is available on pedal timpani but not on the hand-tuned type is the glissando. As in string writing, the indication is a line between the notes (both of which must be within the range of one timpano, of course). Examples of effective timpani glissandos can be found in Bartók's *Music for String Instruments, Percussion, and Celesta* as well as in certain other Bartók works.

Tuning gauges have recently been introduced on some timpani manufactured in this country. These give the player a mechanical means of arriving at pitches with a fair degree of accuracy. So far they have

proved useful chiefly for inexperienced players who might otherwise
have difficulty in making pedal changes accurately or quickly enough.

EXAMPLES

Ex. 13

(a) Ninth Symphony

BEETHOVEN

(b) Symphony in E minor (*New World*)

DVOŘÁK

(c) *Don Juan*

STRAUSS

(d) First Symphony

BARBER

(e) Third Symphony

HARRIS

(f) Third Symphony

HANSON

Tempo scherzando ♩.=92

Timp.

p

Eastman School of Music Publication; Carl Fischer, Inc.

(g) *Music for String Instruments, Percussion, and Celesta*

BARTÓK

♩=circa 46

Timp.

Copyright assigned, 1939, to Boosey & Hawkes, Ltd.   By permission of the copyright owner, Boosey & Hawkes, Inc.

THE XYLOPHONE

Italian: Silofono	French: Xylophone	German: Xylophon
(or Xilofono)		(Old name: Strohfiedel)

Ex. 14

Sounding
an 8ve
higher

The xylophone consists of a set of wooden bars of varying lengths, arranged in the same pattern as the notes on the piano, sometimes with a tuned resonator beneath each bar.   It is played with hard mallets, normally two, although three or four may be used to play chords. Forsyth gives a good idea of the tone of the instrument when he speaks of its "hard dry clatter."   The notes are necessarily short and crisp, there being no way of sustaining them (except by means of a roll, which is a little too reminiscent of the old player-piano to be appropriate in serious music).   The xylophone is therefore completely unsuited to music of a lyric or *espressivo* nature.   But it can perform rapid scales, arpeggios, repeated notes, glissandos, and many other figures with surprising ease.   (Incidentally, passages entirely on the "white" keys are more difficult than those involving both black and white keys.)   In certain music it manages to give a saucy, mocking quality; at other times it may simply add a brittle edge to a melodic line or point up certain notes.   (See Debussy's *Iberia,* the section en-titled *Les parfums de la nuit,* for an example of this last use.)

Xylophones are built in various sizes; consequently it is impossible to give one range that will apply to all of them. Some do not include the notes shown in parentheses, and still others have an even shorter compass at the bottom. Notation is on a single staff, in treble clef, one octave lower than the sounds desired. Many books on orchestration recommend writing the xylophone part at actual pitch, and that system has been much used. But it was based on the belief that the instrument's range extended only up to

whereas the top sound on all xylophones is actually c^5, an octave higher than the pitch just shown. In view of this fact, the system of notation recommended here is a much more sensible one, since it avoids the use of an unreasonable number of leger lines in high passages.[2]

Xylophone parts should be written with a key signature, just as other parts are.

THE MARIMBA

The marimba is an instrument closely resembling the xylophone, but its tone is "oilier" and lacking in the spicy brittleness of the xylophone quality. The marimba is almost never used in symphonic writing and is mentioned here only to avoid a possible confusion between the two instruments.

EXAMPLES

Ex. 15

(a) *Petrouchka*

STRAVINSKY

(b) *Song of the Nightingale* (*Chinese Court Festival*)

ROGERS

Permission for reprint granted by Elkan-Vogel Co., Inc., Philadelphia, Penna., copyright owners.

---

[2] For an interesting discussion of this problem and a possible solution involving the use of a new clef, see *The International Musician* for January, 1951, page 22.

(c) *The Young Person's Guide to the Orchestra*

BRITTEN

The Glockenspiel or Orchestra Bells [3]

Italian: Campanelli   French: Jeu de Timbres   German: Glockenspiel
                                         (or Carillon)

Ex. 16

Sounding
two 8ves
higher

Two types of glockenspiel (or orchestra bells) are in use in orchestras today. The first consists of a set of metal bars mounted on a frame (similar to the xylophone's) with a resonator below each bar. The second type, which is more common, includes no resonators or supporting frame; instead, the bars are attached to a portable case, which is opened up and placed on a small table in performance. As far as range, abilities, and the type of part written are concerned, no distinction need be made between these two instruments.

The bright, ringing tone of the glockenspiel is normally produced by striking the metal bars with hard mallets or with metal hammers. A somewhat more subdued quality can be achieved by using soft mallets, but these should be called for specifically in the part when desired (The same directions, in foreign languages, as those given for "soft sticks" in the section on timpani are used.) Although it is possible for the player to hold two mallets in each hand and therefore to play three-note and four-note chords, parts for the instrument usually consist of a single melodic line. Their most frequent function is to add a bright tang to melodies taken by other instruments, but solos are

---

[3] Not to be confused with tubular bells, or chimes, which will be discussed further on.

practical and effective. (A very early example is the extended glockenspiel solo in Mozart's *The Magic Flute*.) The part is normally written two octaves lower than it is intended to sound. However, in Wagner scores and in certain others it is notated only *one* octave below the concert sounds. Glockenspiels, like xylophones, are built in various sizes; not all of them have the complete range shown here.

To compound the confusion, there is a third instrument that sometimes goes by the name of glockenspiel. This is the "bell lyre," which has come into the public eye as a member of most marching bands. It is a vertical and abbreviated version of the true glockenspiel, generally inferior in intonation and too loud and harsh for use in the concert hall.

There is also a keyed glockenspiel which is commonly used in Europe but is rarely seen in this country. This is the instrument for which the formidable looking glockenspiel part in Dukas' *The Sorcerer's Apprentice* was designed, by the way.

EXAMPLES

Ex. 17

(a) *Die Meistersinger*

WAGNER

(b) *Mathis der Maler*

HINDEMITH

Reproduced by permission of Schott & Co., Ltd., London.

THE VIBRAPHONE

Ex. 18

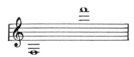

Being a child of the electrical age and therefore a relative newcomer to the instrumental scene, the vibraphone is not listed in any but the

most recent books on orchestration.   Although it has so far been associated more with radio and dance orchestras than with the symphony,
it is mentioned here because it turns up occasionally in serious symphonic music (for example, in Roy Harris' Third Symphony).   It
resembles the xylophone in general pattern.   Metal bars arranged in
"keyboard" fashion on a stand are resonated by tuned tubes below.
But the instrument is distinguished by an ingenious feature: small
metal discs, one at the top of each resonating tube, are made to revolve
by means of an electric motor, producing a kind of pulse or "vibrato"
in the tone (a quantitative rather than a pitch vibrato, however).   The
speed with which the discs revolve can be regulated, with a corresponding variation in the speed of the vibrato.   It is even possible,
of course, to cut out the vibrato effect entirely by turning off the motor
(direction: "fan off").   There is a damper pedal which may be used
to sustain or damp the sound ("damper off" for the sustained effect).

Parts for the vibraphone may be either melodic or harmonic in
character.   Isolated chords (up to four notes) that are allowed to ring
seem to show off the peculiar floating, undulating tone to best advantage in the orchestra.   Either hard or soft sticks may be used (most
often the latter).   The part is written on a single staff, in the treble
clef, at actual pitch.

Ex. 19. Third Symphony

HARRIS

THE TUBULAR BELLS (OR CHIMES)

Italian: Campane   French: Cloches   German: Glocken
                                                                 (or Tiefe Glocken)

Ex. 20

Of the various kinds of bells that have been tried in the orchestra
over the years, the "tubular" bells are the only type now in standard
use.   As their name suggests, they are not "bell"-shaped at all but

cylindrical, like chimes. They are hung from a rack and, when used as a complete set, are arranged like the white and black keys of the piano; that is, the bells that correspond with the black keys are hung behind the others and slightly higher so that there will be space to strike them. But since bell parts often consist of only a few notes, it is usually easier to hang up only those bells actually needed for a given work. Some sets of bells include a pedal by means of which the sound may be damped or allowed to ring. Because of the varying sizes of different makes of bells, the range given here is not an invariable one but may be considered more or less standard, at least in the United States.

The indication "sounding an octave higher" which appears next to the range of the bells needs a note of explanation, for it does not correspond with traditional practice. Heretofore, bell parts have usually been written as if they were sounding at actual pitch, the reason apparently being that bell tones give the illusion of being lower than they actually are. Percussionists now recommend a more accurate system of notation in order that the exact octave in which the passage is to sound will be clear to the player.

Ex. 21

(a) *Iberia*

DEBUSSY

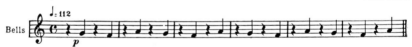

Permission for reprint granted by copyright owner, Durand et Cie, Paris, France; Elkan-Vogel Co., Inc., agents for the U.S.A.

(b) *Háry János* Suite (*Viennese Musical Clock*)

KODÁLY

Copyright assigned to Hawkes & Son, Ltd., 1939. By permission of the copyright owner, Boosey & Hawkes, Inc.

SUGGESTED ASSIGNMENT

A. Know:
    (1) Ranges of timpani of various sizes.
    (2) Which timpani are in common use.

(3) How tuning operation works, on hand-tuned and pedal timpani respectively.

(4) Special effects possible on timpani.

(5) Ranges, transpositions, and special abilities of other instruments discussed in this chapter.

B. Write out *The Star Spangled Banner* and on a staff beneath it write a timpani part. Assume that you have three pedal timpani (either two 28-inch and one 25-inch or two 25-inch and one 28-inch). The timpani need not play continuously.

C. Same assignment as B, but use *America* instead.

(Material for suggested listening is given at the end of Chapter XIV.)

THE PERCUSSION: INSTRUMENTS
OF INDEFINITE PITCH

THE SNARE DRUM (OR SIDE DRUM)

Italian: Tamburo   French: Tambour (Militaire)   German: Kleine Trommel
(Militare)   (or Caisse Claire) [1]

Along with other instruments of indeterminate pitch, the snare drum may be notated, in the score, either on an actual staff or simply on a single line:

Ex. 1

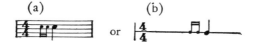

Sometimes a treble clef sign is included, with the staff notation, to distinguish the snare drum part from the bass drum and cymbal parts, which often use bass clef. (Of course the clefs have no pitch significance in these cases.) The snare drum part may be written in the third space or anywhere else on the staff that is convenient. (More will be said about this later.) When two percussion parts are written on the same staff in order to save space, separate stems (one up, one down) are used. Incidentally, the single-line type of notation is best avoided in the player's part, for it seems to be less easy to read than notation on a staff.

The snare drum is at its best in crisp, sharply rhythmic passages. It is played with wooden sticks and involves a technique that differs somewhat from that of any of the other percussion instruments.[2]

---

[1] Strictly speaking, the *caisse claire* is a very small drum; but the name is often used nowadays to mean snare drum.

[2] The "rudimentary" strokes which form the basis of the snare drummer's technique go by such intriguing names as *paradiddle, flamadiddle, ratamacue,* and *flamacue,* each of which imitates the rhythm of the stroke it applies to.

Some strokes which it uses frequently are the following:

The *flam* ____♪♩____ . In the "closed flam," which is the usual form, the first note is played before the beat, unaccented, and joined quickly with the second. This stroke is used to strengthen or lengthen a note. Sometimes it is included by the player even when it is not actually called for in the notation. The "open flam," in which the first note is articulated separately with more of an accent is extremely rare in orchestral playing.

The *drag,* usually ____♫♩____ , in which two very rapid notes precede an accented note. These preparatory notes are not heard separately but merge into a brief "roll" effect that is performed so quickly as to seem almost like a part of the accented note.

The *crushed ruff* ____♪____ in which both sticks are pressed to the head of the drum simultaneously and immediately released, giving a brief "B-r-r." The note has value in this case, in spite of the grace note indication through the flag.

The *four-stroke ruff* ____♫♩____ in which three notes precede an accented note. This stroke is played "open" (with the preparatory notes articulated).

The *roll* ____*tr*~~ ♩____ or ____♪____ .

Comments on the notation of the roll made in connection with the timpani apply here as well. This is one of the snare drum's most effective devices. As anyone who has even seen a tight-rope act will remember, an extended roll on the snare drum has an uncanny way of creating a sense of tension and expectancy. Shorter rolls are used constantly in march rhythms and in other orchestral parts played by the snare drum. As a rule, snare-drum rolls are best ended with a separate detached note.

A special effect which originated in the dance band and occasionally finds its way into the concert hall is the "rim shot." In the symphonic version of this stroke, one stick is placed with the tip on the drumhead and the butt on the rim and is then struck with the other stick. The result is a sharp, dry sound. Another possibility which figures constantly in the dance band but only rarely in symphonic music is the use of wire brushes on the snare drum.

Rhythmic patterns of all kinds and complexities are possible on

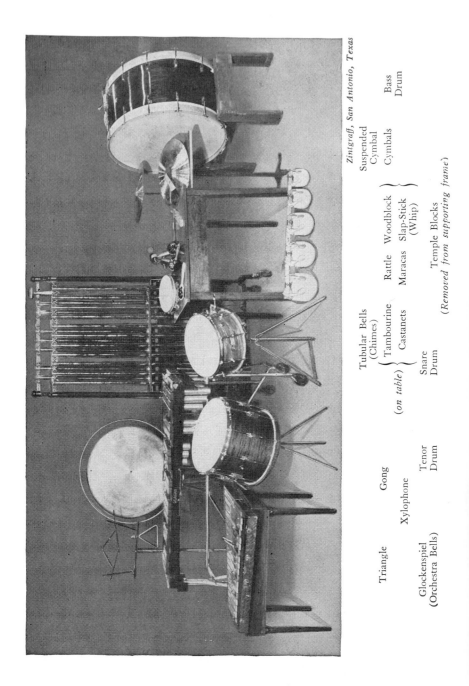

Triangle

Gong

Xylophone

Tenor
Drum

Glockenspiel
(Orchestra Bells)

Tubular Bells
(Chimes)
{ Tambourine
(on table){ Castanets

Snare
Drum

Rattle   Woodblock
Maracas   Slap-Stick
(Whip)

Temple Blocks
(Removed from supporting frame)

Suspended
Cymbal
Cymbals

Bass
Drum

Zintgraff, San Antonio, Texas

212

the snare drum. But it must not be kept going too steadily, for if overused it becomes either ineffective or downright tiresome. No better piece of advice can be quoted than Forsyth's sage comment, "Like almost all the other Percussion Instruments, its principal effect is its entry." Apropos of this point, a general axiom to keep in mind is the fact that instruments of highly individual color are generally effective in inverse proportion to the amount they are used.

The snares of the drum may be loosened, in which case the instrument loses its characteristically brittle quality and sounds rather like a tom-tom. The clearest direction for this effect is "snares off." Another special effect can be achieved by covering the drumhead with a handkerchief (direction: "cover head"). This is, by the way, the crispest sound obtainable on the snare drum. The term "muffled snare drum" has unfortunately been used to describe both these effects; consequently it has become ambiguous and is better avoided altogether.

Certain modern composers, Bartók among them, occasionally specify whether the snare drum is to be played at the edge or at the middle of the head. The latter way produces a crisper sound.

(Examples of passages for snare drum and for other instruments discussed here are given on pages 222 to 224.)

The Field Drum

Italian: Tamburo (Militare)   French: Tambour   German: Rührtrommel

As can be seen, there is a good deal of ambiguity in connection with the foreign names for the field drum, since some of them are used for other, slightly different instruments.

The field drum is longer than the snare drum, and its tone is somewhat deeper and less brittle. It is usually equipped with gut snares. Although it is regularly used in bands, parts for it in orchestral literature are extremely rare. (One example occurs in Hindemith's *Symphonic Metamorphosis of Themes by C. M. von Weber.*)

The Tenor Drum

Italian: Tamburo Rullante   French: Caisse Roulante   German: Rührtrommel

Also longer and larger than the snare drum, but not nearly so large as the bass drum, the tenor drum is used much less frequently than either of these two. It has no snares, and its tone is more somber than that of the snare drum. It is played with wooden or felt-headed sticks.

THE TABOR

French: Tambour de Provence   German: Tambourin
  (or Tambourin)

This is a very long drum, equipped with a single snare in most cases. It is rarely seen in the United States. The part for it in Bizet's second *L'Arlésienne* Suite is labelled "tambourin," and even eminent conductors have been known to make the mistake of having it played on the tambourine. Examples of the use of the tabor in contemporary music can be found in Aaron Copland's *Appalachian Spring* and in his *El Salon Mexico*.

THE BASS DRUM

Italian: Gran Cassa   French: Grosse Caisse   German: Grosse Trommel
  (or simply "Cassa")

Because of its great size and its relatively slow response, the bass drum is obviously not suited to the involved rhythms possible on many of its smaller relatives; simple rhythmic patterns and isolated notes are more practical and effective. Repeated notes had better be no faster than about eighths in moderate time (except in rolls). The instrument is normally played with a single soft beater, though two may be used to produce rolls. A rarely used special effect calls for the use of a wooden snare drum stick in place of the beater. (See Benjamin Britten's *Peter Grimes,* for example.)

Obviously the bass drum is well equipped to add volume or percussive accent. However, one must be a little careful about writing regularly recurring beats for it in serious symphonic music, lest the effect suggest parade music or the Big Top. Its effectiveness in soft passages is too often ignored; at lower dynamic levels it is "felt" rather than heard, and the lay listener may even be unaware that it is playing. Soft rolls, which give a faintly threatening sound not unlike distant thunder, are especially useful for color effects.

Of indeterminate pitch, the bass drum may be notated with or without the bass clef. As with other percussion instruments of indefinite pitch, it is sometimes written on a single line in the score (for reasons of space) but should be notated on a staff in the player's part. It is often written on the same staff with the cymbals, and the two parts are sometimes played by the same person. This arrangement will be explained in the section on cymbals that follows.

THE CYMBALS

Italian: Piatti   French: Cymbales   German: Becken

The notation of the cymbals is the same as that of the bass drum. When the two instruments are written on the same staff or line, the part may look something like any one of the three examples given here:

Ex. 2

There can be no objection to writing both instruments on the same staff, but it is highly unfortunate that both are sometimes played by the same person. One cymbal is attached to the top of the bass drum and the other is clashed against it, while the player uses his other hand to play the bass drum. Speaking about this arrangement, Berlioz says, "This economical procedure is intolerable; the cymbals lose their sonority and produce a noise similar to the sound of a falling bag full of old iron and broken glass."[3] Although this judgment may be a little extreme, there is no doubt that the tone quality of both instruments suffers when they are played in this way. Incidentally, the combination of cymbals and bass drum, playing either simultaneously or in alternation, has figured in so many "war horses" that it has become a bit dated and flat sounding, and it had better be used with caution if at all.

Among the various ways of producing sound on the cymbals, the crash or "two-plate stroke" is by far the most frequently used. The word "crash" must not be construed in this case as meaning only a loud sound, for this stroke can be performed at any dynamic level, from *ppp* to *fff*. One of the most ingenious and effective spots in orchestral literature occurs at the end of the *Fêtes* section in Debussy's *Nocturnes,* where the cymbals are merely rubbed together to produce

[3] Berlioz, *Treatise on Instrumentation.*

a faint "zing." Loud cymbal crashes are much more frequent and are apt to be used for moments of excitement or for climax points. Since there is considerable "ring" to a cymbal crash, it is wise to indicate in actual note values just how long the sound is to last before being damped. (Damping is achieved by touching the cymbals to the player's clothing.) If the sound is to be allowed to ring indefinitely, an easy indication is a small tie that simply ends in the air:⌒

Or the French expression *laissez vibrer* (let vibrate) is sometimes used. If, on the other hand, the note is to be "choked" (made very short), it should be written like this:

(*Sec,* or the Italian equivalent *secco,* means "dry.") "Choke" or "stop" may also be written in.

In the "two-plate roll" the cymbals are struck together repeatedly and rapidly. This is a difficult and infrequently used method which must be called for specifically when it is wanted.

For still another effect, a single cymbal may be suspended from a stand and struck with a stick, usually a wooden snare-drum stick or a hard-headed timpani stick, occasionally a soft stick. As with the cymbal crash, the tone may be damped or allowed to ring. This stroke is usable not only in a *forte* for purposes of excitement or percussive accent but also in a *piano* for a particular color effect. Rolls on the suspended cymbal can produce anything from an almost imperceptible shimmer to a deafening volume of sound. They are particularly useful for accenting a crescendo played by the rest of the orchestra. For a special effect, the suspended cymbal may be played with one or two wire brushes, as it often is in the dance orchestra.

Cymbal parts are occasionally printed in diamond-shaped notes, while commercial arrangements commonly use an X in place of a real note. Although these systems make the cymbal part easy to spot in the score, they have certain disadvantages: the diamond-shaped notes are difficult to make in writing music by hand, and the X's do not show the actual value of each tone. Consequently, ordinary notes appear to be the best solution.

The cymbals we have been discussing here are, of course, of indeterminate pitch. But the *cymbales antiques* (or *crotales*) used by Berlioz and later by Debussy, Stravinsky, and others, are capable of sounding definite pitches. These ancient (or antique) cymbals are much smaller than the kind commonly used and give out a high, bell-like tone.

The Triangle

Italian: Triangolo   French: Triangle   German: Triangel
  (Old name: Sistro)

Single notes, tremolos (rolls), and not-too-complicated rhythms are all effective on the triangle, and the *flam* and *drag* figures mentioned in connection with the snare drum are common. Normally, the instrument is suspended from one of the player's hands and struck with a single steel beater held in the other hand; more complex rhythms may be executed by suspending the triangle from a rack and using two beaters, one in each hand.

The silvery, ringing tone of the triangle is valuable for adding brilliance in either a *forte* or a *piano,* and a triangle roll at climax points can give an extra degree of excitement and intensity. Be careful not to use the instrument too long at a time, however, for its distinctive tone tends to pall quickly.

Actual solos for the triangle are rare, though the well-known one in Liszt's E♭ major Piano Concerto might be mentioned as an example. Notation is either on a staff (with or without treble clef) or on a single line.

Triangles are made in different sizes, and the tone quality varies accordingly.

The Tambourine

Italian: Tamburino   French: Tambour de   German: Schellentrommel
  (or Tamburo Basco)   Basque   (or Tambourin)

The tambourine consists of a small wooden hoop with a calfskin head stretched across one side of it and pairs of small metal plates, called "jingles," attached in openings cut in the hoop. The instrument may be played in various ways:

(1) It may be struck with the fist. This method is suitable for isolated notes and for fairly simple rhythms. It produces the percussive sound of the knuckles striking the head, along with the sound of the jingles. The word "fist" is sometimes written in. Some players prefer to strike the tambourine on their knee to produce the same effect, and in rapid passages alternate fist and knee strokes are sometimes used.

(2) It may be shaken, in which case a "roll" on the jingles results. This is a brilliant sound, useful as an added touch of excitement and color, and especially good in dynamics of *forte* or louder. The notation is either _____ or _____ (preferably the first).

(3) The thumb may be rubbed over the head to produce a roll on the jingles. This effect is especially appropriate for softer dynamic levels, though it can also be played *forte*. Ravel uses _____ for this thumb method and _____ when the tambourine is to be shaken, a simple and efficient way of distinguishing between the two effects.

(4) The tambourine may be laid on a table or flat surface with the head facing upward (or downward for a slightly different effect) and may be played with sticks. The result is a combination of "struck sound" and "jingle sound." When this method is to be used, some such direction as "Played with soft sticks" or "Played with snare drum sticks" must be included.

Of course no one method of playing need be used consistently. It is quite possible to have, say, a "fist" note on the first beat of a measure and a roll on the succeeding beats. Obviously the fourth method takes a moment to set up and cannot be intermingled quickly with the others (except by using two tambourines). The tambourine is frequently used to back up vivid rhythms, or it may simply add color or accent at certain points. Characteristic parts for the instrument can be seen in Rimsky-Korsakoff's *Capriccio Espagnol* and Wagner's *Tannhäuser* Overture, among other works.

THE GONG OR TAM-TAM

Italian, French, and German: Tam-tam

This is a circular piece of hammered or spun metal which is struck with a soft-headed beater. Its tone is most effective when the instrument is allowed to vibrate a moment; therefore, when successive strokes are used, they should be spaced far enough apart to allow for ample vibration on each. However, rolls are possible. Although the gong is not ordinarily damped, *secco* (short) notes are occasionally used. In *The Rite of Spring* Stravinsky introduces a curious effect: the player describes an arc on the surface of the gong with the triangle beater.

Gongs are made in various sizes, and some composers specify "large gong" or "small gong" in their scores.

Possibly by association with the Mysterious East, the tone of the gong is, to Western ears, ominous and faintly spine-chilling. Although this quality has been exploited rather melodramatically by the radio and Hollywood, it has been used with more restraint and with fine dramatic effect by certain serious composers—for example by Strauss in *Death and Transfiguration* and by Tchaikovsky in his Sixth Symphony. (The latter work also involves a suggestion of death at the point where the gong plays, according to the commonly accepted program.) However, the instrument is by no means confined to such macabre themes. Sometimes it is used for an isolated *fortissimo* note, just as one might use a cymbal crash; or a single soft tone may add an unexpected and exotic touch of color to a chord. (See Griffes' *The White Peacock,* for instance.)

Incidentally, *tam-tam,* the European name for gong, must not be confused with *tom-tom,* the name for a snareless drum of a particular type.

THE CASTANETS

Italian: Castagnette   French: Castagnettes   German: Kastagnetten

The sound of castanets is familiar to everyone through Spanish music. But for the sake of those who have never seen them close at hand, they might be described as resembling oversized hickory nuts, chopped in half and partially hollowed out. The name itself means "chestnuts" and was presumably derived from the type of wood used. Today castanets are most often made of ebonite. They were designed originally to be clicked in the hand (that is, with a pair to each hand); but the current practice in orchestras is to use a specially built stick with a pair of castanets attached to it, which can be shaken to give the same clicking sound.

Granted that castanets are "naturals" for music with a Spanish flavor, they can sometimes be included effectively in non-Spanish music when a crisp rhythmic background is in order.

For more detailed information on characteristic castanet rhythms, the reader is referred to Forsyth's *Orchestration.*

THE WOOD BLOCK

The wood block figures occasionally in modern scores, particularly in ballets and in music that is highly colored or strongly rhythmic, or both. It is, as its name implies, a small rectangular piece of wood (or of plastic), solid except for slits cut into it on two sides to give resonating space. Wooden drum sticks or xylophone mallets are used in playing it, and rhythms of all kinds are possible. The tone is dry and brittle—a little reminiscent of horses' hoofs, especially in certain rhythms. Single notes on the wood block have an impudent, unexpected quality that may verge on the comic.

CHINESE TEMPLE BLOCKS

Chinese temple blocks are a series of hollow wooden blocks, roughly circular in shape and painted in fantastic dragonhead patterns. Wooden or felt sticks are used in playing them. They may come in any number from two to five (five being the standard number) and are graduated in size, so that the pitch varies from one to the other. The tone is similar to that of the wood block, but a little "rounder" and hollower. Although temple blocks are tuned to a pentatonic scale, no attempt is made to notate actual pitches in writing for them. But since some system must be used to distinguish one block from another, a note (any note) is usually assigned to each block and the part written accordingly. The pitches chosen may be a series of scale tones or the notes of an arpeggio; it does not matter, as long as they are arranged in the same relative order of pitch as the temple blocks.

LATIN-AMERICAN PERCUSSION INSTRUMENTS

Some of the instruments frequently used in Latin-American music are the following:

The *claves,* two short sticks which are struck together. One is held in such a way that the cup of the hand resonates the sound.

The *maracas,* two hollow gourds with handles attached and dried seed (or buckshot) inside. They are shaken to produce the characteristic rhythms of the Rhumba, the Beguine, and other dances. Claves and maracas are nearly always used together. Following is a characteristic passage for them:

Ex. 3

The *guiro*, a serrated gourd which is scraped with a stick.

Bongos, one-headed drums open at the bottom and played with the fingers.

Timbales, like the bongos but larger.

OTHER PERCUSSION INSTRUMENTS

There are, in addition to the instruments already mentioned, others which are very rarely used. In this category might be listed the ratchet or rattle (German: Ratsche) and the wind machine, both found in the Strauss tone poems; the slap-stick or whip (see Copland, Third Symphony, and Mussorgsky-Ravel, *Pictures from an Exhibition: "Gnomus"*); cow-bells, used by Milhaud in his *La Création du Monde;* sleigh-bells, which figure in the Mahler Fourth Symphony and in Respighi's *Roman Festivals,* for example; and the "anvil," which is really a small steel bar made so as to sound like an anvil, and which appears in scores by Verdi, Berlioz, Mahler, Wagner, and others. The list could be extended still further by the addition of such realistic sounds as the clanking of steel plates in Mossoloff's *Iron Foundry* or the recorded song of a nightingale in Respighi's *Pines of Rome.*

THE PERCUSSION SECTION AS A WHOLE

Percussion parts fall into two broad categories:

(1) Those which point up the actual thematic or structural aspects of the music (timpani parts, for example, are most often of this sort).

(2) Those which are included chiefly for color purposes. But since the possibilities in both categories are almost infinite, an attempt to catalog them completely would be futile. Furthermore, each composition to be scored is an individual case with its own peculiar demands and possibilities. The best solution is to fix the sounds of the various percussion instruments in one's aural memory and draw on them as imagination and taste dictate.

It might be pointed out here that the dynamic range of the percussion section is greater (at both loud and soft extremes) than the dynamic range of the rest of the orchestra. This relationship can be illustrated on paper in the following manner:

Dynamic range of the percussion:

Dynamic range of the rest of the orchestra:

EXAMPLES

Ex. 4

(a) *Scheherazade*

RIMSKY-KORSAKOFF

(b) *Bolero*

RAVEL

Permission for reprint granted by copyright owner, Durand et Cie, Paris, France; Elkan-Vogel Co., Inc., agents for the U.S.A.

(c) *American Festival* Overture

WILLIAM SCHUMAN

Copyright, 1941, by G. Schirmer, Inc.

(d) *Fire Bird* Suite

STRAVINSKY

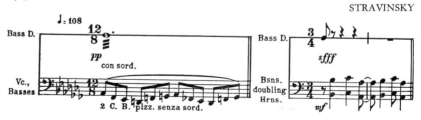

(e) *El Salon Mexico*

COPLAND

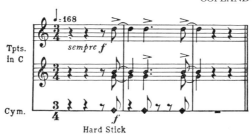

Copyright, 1939, by Hawkes & Son (London) Ltd. By permission of the copyright owner,
Boosey & Hawkes, Inc.

(f) *Capriccio Espagnol*

RIMSKY-KORSAKOFF

(g) *Carmen*

BIZET

(h) *The White Peacock*

GRIFFES

(i) *Bolero*   RAVEL

(j) *Capriccio Espagnol*   RIMSKY-KORSAKOFF

(k) *Symphonic Metamorphosis of Themes by C. M. von Weber*   HINDEMITH

(This passage is for percussion alone and continues for eight more measures.)

THE ARRANGEMENT OF PERCUSSION PARTS

In the score, timpani are generally listed first among the percussion instruments. Then follow the instruments of indefinite pitch—in any order—and finally the glockenspiel, xylophone, celesta, and piano (although few scores use all these instruments). Because the celesta and the piano are not usually played by members of the percussion section, they are discussed in another chapter along with the harp.

Most professional orchestras have at least three percussion players (including the timpanist). The usual plan is to hire extra percussionists for works that require them, although the orchestra's budget unfortunately enters in here, and percussion parts have been known to go unplayed for economic reasons. With a little judicious planning, it is usually possible to arrange the percussion parts so that one player can play several instruments (successively, of course!).[4] For purposes of illustration let us suppose that at a certain point the triangle must play a few notes; eight bars later there is a passage for snare drum, and sixteen bars after that the xylophone has a solo. There is no reason why the same player cannot handle all three instruments in turn. As for the player's part in that case, the three instruments could all be written on the same sheet, or the snare drum and triangle might be written on one part, the xylophone on another. In the latter case, there should be a cue in the snare drum-triangle part to show the player where the xylophone solo occurs. (Cues are discussed in greater detail in Chapter XIX.) There is no hard and fast rule for the grouping of percussion instruments in either score or parts, because each score presents individual problems and the best solution can be determined only by "horse sense." However, snare drum and triangle are often written on the same staff, usually with triangle notes on the

top space and snare drum notes on the third space

---

[4] However, it is possible for one percussionist to play certain *pairs* of instruments at the same time if need be. For example, a player can strike the triangle with one hand and shake the tambourine with the other, or play the bass drum with one hand and the gong with the other.

As has already been mentioned, bass drum and cymbals frequently share the same staff. It is normally impractical to write two percussion instruments of *definite* pitch on the same staff. Timpani parts are nearly always separate; that is, they have a staff to themselves in the score, and a separate player's part.

Probably the most practical plan (especially if a good many percussion instruments are involved) and one which has been used by Hindemith, Hanson, Britten, Lambert, and others is to arrange the percussion parts with a specific number of players in mind and to show each player's part on a separate staff (even in the score, in some cases). For example, in *The Rio Grande* Lambert calls for five percussion players (including the timpanist) whose parts are labeled 1 through 5. When all five are playing, the parts look like this:

Ex. 5. *The Rio Grande*

Copyright, 1928, Oxford University Press; reprinted here by permission of the copyright owner.

(It happens that the timpani part has been put at the bottom here instead of in its usual place above the other percussion.) If only certain players are involved, the parts are designated by number:

Ex. 6. *The Rio Grande*

LAMBERT

Under this system, each percussionist may be called on to play several different instruments in the course of his part (each new instrument being indicated at its entrance, of course). This whole arrangement has decided advantages. For one thing, it solves in advance the problem of distributing the parts in a practical way among a given number of players—a problem which must otherwise be solved by the percussionists in rehearsal, often with a good deal of frenzied rushing from one instrument to another. Also, it saves copying of several different percussion parts for the players if the following procedure is used: all the percussion parts (excluding the timpani in most cases) are written on the same sheet and copies of that sheet—as many as are needed for the players—are then made by the "Black and White" process or some other method of reproduction. (See Chapter XIX.) This system has the further advantage that each percussionist has all the parts before him and can therefore relate his own part to those of the other percussionists.

Whatever arrangement of percussion parts is used, the number of players required should be indicated at the beginning of the score, along with the list of instruments. In a few rare instances, as many as six or seven percussion players are called for. An extreme example is Respighi's *Roman Festivals,* which lists fourteen percussion instruments, ten of which play at once at one point! But that sort of thing is obviously impractical as a general rule. It is, in fact, the kind of instrumentation that the aspiring composer had better not imitate if he expects to get his scores performed.

SUGGESTED ASSIGNMENTS

A. Be able to list the percussion instruments discussed here (except the Latin-American instruments and those included under "Other Percussion Instruments," page 221) and to translate the foreign names for them into English.

B. Know:

(1) The strokes commonly used on the snare drum.

(2) The various ways of playing cymbals and tambourine.

(3) Special abilities of each of the instruments.

(4) Proper notation in each case.

SUGGESTED LISTENING

PERCUSSION (INCLUDING TIMPANI)

Timpani Studies by Alfred Friese, with Edwin McArthur, pianist, and Dr. Philip James, narrator (recorded by Benjamin Sachs, Artist Recordings, 939 Eighth Avenue, New York). The most valuable portion of this album is that which presents numerous solos and prominent passages for timpani from standard orchestral literature, with the orchestra parts reduced for piano.

Rimsky-Korsakoff, *Capriccio Espagnol; Scheherazade.*

Debussy, *Iberia.*

Ravel, *Daphnis and Chloe* Suite No. 2; *La Valse; Rapsodie Espagnole.*

Kodály, *Háry János* Suite.

Respighi, *Pines of Rome; Fountains of Rome; Roman Festivals.*

Stravinsky, *Les Noces; L'Histoire du Soldat; The Rite of Spring.*

Bartók, *Music for String Instruments, Percussion, and Celesta;* Sonata for Two Pianos and Percussion; Concerto for Orchestra.

Hindemith, *Symphonic Metamorphosis of Themes by C. M. von Weber.*

Chavez, *Sinfonia India.*

Hanson, *Merrymount Suite.*

Lambert, *The Rio Grande.*

Copland, *El Salon Mexico; Appalachian Spring.*

Britten, *The Young Person's Guide to the Orchestra,* Theme E and Variation M.

Shostakovitch, Fifth Symphony.

Piston, Suite from the ballet, *The Incredible Flutist.*

Varèse, *Ionisation* for eleven percussion instruments.

Instruments of the Orchestra (Victor, 20523 B).

Chapter XV

THE HARP, CELESTA, AND PIANO

THE HARP, celesta, and piano have been allotted a special chapter because they do not belong to any of the four orchestral groups already discussed. True, the harp and the piano do have strings, but they are not classed as stringed instruments because their tone is not produced by bowing. Although the celesta is listed with the percussion group in some orchestration books, it is not normally played by a member of the percussion section; most orchestras have a separate player who performs either celesta or piano parts as required.

THE HARP

Italian: Arpa   French: Harpe   German: Harfe

Ex. 1

The harp differs from other instruments in being built on a non-chromatic basis; that is, instead of having twelve strings (one for each semi-tone) within each octave as one might expect, it has only seven. When the instrument is in its "home" key, these are tuned to the notes in the scale of Cb major: Cb, Db, Eb, Fb, Gb, Ab, and Bb. At the base of the harp are seven pedals, each one controlling all the strings of a particular letter-name on the instrument and capable of raising those strings either a half step or a whole step in pitch. For example, if the appropriate pedal is pressed halfway down (where it can be secured in a notch) all the strings that formerly sounded Cb

229

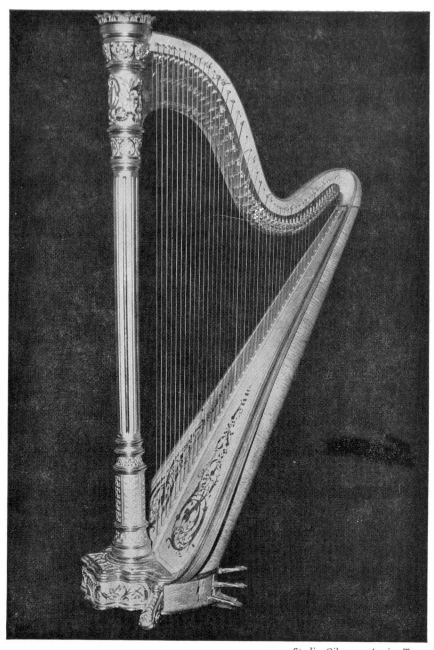

Harp

will now sound C♮; if we depress the same pedal still further to a
bottom notch, the same strings will sound C♯. Using another pedal,
the D♭'s in all octaves can be raised to D♮'s or to D♯'s; and so on,
with all the strings. It is obviously impossible to tune the strings of
one letter name differently in different octaves.* The reason for using
the forbidding key of C♭ major as the basic key of the harp may now
be apparent: it is the only one in which each pitch can be raised two
semi-tones without the use of double sharps (or double flats to begin
with); the three pitch possibilities of each string can be expressed
by a flat, a natural, and a sharp.

The pedals are arranged in semi-circular fashion around the base
of the harp, three on the left, four on the right, in the following
sequence:

D C B | E F G A

The three on the left are operated by the harpist's left foot; the
other four, by the right foot. It takes only an instant to depress
or release a pedal, and two pedals may be changed at the same time
as long as they are on different sides of the instrument; for example,
B and G, or D and A, or C and F. Harpists do occasionally take the
E pedal with the left foot in cases of absolute necessity; that is, in
order to achieve a double change of pedals on the right side quickly.
But the opposite arrangement (use of the right foot for pedals on the
left side) is so awkward as to be impractical. Fortunately, these
fine points need seldom be considered, since it is usually possible
to make pedal changes one at a time rather than simultaneously.

The "setting" of the pedals at the beginning of a work should be
indicated in the harp part; and each pedal change should be written
in, preferably at the point where it is actually to be made. (Changes
can often be made most conveniently in rests that occur several beats
or even several measures before the point where the actual sound is
wanted.) To illustrate: suppose that we have a piece in the key of
E♭ major. It happens that the harp does not play for the first twelve
measures. The beginning of the harp part, including pedal setting
and necessary changes, might look like Example 2.

---

* The only exceptions are the bottom C string and the top G string. These are **not**
controlled by the pedal mechanism and must be tuned independently by hand.

Ex. 2

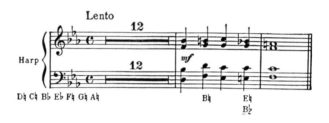

It can easily be seen why the harp does not lend itself to music of a chromatic nature. Constant pedal changes become overtaxing for the player, and in highly chromatic music that moves along at a faster speed than that in Ex. 2, it may be completely impossible for the harp to make pedal changes fast enough to "fit in" with the harmony. In such cases there are several possible solutions:

(1) Omit the harp altogether. It should not play constantly anyway, and there is no point in trying to force on the instrument a type of music that is basically foreign to its nature.

(2) Use two harps, letting them take turns at playing. Each harp will then have rests during which the necessary pedal changes can be made. Strauss, Debussy, and others often use two harps, not only for the reason just discussed but to give greater volume when both are playing at once.

(3) Write the part (for one harp) in such a way that the chromatically changed notes are omitted as much as possible, assuming that other instruments are playing along with the harp and will make the harmony sound complete. Using this third approach, the passage above might have been written:

Ex. 3

This version involves no pedal changes and will be about as effective as the first way—provided, of course, that other instruments are playing the notes omitted from the harp part. The harp is, after all, primarily a color instrument in the orchestra; and as long as its rich, warm quality is heard, the omission of a note here and there will not be apparent in such a case, although the same would obviously not be true in a passage for harp alone.

(4) Omit the *chords* involving chromatic alterations and let the harp take, say, the chord on the first beat of each measure. Or give it some other pattern, depending on where and how often the harmony changes. In our own example, it might well play the first and third beats:

Ex. 4

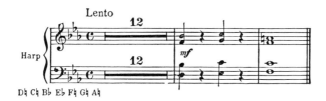

This same type of simplified part is often used in passages which involve rapid melodic lines that would not be practical or effective on the harp.

Notice that the key of a piece is not always an accurate index of the pedal setting at the beginning. For instance, in the fragment we have been using as an illustration, the key is Eb, which might suggest that Ab would be wanted as part of the pedal setting. But the first time an A of any kind occurs, it is an A♮. Therefore we may as well have the A♮ tuning prepared at the beginning.

Harp parts may be written either with or without a key signature. If the part is fairly diatonic, a key signature appears to be the most sensible solution. But if the harp has a part which would require constant cancellations of the signature, then it may as well be written without key signature, the accidentals being written in.

Two notes which sound the same but are spelled differently are spoken of as being "enharmonic." If we think back to the possible tunings of each harp string, we will discover that there are a good many possibilities for enharmonic notes where the strings overlap in pitch. For example, if we have the B pedal in the middle notch so that the string will sound B♮, and the C pedal in the top notch to produce Cb, the two strings will give the same pitch. The whole list of enharmonic possibilities is as follows:

Cb–B♮	Eb–D♯	Gb–F♯
C♮–B♯	E♮–Fb	G♯–Ab
C♯–Db	E♯–F♮	A♯–Bb

The word "homophones" is sometimes used to describe these en-harmonic tones on the harp.   They are useful in various ways, but most frequently in connection with glissandos.

In performing a glissando, the player draws his hand quickly across the strings, touching each string included within the "sweep."   Be-cause it is not possible to skip over any of the strings, each one must be tuned in such a way as to fit into the musical scheme at that point. The glissando may consist of a scale or a chord.   If a scale is used, there is no particular problem, since the strings can be adjusted to give any major or minor scale, each string sounding one note of the scale.   But suppose that we want a chord, say a dominant 9th sound on C, to be played as a glissando.   We could prepare C♮, E♮, G♮, Bb, and D♮ on the strings of those letter names.   There is then the problem of what to do with the F and A strings.   Can they be made to fit into the chord, and if so, how?   By putting the F pedal in the top notch, the string can be made to sound Fb, equivalent to E♮ in pitch; by depressing the A pedal to the bottom, we can make that string sound A♯, or the same as Bb.   Our complete pedal setting, then, would be: C♮, D♮, E♮, Fb, G♮, A♯, Bb.   When the player's hand is drawn rapidly over the strings, the fact that certain pitches are sounded twice will not be apparent to the ear.   The result will simply be a dominant 9th sound on C without any extraneous tones.   To give another illustration, suppose we want a diminished 7th chord on F♯ to be played as a glissando.   The pedal setting in that case would be: F♯–Gb, A♮, B♯–C♮, D♯–Eb.   (The letters have been listed here in such a way as to show the enharmonic pairs.)   Obviously, not all chords can be played as glissandos.   In the case of a G major triad, for example, the A string cannot possibly be raised to the enharmonic equivalent of B nor lowered to the enharmonic equivalent of G; like-wise, the E and F strings cannot be made to fit into the chord.   The only solution, in such cases, and one that is commonly used, is to include "extra" notes.   With the G major triad, the A string could be tuned to A♮, the E string to E♮, both extra; the C pedal would be tuned to Cb

(＝B♮) and the F pedal to F♭ (＝E♮). The notes played by the harp, then, would be: G♮, A♮, B♮, C♭, D♮, E♮, F♭. Although this is a more highly colored sound than the pure G major triad, the added notes would not sound as "extraneous" as might be expected. Of course another solution here would be simply to abandon the attempt at a chord glissando and use the notes of the G major scale as a glissando. Either way would give the requisite "splash."

Glissandos may be begun and ended anywhere on the harp, may be made in either direction, and may cover as much of the instrument as desired. They are usually at least two octaves or so in length, since it is difficult to work up much sound or sense of sweep within shorter distances; sometimes they cover nearly the entire range of the instrument. Various methods of notation have been used, but the clearest and most satisfactory one (as applied to ) seems to be the following:

Ex. 5

Of course the proper pedal settings must have been indicated previously. It is possible to play up to six notes (three in each hand) in an ascending glissando and up to eight notes in a descending glissando. A triple glissando is included in the examples that follow.

Ex. 6

(a) *Daphnis and Chloe* Suite No. 2

RAVEL

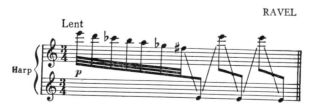

(b) *Fire Bird* Suite

Notice that in glissandos the actual notes (including any enharmonic sounds) need be written out for only one octave. If the strings are tuned to sound these pitches in one octave, they must sound them in all octaves. Consequently it would be superfluous—as well as a great nuisance—to write out every note in the glissando. The matter of time values is not of any great importance; orchestrators seem to use anything from sixteenths to sixty-fourth notes. Usually there are so many notes that the actual mathematical values would be hard to notate accurately anyway.

There is no denying the fact that the glissando is basically one of the most intriguing and effective sounds in the harp's repertory. But it has been so overused (particularly in radio and film music) that it has lost some of its freshness and charm; it is best used sparingly nowadays.

Normally, the harp's tones are allowed to ring after being plucked, and they have considerable sustaining power. When that effect would cause a blur or be inappropriate to the music, the player may be directed to damp the sound with his hands. For a series of notes or chords, each one to be damped immediately after it is played, the French expression *sons étouffés* ("damped sounds") is commonly employed. Sometimes the single word *étouffez* is placed at the end of a passage or after a glissando, to show that the sound must not be allowed to ring. The contrary direction is *laissez vibrer* ("let vibrate").

As was intimated earlier, the harp is by nature more harmonic than melodic in feeling. As a rule, melodies played on it sound thin and ineffectual, though it occasionally doubles a slow melodic line for a special color effect. Arpeggios and chords are its most frequent assignments. Some typical and effective arpeggio figures are shown on the next page.

Ex. 7

(a) *Prelude to The Afternoon of a Faun*

DEBUSSY

(b) *The White Peacock*

GRIFFES

(c) *Requiem*

BRAHMS

Because of the angle at which their hands engage the strings, harpists do not use the little finger of either hand in playing. That means that chords involving more than four notes to a hand cannot be played, except by using a very pronounced roll or arpeggio effect. Incidentally, the stretch of a 10th on the harp is roughly equivalent in difficulty to the stretch of an octave on the piano and may be considered a safe practical limit.

It is traditional to roll all chords slightly in harp playing; a vertical wavy line in front of a chord should be used only when a much more decided roll is wanted. If a chord is to be played without any roll whatever (that is, with all the tones starting at exactly the same time), a bracket the length of the chord should precede it (Example 8).

Ex. 8

Double 3rds and 6ths are quite feasible, either harmonically or melodically performed:

Ex. 9

Rapid repeated notes on the same string are not very practical; a sudden return to the string only damps out the vibrations of the previous note before they have had a chance to get well started. Here is another case in which the enharmonic possibilities of the harp prove useful. By tuning two strings to the same sound and playing them alternately, we get the effect of a repeated note, but each string has twice as long to vibrate as it would if used by itself:

Ex. 10

Obviously, two strings will produce more sound than one. It is for that reason that we sometimes find a single sound written for two enharmonically tuned strings, as in the following:

Ex. 11. *Daphnis and Chloe* Suite No. 2

RAVEL

Although the changing of pedals is part of the harpist's business, it is only humane and reasonable to avoid unnecessary pedal changes. This can often be done by using a "false" spelling for certain notes. For instance, Example 12, as written, requires constant changing of the B pedal and a double change of the D and B pedals. (The double change is especially bad since both pedals are on the same side of the instrument.)

Ex. 12

If the passage is written as follows, different strings are involved, and no pedal changes are necessary:

Ex. 13

From the standpoint of harmonic spelling, this last way is obviously incorrect. In fact, the whole system of false notation produces results that would send a harmony teacher to an early grave. Nevertheless, its use is justified in harp writing by the fact that it makes for greater ease in performance.

The bottom notes of the harp are dark and sonorous in quality, the middle register rich and warm. Although the higher strings do not have much volume or sustaining power, their dry, slightly percussive quality enables them to come through more clearly than might be expected. It should be remembered, though, that whatever register the harp is playing in, it cannot compete with large masses of sound if it is to be heard prominently. Because harp strings are slightly more resonant in their "flat" position—in the top notch—flat keys should be chosen in preference to sharp keys where there is a choice. For example, if the rest of the orchestra were playing in B major, it would usually be best to write the harp part enharmonically in C♭ major.

Harmonics can be produced on the harp: (1) by touching the string lightly in the middle with the lower part of the left hand and plucking the string with the left thumb; or (2) by touching the string lightly in the middle with the knuckle of the index finger of the right hand, and plucking the string with the right thumb. The note that results is the first overtone, an octave higher than the normal pitch of the string. (Although harmonics involving higher overtones are possible, they are almost never used.) Harmonics have an attractive crystalline, bell-like quality; but as they have little volume, there is no point in using them except in passages where the background is extremely light. They are useful for single notes or, rarely, for short melodic lines that move slowly enough to allow for the special technique involved in playing the notes as harmonics. It is possible to play two harmonics at once with the left hand, but not with the right. Therefore, three-note chords of harmonics are available. The middle register of the harp is much the best one for harmonics. As regards the notation of them, there are, unfortunately, two different systems in current use: (1) the harmonic is written at its actual pitch; or (2) it is written an octave lower than the pitch desired. In both cases, a small circle above the note is the indication for a harmonic. The first way seems the simpler, but since the second has been used more often, any harmonics had better be accompanied by a note in the harp part telling which method is being used. In Example 14, the harmonics are intended to sound an octave higher than the written notes.

Ex. 14

(a) *Fire Bird* Suite

STRAVINSKY

(b) *Prelude to The Afternoon of a Faun*

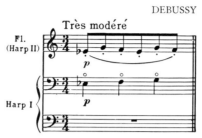

DEBUSSY

(c) *Daphnis and Chloe* Suite No. 2

RAVEL

There is not space here to describe all the other special effects possible on the harp. Many of them have been widely used in solo music for the instrument (particularly in pieces by the eminent harpist Carlos Salzedo) but have been little exploited in symphonic music. However, one or two of the most important might be mentioned. There is, first, the brittle, somewhat metallic sound produced by playing with the fingernails. The usual symbol for this effect is, logically enough, a small crescent-shaped sign like a fingernail. The back of the nails may also be used in playing glissandos, to give what the Salzedo school calls a "falling hail" effect. Then there is the special tone quality that results from playing close to the sounding board. (*Sons près de la table* or simply *Près de la table* is the French direction.) Particularly when played with the nails, notes taken close to the sounding board have a surprising way of suggesting muted trumpets playing at a distance. Another effect which Strauss sometimes calls for is a soft tremolo performed by the two hands in alternation. The usual marking is, *bisbigliando,* meaning "whispering," though this same indication sometimes accompanies effects other than the tremolo.

Instead of writing out the letter names and accidentals for pedal setting, harpists generally use a small diagram which is really a "picture" of the pedals. A horizontal line corresponds with the middle notch on all pedals. Small marks above, through, or below this line show whether the pedals are in the top, middle, or bottom notch, respectively. For example, the pedal setting Db, C#, Bb, E♮, Fb, G#, Ab would be indicated as follows:

This system has been little used in orchestral scores but appears to be as clear as the traditional method.

THE CELESTA

Italian: Celesta   French: Celesta   German: Celesta

Ex. 15

In appearance the celesta is rather like a small piano. It has a keyboard like the piano's (though much shorter)and a "damper" pedal which, when depressed, allows the tone to ring. But in place of strings, the instrument is equipped with small steel bars, each one with its own wooden resonator. These give out a delicate, bell-like tone. Gordon Jacob remarks, picturesquely, that the tone of the celesta always reminds him of the taste of a ripe plum.[1] In spite of its charm, however, it has little power and is drowned out by anything but the lightest of backgrounds.

The celesta is most often used to add a silvery edge to a melodic line. At other times it may merely provide "shimmer" via an arpeggio or some other figuration, as in the Ravel example below. On rare occasions it may take a melody or a complete harmonic passage by itself, as in the Tchaikovsky example.

---

[1] Gordon Jacob, *Orchestral Technique.*

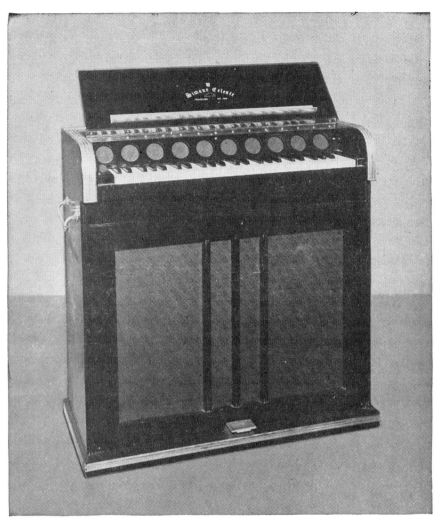

Zintgraff, San Antonio, Texas

Celesta

EXAMPLES

(Celesta sounding an octave higher)

Ex. 16

(a) *Nutcracker* Suite

TCHAIKOVSKY

(b) *Schelomo*

BLOCH

Copyright renewal assigned, 1945, to G. Schirmer, Inc.

(c) *Daphnis and Chloe* Suite No. 2

RAVEL

Permission for reprint granted by copyright owner, Durand et Cie, Paris, France; Elkan-Vogel Co., Inc., agents for the U.S.A.

THE PIANO

Italian: Pianoforte   French: Piano   German: Klavier

Ex. 17

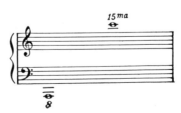

The piano is not, strictly speaking, an orchestral instrument, but it is occasionally used in the orchestra for purposes of color or special effect. Its upper register can add sparkle or a bright clang, while the bottom notes are sometimes employed for their dark, faintly gong-like quality or to add percussive force and body to a bass line. The middle register, being more neutral in color, is less interesting in the orchestra. Furthermore, use of the piano for middle-register harmony parts is apt to be unpleasantly reminiscent of small radio and salon orchestras in which the piano must often take the place of missing horns, bassoons, and other instruments. Also to be avoided, as a rule, is the "fussy," rich-textured sort of writing that figures in piano concertos of the romantic period. Something simple and striking will be far more effective. In fact, parts for the piano as an orchestral instrument seem to be successful to the extent that they get away from overfamiliar "solo piano" patterns.

It should perhaps be emphasized that the piano is called for only rarely in orchestral writing, even in contemporary works. When it is included, it is best used in small doses like other "special" orchestral colors. Excellent examples of its use in modern music can be found in Prokofieff's Fifth Symphony and in Copland's Third Symphony.

EXAMPLES

Ex. 18

(a) *Fire Bird* Suite

STRAVINSKY

(b) First Symphony

(c) *Pines of Rome*

By permission of G. Ricordi & Co., copyright owners.

THE PIPE ORGAN

Although there is not room here to go into the complicated workings of the pipe organ, that instrument should possibly be mentioned as another "extra" since it figures in a few orchestral scores (Scriabin's *Poem of Ecstasy* and Respighi's *Pines of Rome,* to mention only two). Most often it is reserved for grandiose climaxes, where it supplies added volume and its own majestic tone quality. Occasionally the pedals (especially with 16-foot and 32-foot stops) are used alone to double the lower orchestral instruments for an extra-dark, ponderous effect. Music for the organ is written on three staves, the upper two for the "manuals" or keyboards, the bottom one for the pedals.

SUGGESTED ASSIGNMENTS

A. Know:
    (1) Ranges of harp, celesta, and piano.
    (2) Function of pedals on harp and order in which they are arranged.
    (3) Enharmonic possibilities, false spelling.
    (4) Proper notation of glissandos.
    (5) Special effects on the harp.
    (6) Transposition of celesta.
    (7) Effective uses of celesta and piano in the orchestra.

B. (1) Give the pedal setting that would be used if each of the following harmonies were to be played as a glissando on the harp. If any of the chords are impossible as a glissando (without the addition of extra notes) indicate that opposite the appropriate number.

Ex. 19

(2) List the dominant 7th chords possible as glissandos on the harp and show the pedal setting for each.

SUGGESTED LISTENING

HARP

Berlioz, *Fantastic Symphony,* 2nd movt. (*Un bal*).

Wagner, *Love Death* from *Tristan and Isolda; Immolation Scene* from *Die Valkyrie.*

Franck, Symphony in D minor, 2nd movt.

Tchaikovsky, *Romeo and Juliet; Waltz of the Flowers* from the *Nutcracker* Suite.

Rimsky-Korsakoff, *Capriccio Espagnol,* near beginning of section IV (*Scena e Canto Gitano*).

Debussy, *Afternoon of a Faun; Nocturnes:* II. *Fêtes; Iberia; La Mer.*

Ravel, *Introduction and Allegro; Daphnis and Chloe* Suite No. 2; *La Valse; Rapsodie Espagnole; Le Tombeau de Couperin; Pavane pour une Infante Défunte.*

Widor, *Chorale and Variations* for harp and orchestra.

Stravinsky, *Fire Bird* Suite; *Orpheus,* First Scene and Third Scene.

Bartók, Concerto for Orchestra, particularly Section III (*Elegia*) and latter part of Section II (*Giuoco delle Coppie*).

McDonald, Suite *"From Childhood"* for harp and orchestra.

Dello Joio, Concerto for Harp and Orchestra.

White, *Sea Chantey,* for harp and orchestra.

CELESTA

Tchaikovsky, *Dance of the Sugar Plum Fairy* from the *Nutcracker* Suite.

Strauss, *Der Rosenkavalier,* number 303 (near the end) and following, also other passages.

Debussy, *Iberia,* Section II (*Les Parfums de la nuit*).

Ravel, *Daphnis and Chloe* Suite No. 2; *Rapsodie Espagnole.*

Stravinsky, *Petrouchka* (celesta played 4-hands at figure 15).

Bloch, *Schelomo.*

Griffes, *The White Peacock.*

Bartók, *Music for String Instruments, Percussion, and Celesta.*

Shostakovitch, Fifth Symphony, end of 3rd movt.; Sixth Symphony, 1st movt., at number 28.

PIANO

Saint-Saëns, *The Carnival of Animals.*
Stravinsky, *Fire Bird* Suite; *Petrouchka; Symphony of Psalms;* Symphony in Three Movements; *Les Noces.*
Prokofieff, Fifth Symphony.
Respighi, *Pines of Rome; Roman Festivals.*
Shostakovitch, First Symphony.
Copland, *Rodeo; El Salon Mexico; Appalachian Spring.*
Lambert, *The Rio Grande.*

Chapter XVI

SCORING FOR FULL ORCHESTRA

SO FAR we have dealt almost entirely with the scoring of chordal and homophonic music. In this chapter the first project to be undertaken, by way of illustration, is the orchestration of excerpts from a typical polyphonic composition, a Bach fugue. The whole question of scoring purely polyphonic music has been put off until now so that we would have the entire orchestra to work with. In a sense, this is one of the more difficult aspects of orchestration. In linear music everything is "out in the open"; there are no rich masses of harmony, no easy "effects" to fall back on, and the relative weight of each line must be calculated with special care.

One of the main objectives in scoring music of this kind is to bring out the individual voices clearly. Here the orchestra has a certain advantage over the piano: whereas the piano has only one color to offer, the orchestra has many, and by allotting a different color to each voice we can give the lines a clarity and independence—a kind of third-dimensional feeling—that is impossible on the piano. For example, if three voices are involved, we might give one to oboe, one to clarinet, and one to bassoon. But it is not always necessary to use sharply contrasting colors. The three voices might also be given to violins, violas, and cellos, respectively, in which case the differences of timbre, although less decided, would still afford a small color contrast between the parts. While it is possible to use instruments of different sections on the various parts, one must be careful to choose instruments which can be made to balance properly. It is also possible to contrast one composite color with another composite color—or with a pure color.

Doublings of the top voice an octave (or even two octaves) higher and of the bottom voice an octave lower are useful and effective in arrangements of polyphonic music. But octave doublings of the inner

249

voices are apt to be less successful, for they often involve a crossing of parts that may cause a "muddled" effect. When that happens, they had better be avoided.

Obviously, an instrument or group of instruments that begins a particular voice should follow through on that voice to the end of the phrase or musical thought. In fugues, for example, it is usual to retain the same instrument on each voice at least up to the point where all the voices have announced the subject. After that, changes in scoring on the various parts are definitely in order, at points where the structure of the music seems to warrant them. Re-entrances will be doubly effective if they can be scored in a timbre that has not been heard for several bars. To state the case another way, if an instrument is to make an important entrance, try to give it at least a few measures of rest beforehand.

With these brief remarks as a prelude, let us go on now to the fugue we are to use for our sample scoring. The first excerpt is the beginning or exposition of the fugue. Instead of including a separate example to show the actual orchestration, we have simply indicated here in the piano version the instruments that might be chosen. As no dynamics are given in the original, we have had to invent our own. The third and fourth announcements of the subject have been marked a bit louder than the first two in order to bring them out in relation to the upper voices.

Ex. 1. Fugue II (Book II of *The Well Tempered Clavier*)

BACH

Probably pure colors are best here at the beginning, mixed tone being reserved for later sections. By the same token, although it would be possible to give this opening section to brass instruments, it is much more effective to save them—or at least some of them—for the heavier, more emphatic announcements of the subject that usually occur later in the fugue.

The next excerpt is an ingenious *stretto* from about the middle of the fugue (in a *stretto* the subject overlaps itself). Here the subject appears in three different versions: (1) in the original form; (2) in augmentation (with note values doubled); and (3) in inversion (with the direction of the intervals reversed). If the musical content of this passage is to be made clear, each voice must stand out sharply on its own; and that effect, in turn, can best be achieved by using a different color on each voice. Here again, we have merely suggested one of the many possible ways in which the excerpt could be transcribed.

Ex. 2

The third excerpt consists of the last five and one half bars of the fugue, again an impressive *stretto*. (Each entrance of the subject or a portion of it is marked with an "S" here.)

Ex. 3

Although this fugue is usually played legato, a marcato effect seems appropriate, or at least possible, in this concluding section for the sake of greater "punch," and that interpretation has been used in the orchestral version that follows. We shall probably want to bring our full orchestra, including brass, into play here. As the voices seem to be about equally important and must therefore be balanced, it will be necessary to distribute them among the brass instruments, strings and woodwinds being doubled with these parts, either in unison or at the octave. However, instead of using the entire orchestra from the beginning of the passage, strings and woodwinds have been added one or two at a time, in order to accentuate each entrance of the subject and also to achieve a cumulative effect in leading to the *tutti* at the end. It would have been possible to reverse the orchestration by starting the final *stretto* with strings and woodwinds and adding brass at each entry of the subject.

It must not be concluded from these comments that the brass should be included only in *fortissimo,* heavily scored passages or that all the brass instruments must play if one plays. It is quite possible to use a single brass instrument on one voice with woodwinds and/or strings on other voices as long as the dynamics are adjusted to give proper balance.

As another example of polyphonic music scored for full orchestra, an excerpt from the Prelude to *Die Meistersinger* is given following the Bach scoring.

Ex. 4. Fugue II (Book II of *The Well Tempered Clavier*) (Arr. by K. W. K.)

253

Ex. 5. Prelude to *Die Meistersinger*

WAGNER

As we turn now to the scoring of other types of music for the complete orchestra, there is little new in the way of general principles that need be added. If the music is chordal, we can apply the material learned in Chapter X, the only difference being that a succession of chords is involved instead of a single isolated chord. The important question of voice-leading between the chord tones consequently enters in here too.

Suppose that we had set out to score the Brahms Rhapsody in E♭ major (Op. 119, No. 4), the beginning of which is a good example of chordal music. The first two measures are as follows:

Ex. 6. Rhapsody, Op. 119, No. 4

BRAHMS

Although, as we have seen, "scoring for orchestra" does not necessarily involve making constant use of all the instruments on hand, this particular example seems to suggest the full orchestral *tutti*. It also suggests a fairly brilliant coloring. We shall want to fill in the gap between the two hands, of course. It would probably be wise to sketch the orchestration (for at least the first chord or two) before writing out the actual score. Such a sketch, showing the layout of each section, might look like this:

Ex. 7

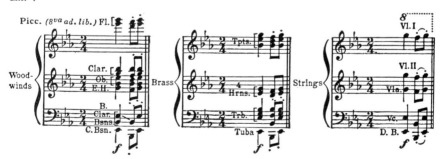

We would undoubtedly want to use timpani as well, either on the first beat of each measure

Ex. 8

(a)

or on the complete rhythmic pattern

(b)

(assuming that three timpani are available). Having once set up this arrangement of instruments, our only problem is to let each note progress to the appropriate note in the next chord, so that good melodic lines will result for the individual instruments. Of course there will be different arrangements of the instruments as the musical structure changes. An excellent exercise would be to write out the first ten measures (or more) of this piece in full score, using the sketch given here as the basis for the beginning.[1]

The excerpt from Strauss' *Death and Transfiguration* that follows is a good example of primarily chordal music scored for full orchestra. Incidentally, it illustrates the fact that full scoring need not be reserved for very loud passages; in this case the dynamic marking is *pianissimo.*

---

[1] Transposition of the piece to a slightly lower key would allow the trumpets to enter in a more comfortable register.

Ex. 9. *Death and Transfiguration*

257

Another example of chordal texture is the Mussorgsky-Ravel excerpt (Example 10). Here the original piano version is included
at the bottom for purposes of comparison and is not meant to be
played in the orchestral version.

Ex. 10. *Promenade* (from *Pictures from an Exhibition*)

MUSSORGSKY-RAVEL

259

The scoring of homophonic music was discussed in Chapter XII. There we used an orchestra consisting of woodwinds in pairs, horns, and strings. If a larger orchestra is involved, the problem is not altered as far as essential principles are concerned; the inclusion of additional woodwinds and of a full brass section merely gives us greater potential volume, increased range in the woodwind and brass sections, and new colors which may be used in a solo capacity. Some examples of homophonic music scored for full orchestra are shown next. (The first example makes use of the "full orchestra" of Beethoven's day, one which included no trombones.)

In Example 11 the melody is taken by first violins and first horn in octaves, with the second horn harmonizing in the same rhythm and bassoons joining in presently to double these two voices in a lower octave. The upper woodwinds have sustained harmony parts; second violins and violas take "string-istic" accompaniment figures, while trumpets, timpani, and lower strings reiterate the A pedal point.

In Example 12 the chief melodic line in octaves is given to a doubling of woodwinds, brass, and strings, with harmonic background and moving bass also distributed among the three sections.

Example 13 (a) demonstrates an arrangement which is uncommon in piano music but fairly frequent in the orchestra: the melody is in the bottom voice with harmonies above. Here, again, an octave doubling made up of brass, strings, and woodwinds is used for the melody. In this case the brass will predominate.

In Example 13 (b) the two melodic lines, played by trumpets and (in the last two bars) by trombones, are in middle voices, with harmonic parts above and below. Because of the power of the trumpet and trombone, two of each give enough sound to come through the rest of the orchestra.

In Example 14, the most important melody is given to the strings, a countermelody to the woodwinds, and a second countermelody to the upper brass. Except for an E pedal-point which is shared by the lower brass and the double basses, this excerpt illustrates on a broad scale the principle we discussed in connection with polyphonic music, that of allotting a separate color to each voice to achieve the maximum distinctness and independence of line. Here we have not merely separate colors, but separate *sections* on the various parts. It might be argued that this example is actually polyphonic rather than homophonic in texture. The truth is probably that it lies somewhere between these two types; we are dealing in lines, to be sure, yet the countermelodies in woodwinds and brass seem to have the character more of ornamented harmony parts than of independent voices on a par with the melody in the strings.

This case brings up the point that music does not always fall exclusively into one of the three categories we have mentioned frequently in this book: chordal, homophonic, or polyphonic. We have used these categories in order to point out certain broad approaches to scoring. But there are hybrid types, and it is not uncommon to find two or more types occurring at once. For example, we often have an important melodic line against a harmonic background (homophony) along with countermelodies that introduce a partially polyphonic effect. And some harmonic music consists of individual lines which move in an independent and musically interesting way, so that a polyphonic element is present.

When countermelodies are involved, one must be careful to "weight" the principal idea strongly enough—either by dynamics or sheer number of instruments—so that it will not be eclipsed by the secondary counterpoints. Many a beginning arranger has discovered that miscalculations in this respect result in a jumble of sound in which the chief point of the music is lost. Notice, by the way, that in Example 14 the trumpets and horns are marked one degree softer than the woodwinds and strings in order to compensate for the greater power of the brass.

In Example 15 the woodwinds and horns take the melody and its parallel harmonization, while the strings play a countermelody and the brass also has subordinate parts.

Ex. 11. Seventh Symphony

BEETHOVEN

Ex. 12. Symphony in D minor

FRANCK

263

Ex. 13. Symphony in E minor (*New World*)

(a)   (b)

DVOŘÁK

TCHAIKOVSKY

Ex. 15. *Les Préludes*

LISZT

In orchestral scoring, crescendos and diminuendos can be achieved not only by actual dynamics but by the gradual addition or subtraction of instruments. For the crescendo, instruments are introduced one or two at a time, usually softly, so that the listener is generally unaware of the separate entrances and senses only the gradual build-up as more and more instruments join in and increase in volume. For the reverse effect, individual instruments make a diminuendo and drop out successively. Although these devices did not happen to figure in any of the examples in this book, they are seen quite frequently in scores and are extremely valuable.

Other Exercises

A word might be added here about certain exercises which have not been mentioned before. One consists in "de-orchestrating"; that is, reducing an orchestral score for piano, or for piano four hands, or for two pianos (possibly even for organ in the case of students who are organists). Almost any orchestral music may be chosen for this purpose, though for the first attempt it would probably be wise to select a relatively uncomplicated score, say a Mozart or Haydn symphony. This is an excellent way to achieve an intimate acquaintance with a score and with the composer's characteristic use of instruments.

Piano reductions of many scores are available commercially. Another exercise consists in arranging such a reduction for the same orchestra which the composer originally used. The completed scoring can then be compared with the original orchestral version.

A somewhat similar exercise, mentioned earlier, is that of scoring a work which was written originally for piano and later issued in orchestral form. (A list of such works is given at the end of Chapter XI.) The student's version can then be compared with the published orchestral version. The same process might of course be applied to songs or chamber works which were subsequently orchestrated by their composers or others.

Finally, there is score-reading at the piano—or at two pianos, with one player taking the woodwind and brass parts and the other taking the string parts. In any case, it is wise to begin with fairly simple material and progress to more complex.[2] Although this is a rather

---

[2] In this connection, Martin Bernstein's *Score Reading* (M. Witmark, 1932) provides an excellent series of graded excerpts and is highly recommended. A revised edition of the book has recently been issued.

special technique which can be learned only by repeated practice over a period of time, a few advance hints may be of some help:

(1) It will not always be possible to play all of the notes; sometimes octave doublings, secondary counterpoints, and the like will have to be omitted.

(2) In widely spaced chords, string figurations, and other passages which are awkward pianistically, some rearrangement of the notes will be necessary. This process is the reverse of the one we discussed in the chapter on transcribing piano music.

(3) Try to keep going in spite of minor slips or omissions. It is more important to keep the music moving along at a steady pace (not necessarily up to tempo, however) and to aim at the general effect of the original than to worry too much about individual notes— although accuracy should be striven for, of course.

Suggested Assignments

The following are suitable as exercises in scoring for full orchestra (although not all of them call for consistently heavy scoring). If it is possible to have a school or local orchestra try out student projects in orchestration, the instrumentation of that orchestra should be learned in advance and used for the pieces to be played.

(1) Bach, any of the chorales.
(2) Bach, Fugue in Bb minor (No. 22, Book I of *The Well Tempered Clavier*).
(3) Bach, Fugue in G minor (No. 16, Book I of *The Well Tempered Clavier*).
(4) Beethoven, *Sonata Pathétique,* Op. 13; first 6 bars.
(5) Brahms, Rhapsody in Eb major, Op. 119, No. 4; first 10 bars or first 64 bars.
(6) Chopin, Polonaise in A major, Op. 40, No. 1; first 8 bars (or more).
(7) Mussorgsky, *The Great Gate of Kiev* from *Pictures from an Exhibition;* first 21 bars (or more).
(8) Mussorgsky, *Ballet of the Chickens in their Shells* from *Pictures from an Exhibition* (this offers a good chance for the use of special color effects: harp, celesta, percussion, etc.).
(9) Schubert, Sonata in A minor, Op. 143, first movt.
(10) Rachmaninoff, Prelude in G minor.
(11) Griffes, *The White Peacock* from *Roman Sketches.*
(12) Griffes, Scherzo, Op. 6, No. 3.
(13) Prokofieff, March, Op. 12, No. 1 (this offers a good chance for the use of percussion and "extras").
(14) Debussy, *The Sunken Cathedral,* No. 10 in the first book of Preludes (this offers a good chance for the use of impressionistic color effects).

Chapter XVII

INFREQUENTLY USED INSTRUMENTS

THE SAXOPHONES

Italian: Sassofono	French: Saxophone	German: Saxophon
Sassofoni	Saxophones	Saxophone

Ex. 1

Bb Soprano, sounding a major 2nd lower.
Eb Alto, sounding a major 6th lower.
Bb Tenor, sounding a major 9th lower.
Eb Baritone,[2] sounding an 8ve and a major 6th lower.
Bb Bass, sounding 2 8ves and a major 2nd lower.

All the saxophones have the same *written* range and all are notated in the treble clef, but each size transposes differently. The written note would sound as follows on each of the saxophones:

Ex. 2

Therefore, in terms of actual sound we have five different ranges:

Ex. 3

Awkward as this system may seem, it has the advantage of enabling the player to use the same fingering on any one of the saxophones.

---

[1] Many alto saxophonists are able to play the high F# or even G, although these notes are more difficult.

[2] Some baritone saxophones do not have the top F.

Let us suppose that we are scoring a piece for a combination that includes saxophones. We have decided that a particular melodic line lies comfortably within the range of the tenor saxophone and will sound well on that instrument. The part begins like this:

Ex. 4

In order to notate the passage correctly we must transpose up a major 9th (an octave plus a major 2nd). The written part will then begin with these notes:

Ex. 5

To write a part for the baritone saxophone we must think up an octave plus a major 6th from the actual sounds—and so on for the other saxophones.

A very small "sopranino" saxophone and a "contra-bass" saxophone are listed in some orchestration books, but these are simply not in current use. Likewise all but extinct is the "C-melody" saxophone which had a considerable vogue at one time. Even the bass and soprano instruments are little used today, although the latter has found favor with certain dance orchestras. (Incidentally, there are two types of soprano saxophone, one a miniature counterpart of the larger saxophones, the other straight like a clarinet.) But the alto, tenor, and baritone members of the family are in constant use in commercial arranging.

In the symphony orchestra, saxophones are employed only rarely. Examples that can be cited are the parts for them in Ravel's *Bolero* and the wonderfully effective solo for alto saxophone in the same composer's orchestration of Mussorgsky's *Pictures from an Exhibition* (in the section entitled *The Old Castle*). School orchestras, however, sometimes use saxophones as substitutes for horns, bassoons, or other instruments that happen to be missing; and some scores for school use include actual parts for saxophones.

In general, the entire compass of the saxophone is usable, although the bottom three or four semitones tend to be slightly inferior and are better avoided. In writing for inexperienced players it is wise to avoid the extreme upper register as well. The instrument is remarkably agile technically. Almost every sort of figure is practical on it; but, being of the single-reed family like the clarinet, it is not well suited to playing rapid repeated notes. The bass saxophone, because of its greater size and ponderous operation, cannot be expected to perform quite as nimbly as the others, especially in the bottom 5th or so of its register.

It seems only fair to point out, in defense of the saxophone and its symphonic possibilities, that it need not have the blatant, "wailing" quality nor the wide, bleating vibrato that we hear so often in the dance band. That is merely one style of playing; the instrument can be made to produce a much more refined and sensitive tone, one that is more appropriate for serious music. Even so, it seems unlikely that the saxophone will ever become a regular member of the symphony orchestra.

The examples that follow show two different ways of arranging a chorale excerpt for groups of saxophones. The soprano and bass saxophones have not been included in these scorings, since they almost never figure in symphonic orchestration. The original key of the chorale was E minor; but other keys have been chosen here with an eye to good key signatures and comfortable playing ranges for the saxophones.

Ex. 6. *Jesu, meine Freude*

BACH

(a)

(b)

Actual Sounds

2 Alto Sax.

1 Tenor Sax.

1 Baritone Sax.

THE FLUTE IN G

Ex. 7

Sounding a perfect 4th lower

Strangely enough, the flute in G is known both as "alto flute" and as "bass flute." The first name appears to be the more logical of the two and is preferred.[3] Since the instrument has the same written range as the ordinary concert flute but sounds a 4th lower, its sounding range extends down to the G below middle C. Its tone is rich and velvety, although not quite so good in the top octave as in the middle and lower parts of its range. There is not much point in using the highest register anyway as the concert flute can ordinarily take these notes more successfully. All that was said in an earlier chapter about the technical possibilities of the flute applies here. The G flute appears conspicuously in Ravel's *Daphnis and Chloe* Suite No. 2 and in Stravinsky's *The Rite of Spring,* among other works.

THE OBOE D'AMORE

Italian: Oboe d'Amore   French: Hautbois d'Amour

Ex. 8

Sounding a minor 3rd lower

---

[3] At one time there was an actual bass flute, capable of going an octave lower than the concert flute, but it is no longer used, at least in this country.

Used in Bach's day and revived by Strauss in his *Sinfonia Domestica,* the oboe d'amore is an extreme rarity today.   It is like the oboe as to fingering, but its tone is sweeter and less biting.   Because it is midway in size between the oboe and the English horn, it is sometimes described as a mezzo-soprano oboe.   In Bach's works, the part for it is written at actual pitch, but in modern scores the transposition given here is used.

THE HECKELPHONE

Ex. 9

This instrument, invented by Heckel in 1904, is an oboe pitched an octave lower than the normal oboe.   It is longer than the English horn and has a larger distension at the bell.   Its tone quality is extremely reedy and full, particularly in the lower register.   Except for Strauss (in *Salome*) and Delius, few composers have written for the Heckelphone, but it is now finding some use in commercial orchestral arranging.

THE Eb CLARINET

Ex. 10

This is a small clarinet which has found great favor with military bands but little with orchestras.   One reason for this state of affairs is the fact that its tone lacks the mellow warmth of the Bb clarinet and is, instead, rather hard and inelastic.   On the other hand, this very quality has now and then been exploited with striking effect in orchestral writing, as in Berlioz's *Fantastic Symphony* (the section entitled *Dream of a Witches' Sabbath*), in Strauss's *Ein Heldenleben* (in the "critics" section) and in Ravel's *Daphnis and Chloe* Suite No. 2. Because its practical upward compass, in actual sounds, is slightly greater than that of the Bb and A clarinets, it can take passages which would be too high for them. However, unless both instrument and player are first-rate, high passages for the E♭ clarinet are apt to be unpleasantly shrill or out of tune or both.

Strauss writes for a small clarinet in D, which has the same written range as the E♭ clarinet but sounds a major 2nd higher than written. The D clarinet is all but unknown in the United States, and the few parts for it (such as the important one in *Till Eulenspiegel*) are usually played on the E♭ instrument.

THE BASSET-HORN

Italian: Corno di Bassetto   French: Cor de basset   German: Bassethorn

Ex. 11

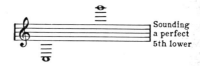

The Basset-Horn is not a horn at all but derives the second part of its name from a man named Horn who introduced the instrument. However, through an understandable confusion, "Horn" was translated literally as "Corno" by the Italians. The Basset-Horn was a forerunner of the E♭ alto clarinet, an instrument which has been much used in bands. Examples of parts for Basset-Horn may be found in Beethoven's *Prometheus* and in Mozart's *Requiem* and several of his operas. Strauss later revived the instrument for use in *Elektra*. As a point of interest, it may be recalled that George Bernard Shaw used "Corno di Bassetto" as a pen name during his early days as a critic.

THE SARRUSOPHONE

Ex. 12

An invention of a French bandmaster named Sarrus, the sarrusophone is a double-reed instrument very similar to the bassoon in construction but made of metal instead of wood. It came originally in six different sizes, pitched alternately in B♭ and E♭. Of these, the only one used in the orchestra was the largest, which sometimes substituted for the contra bassoon. In order that the player might read from the contra-bassoon part without having to transpose, a contra-bass sarrusophone in C was introduced, and it is this instrument whose range and transposition are given here. The sarrusophone in E♭ is still made today, however. Although the sarrusophone has had a considerable vogue in France, it appears only rarely in American orchestras. A part for it may be seen in Ravel's *Rapsodie Espagnole.*

THE TRUMPET IN D

Ex. 13

The trumpet in D is smaller than the B♭ or C trumpets. Its chief virtue is obviously its ability to play parts that would be uncomfortably high for the larger instruments. Consequently the lower register is apt to be little used. Parts for D trumpet can be seen in Stravinsky's *The Rite of Spring* and in Ravel's *Bolero,* among other works. Because D trumpets are scarce, however, it is ordinarily impractical to score for them.

THE TRUMPET IN F

Ex. 14

Forsyth says, "The Valve-Trumpet in F is in size and build the only representative of the old family of Trumpets, and its tone quality differs materially from that of the Trumpets in C, B♭ and A." Trumpets of the "old family" were larger than the modern instruments, and their tone was broader and more heroic. Parts for the F trumpet are found in scores by Wagner, Franck, Strauss, and others, but since the instrument is not in current use, these parts are now played on the B♭ or the C trumpet. There is also a *small* trumpet in F, which is occasionally used today for very high trumpet parts.[4]

THE BASS TRUMPET

Ex. 15

In C, sounding
an 8ve lower
In B♭, sounding
a major 9th lower

Although never used in symphonic scoring today, the bass trumpet is mentioned here because it figures in certain Wagner scores.

THE WAGNER "TUBAS"

Ex. 16

(a)   (b)

Sounding
a major
2nd lower

Tenor

Sounding
a perfect
5th lower

Bass

Wagner had these instruments constructed for use in his music dramas. Forsyth points out that they might more logically go by some other name, inasmuch as they are really modified horns. They have been little used by other composers, though Bruckner wrote for them and there are parts for B♭ tenor tuba in Strauss's *Ein Helden-leben* and *Don Quixote* as well as in Holst's *The Planets*. However, in actual practice today, these parts are often played on a euphonium (or "baritone"), an instrument which is a regular member of the band.

THE VIOLA D'AMORE

Italian: Viola d'Amore   French: Viole d'Amour   German: Liebesgeige

Ex. 17

(a)   (b)

Range

Tuning of
strings

---

[4] There are one or two instances of the use of trumpet in F *basso* (sounding a 5th lower) in the works of Wagner and Rimsky-Korsakoff, and Strauss has written for a trumpet in E♭ basso.

This curious instrument differs in several important respects from the ordinary viola. It is larger and heavier, and has seven strings tuned as shown. Beneath each of these is another string which vibrates sympathetically with the one above (but which is not touched by the bow). A serious limitation is the fact that the tuning of the strings centers so exclusively around the D major triad that passages which do not involve these notes are less resonant and effective. Also, the uneven spacing of the open pitches brings about some irregularities of fingering. Bach and Meyerbeer wrote for the viola d'amore; Charles Martin Loeffler included a part for it in *Le Mort de Tintagel,* and Hindemith has even written a concerto for it (*Chamber Music No. 6 for Viola d'Amore and Chamber Orchestra*).

Suggested Assignments

A. Know:
  (1) Written range of all the saxophones.
  (2) Transposition of the various sizes.
  (3) General abilities and limitations of saxophones.
  (4) Transposition of Flute in G, Eb Clarinet, Trumpet in D, and Trumpet in F.
B. Score the first 6 bars of *America* for:
  (1) Two alto and two tenor saxophones.
  (2) Two alto, one tenor, and one baritone saxophone.
(Use other keys if you feel that the original key (F) is unsatisfactory.)

Chapter XVIII

HINTS ON SCORING FOR HIGH
SCHOOL ORCHESTRA

FROM time to time in the course of this book there have been brief comments on the subject of arranging for school orchestra. It may be helpful to gather together some of these remarks and to expand a bit on the problem as a whole. However, this chapter should be considered more as a collection of pointers than as a full-fledged treatise on the subject.

To begin with, it must be realized that there is a tremendous variation from school to school in the instrumentation and playing abilities of orchestras and that consequently there is no one formula for scoring that will apply to all of them. At one extreme are the strangely assorted little groups, of very limited ability, that we are likely to find in the smaller schools, especially in less prosperous communities. At the other extreme we have the orchestras of semi-symphonic proportions and capabilities which have been developed in certain of the larger high schools. Somewhere in between these two types lie the majority of high school orchestras.

There is also a great variation in the instrumentation used in published arrangements for school use. These may, however, be divided into two broad categories: (1) Those designed for the smaller and less competent groups (particularly at the junior high school and elementary school levels) and involving an instrumentation similar to that shown in column (a) following; and (2) those aimed at the more complete and highly skilled groups and calling for an instrumentation which approaches that of the average symphony orchestra, similar to column (b).

(a)	(b)
1 flute	2 flutes
1 oboe	2 oboes
2 clarinets in Bb	2 clarinets
1 bassoon	2 bassoons
2 horns in F	4 horns in F
2 trumpets in Bb	2 trumpets in Bb
1 trombone	2 or 3 trombones
timpani (2)	timpani (2)
other percussion	other percussion
piano	
strings	strings

Some scores also include parts for saxophones, usually two altos and one tenor. These are generally marked *ad libitum,* to be included or not at the discretion of the conductor. They are often duplications of the horn parts which can be used to replace or bolster the horns. Also, the tenor saxophone can be helpful in doubling bassoons and/or cellos. As might be expected, cornets are sometimes substituted for trumpets in actual practice. A piano part (which may be placed either where shown or at the bottom of the page) figures frequently in the first type of arrangement but less often in the second. It is usually a condensation of the score (or salient elements of it) and may actually be played or not, depending on whether it is needed to replace missing instruments, to reinforce weak instruments, or to reinforce the orchestra as a whole. Many of the orchestras which use the (b) arrangements do not actually have on hand all the instruments included in the score. Second oboe, second bassoon, and third and fourth horns are the instruments most likely to be missing, even in otherwise well-equipped orchestras.

More will be said on this subject shortly, but first we must consider another important point, the influence of the band on school arranging. Because of the popularity of bands today, we should nearly always be safe in assuming that where there is an orchestra in a high school, there has been a band first. This means three things: (1) that band instruments are readily available for use in the orchestra; (2) that there are plenty of players for these instruments; and (3) that these players, as a group, have already had considerable experience on their instruments and will therefore be more skilled than most of the other players in the orchestra, at least in the initial stages. If we interpret this situation in terms of actual instruments, we find that most schools have plenty of performers on flute, clarinet, saxophone, trumpet, trombone, and percussion, all of which figure in the band. Ordinarily at least two horn players are available; but not all schools have four who are strong enough to handle independent parts. The orchestral instruments which are conspicuously missing from this list are the oboe, bassoon, and strings. String players can usually be recruited, except for viola players, who are extremely scarce. But oboists and bassoonists present more of a problem. It is not merely a matter of training the players; the high cost of the instruments is also a stumbling block, particularly in the case of the bassoon.

As a result of all these considerations, important passages and even solos can be given to flute, clarinet, trumpet, or trombone with a reasonable assurance that players for these parts will be on hand. But solos for oboe, bassoon, or horn are risky and, when used, are generally "cued" in another part so that the passage can be played by another instrument if necessary. Oboe solos may be cued for trumpet (usually muted) or for clarinet, flute, or violins, depending on which is convenient. Sometimes they are cued for two or more of these, in which case the conductor will decide which instrument is to do the substituting. Bassoon parts may be cued for trombone or cellos, while horn passages may be taken over by trombone, trumpet, or strings—or saxophones, if used.

However, solos are much less frequent in scoring of this type than in full-fledged symphonic orchestration. Even independent parts are used less often, whereas doublings between winds and strings are more frequent. Flutes, oboes, and clarinet double the upper strings much of the time (flutes sometimes an octave higher); bassoon plays in unison with cellos, and so on. The advantages of this type of arrangement are obvious: if one instrument is missing or weak, another will play the part. Also, inasmuch as high school players seldom have the tone, the technique, or the assurance of more mature performers, doubling helps to give body and a more solid effect.

Some orchestra directors even use the following plan in making arrangements for their groups: each instrument has a part written for it throughout the piece, instruments being allotted according to a kind of "type-casting" system such as this:

Melody	Upper Register Harmony Parts	Middle Register Harmony Parts	Bass
Flute	(1st Clarinet?)	Horns	Bassoon
Oboe	2nd Clarinet	2nd Violins	Trombone
1st Clarinet	(and/or 2nd Violins)	(and/or 2nd Clarinet)	Cellos
1st Trumpet	2nd Trumpet	Violas	Basses
1st Violins			

(The orchestra used here for purposes of illustration is of the small (a) variety; the same approach is sometimes—though less often—employed in scoring for larger groups.) When the time comes to play the arrangement and the conductor is sure what instrumentation he will have, he can cut out certain instruments wherever he feels that to be advisable, in order to get away from a constantly heavy scoring and to introduce a lighter texture and pure colors. Although this system may seem at first to be roundabout, and although it is certainly an unimaginative one, it has certain points in its favor: (1) It insures that there will at least be enough volume, where volume is needed, and that each voice will actually be played—barring hopelessly deficient instrumentation. (2) It eliminates the need for writing cues as such (the cues being "built in," so to speak), and it allows for the maximum number of possibilities in substitution. In the case of orchestras which vary radically in make-up from year to year, this type of arrangement may be more useful than one with only limited cross-cueing. (3) Arrangements made according to this plan can often be used for smaller instrumental ensembles, such as woodwind quartet or quintet, brass quartet, or small string group. That is, it is possible to plan the scoring so that certain groups of instruments playing by themselves will sound complete and satisfactory. (4) In working with an orchestra, it is easier to delete parts than to add them. For example, the conductor can, if he wishes, simply tell a player not to play a particular passage; but if he should decide, in rehearsal, that he wanted to add that instrument, he could not do it without writing out a new part—assuming that the instrument was not cued at that point.

On the other hand, there are some serious disadvantages to this system. For one thing, it tends to involve much heavy doubling, which, in turn, brings about a constantly mixed tone that becomes monotonous. Also, because the arrangement must be contrived in such a way as to sound well whether it is played by a large or a small group, instruments are often not used in the most interesting or effective way. (It is chiefly this same limitation that keeps "stock" dance arrangements from being as interesting or colorful as "special" arrangements.) This whole method is one born of practical necessity rather than artistic choice; obviously there is no point in adopting it in the case of orchestras which have a more or less complete and constant instrumentation.

Of course there is nothing hard and fast about the allotment of instruments to various voices in the chart shown on page 281. In the first place, it applies, as given here, chiefly to homophonic music, and even within that category it would have to be altered from piece to piece to fit the individual structure of each. If a countermelody were present, that might involve changes in the distribution of the voices, and if the music were entirely contrapuntal, a different classification of the musical elements would be needed. But the arrangement shown is usually appropriate for school songs, the type of music that high school instrumental directors are most often called upon to arrange.

Some technical points to keep in mind in scoring for school orchestra are given next, arranged by section.

Woodwinds

Be sure to give the flute plenty of rests. This is a good principle to follow even in writing for seasoned flutists, and it is doubly important in the case of young players, whose breathing powers are not as fully developed. Remember that the flute is by nature weak in its bottom octave and must be written higher if it is to add anything in a *tutti* or to come through any but the lightest background in a solo. However, had better be considered the upward limit.

The oboe, also, must have sufficient rests. Keep its part well within the easiest register, roughly .

First clarinet parts may be of considerable technical difficulty; but second clarinet parts are best kept simpler to accommodate the less skilled players who will probably be assigned to them. Keep in mind the fact that particularly in the hands of an inexperienced player the clarinet becomes "squealy" above about $\begin{array}{c}\text{♩}\end{array}$.

Some directors have found it helpful to include a bass clarinet or contra-bass clarinet borrowed from the band to reinforce the bass parts. However, parts for these instruments do not appear in published orchestra scores for school use.

The bassoon part had better not go above $\begin{array}{c}\text{♩}\end{array}$ or so and should not involve very fast or intricate passages. It is normally written in the bass clef—almost never in the tenor clef as in certain passages in symphonic scores. This is a debatable practice, inasmuch as players who go on to more advanced work are totally unprepared to read the passages in the tenor clef which they are certain to en-counter. The same question comes up in connection with tenor trombone and cello parts.

Brass

Horn parts should be kept within a written range of about

$\begin{array}{c}\text{♩}\end{array}$.

Notes above the F are risky, while passages that go below A or G are more difficult for young players and ungrateful to play. Besides, as intimated earlier, not all school orchestras include an actual fourth horn player. Even when four players are available, it sometimes happens that one or more of these are too inexperienced to manage separate parts, and in such cases a frequent solution is to use only two horn parts (I and II as a rule) with two players to each part. Probably the safest approach to horn writing for school use is to score for four horns but to plan their parts in such a way that the music will sound satisfactory if only the parts for Horns I and II are played.

High school trumpet players, on the other hand, are apt to be quite proficient, and the same is true to a slightly lesser degree of the trombonists. In fact, there are few limitations that apply to writing for these players—apart from the natural limitations of the instru-ments themselves, which have already been discussed. Remember especially that entrances on high notes should be avoided. (See page 151.) Trombone parts, like bassoon parts, use the bass clef as a rule.

PERCUSSION

Many schools now own pedal timpani, and there is every reason to suppose that in a few years all schools will have them. Remember that even if pedal timpani are available, it is unreasonable to demand extremely fast changes or a great number of changes in quick succession from an inexperienced student player, though a tuning gauge will allow for more accurate and rapid tuning than would be possible otherwise.

Thanks to the band, there is rarely any dearth of players for the snare drum, bass drum, cymbals, and the other percussion instruments. Many school orchestras include a set of chimes, a glockenspiel, and a xylophone (or a marimba). Vibraphones are considerably scarcer, however.

HARP, CELESTA, AND PIANO

Since harps are the exception rather than the rule in high school orchestras, they are not normally given a part in published arrangements for those groups. Of course schools which have a harp and a competent player can make very effective use of the instrument in arrangements of their own.

Because of its rarity, the celesta may as well be ruled out for school use. Parts written originally for it can be played on the piano (an octave higher than written).

The role of the piano in the school orchestra has already been mentioned. It is chiefly a "utilitarian" role, rather than a coloristic one as in symphonic scoring.

STRINGS

While some scores for school use employ the standard string grouping, others subdivide the first violins into two parts (labeled "A" and "B") and still others into three parts ("A," "B," and "C"). The chief point of this arrangement is to provide parts of graded difficulty; those members of the first violin section who would not be able to manage the more difficult spots can take "B" or "C." When the first violins are not subdivided in this way and they are called on to play a high passage, it is a wise idea to divide the group into octaves so that the less experienced players can take the lower (easier) octave. A general axiom in writing string parts for school use is that passages in first position are most practical and that it is best not to go higher than third position. The following notes may be considered safe upward limits for high school players of average ability:

Ex. 1

If higher notes are required in the first violin part, they may be allotted to one or two of the better players while the rest of the group plays the lower octave. (In most string sections there will probably be at least a few violinists who can perform passages in fifth position successfully.)

Since viola players are scarce and generally beginners on the instrument, it is unwise to depend on the violas alone for any important line. Scores are usually planned so that the viola part is doubled by other instruments, normally by Violin C when the "A, B, C" arrangement of violins is employed.

The tenor clef is almost never used for the cellos in school music.

Only the easier multiple stops should be called for, preferably those making considerable use of open strings, especially in the case of triple and quadruple stops.

Harmonics are seldom seen in school scoring, although the natural harmonics on the E string of the violin may occasionally prove useful for color effects or for very high notes that would be too difficult if played in the ordinary way.

Because the string groups are likely to be small, the players inexperienced, and the instruments of generally inferior quality, *divisi* passages should be used sparingly (and not at all for the violas). Division into more than two parts had better be ruled out altogether, unless the string section is well above average in size.

As to the size of string sections, a word should be added about the number of string parts included in published arrangements. Some publishers make a practice of including only one of each string part, any additional parts being ordered separately. Other firms classify their arrangements in three "sets" of different sizes, according to the number of string parts contained in each. The proportions used by one leading publisher are as follows:

	Set A	Set B	Set C
1st Violins	2	6	8
2nd Violins	2	6	8
Violas	1	3	5
Cellos	1	3	5
Basses	1	3	5

It must be remembered that these figures represent parts and that as two string players normally read off the same stand, the number of string players will be roughly twice as large as the number of string parts.

Four general hints on scoring for school groups might also be offered here:

(1) Avoid very fast passage work or complicated rhythms.

(2) Choose easy keys, preferably those involving no more than four sharps or three flats.

(3) Stay well within the "practical" range for each instrument.

(4) Make every effort to write parts which will be grateful and enjoyable for the players, parts which have genuine musical appeal and which are challenging enough to be interesting yet not so difficult as to be impractical.

Examples 2 and 3 are from scores for high school orchestra. The first, from an arrangement of a Haydn symphony, illustrates the use of cross-cues as well as a number of other points that were mentioned in this chapter. The second is from a small symphony by George Frederick McKay written expressly for school orchestras. It is a good example of effective and successful writing in a contemporary idiom for players of limited ability. The following note appears at the beginning of the score: "The inclusion of saxophones in the instrumentation is merely for practical effectiveness in making parts available where these instruments are part of the ensemble. Ordinarily they should be omitted." This approach to the use of saxophones seems to be a realistic and sensible one.

Both these examples are published in full score rather than in the condensed form which has been much used—and abused—in school band and orchestra music. Condensed scores are written on three or four staves and give a sketch of the music at actual pitch, with general indications as to how the various parts are scored. The obvious weakness of that system is that the conductor cannot tell from the score exactly what notes are to be played by each instrument and that there is consequently a good deal of room for error and confusion. For this reason, the use of condensed scores is not recommended. Fortunately, the current trend (in school orchestra music, at least) seems to be toward a consistent use of the full-score type of notation.

Ex. 2. Symphony XV (*La Reine*) in Bb major (Arranged by Mayhew Lake)

HAYDN

McKAY

Suggested Assignment

Choose a song from a school song book and score it for high school orchestra (instrumentation to be specified by the instructor). Keep in mind the points discussed in this chapter and include cross-cues wherever advisable.

Chapter XIX

ON WRITING SCORE AND PARTS

UNFORTUNATELY, most students (like many composers) cannot afford to hire a professional copyist and must write out their own scores and parts. This aspect of orchestration may appear to be mere "hack-work" requiring no special knowledge; actually, it involves some problems that students have seldom had occasion to learn before. Therefore this list of pointers on the subject is included here.

CONCERNING THE SCORE

Anything from 12-line to 24-line manuscript paper may be used, depending on the size of the orchestra involved.

Naturally, an ink score is much preferable to one in pencil and would be expected by the conductor of any professional orchestra.

As explained earlier, dynamics must be shown beneath each part, but it is usually sufficient to show tempo indications in only two places on the page, at the top and just above the violins. Sometimes they are also shown at the bottom of the page.

Time signatures may be written in each part, or two or three time signatures written in large elongated figures may be used instead. The latter system is preferable in certain modern music where the time signature changes frequently, for the larger figures are more easily visible to the conductor.

In order to save time in student scoring, it is possible to omit whole rests and to leave the measures blank instead. But rests of a fraction of a measure must always be shown. Of course whole rests are included in printed scores and in manuscript scores intended for professional use.

When a single melodic line appears on a staff that is shared by two woodwind or brass instruments, be sure to indicate whether the passage is to be played by both instruments or by the first or by the second ("a 2" or "1." or "2.").

When only a portion of the orchestra is playing, either one of two systems may be used: (1) All the instruments are listed on each page, with rests (or blanks) for those that are not actually playing. (2) Some or all of the instruments that are resting are omitted from the listing on the page. Since fewer staves are required this second way, it is sometimes possible to put on one page what would have taken up two full pages under the other system; that is, the page is divided into an upper score and a lower score. While this method saves paper, it has the disadvantage of not keeping the instruments in the same relative places on the page and therefore makes score-reading a bit more difficult. In any case, the *first* page of a score should show all the instruments to be used.

The sections of the orchestra can be more clearly distinguished from each other if there is a gap in the bar lines between each section. The horns may have a separate bar line or be grouped with the brass.

"Rehearsal letters" (or numbers) must be included in both score and parts so that the conductor can tell the orchestra where to start when particular passages are to be rehearsed. Sometimes these letters or numbers are placed at likely "starting points" throughout the score. Another method is simply to write in the number of the measure above the staff every 10 or 20 bars (or as often as desired). In either case, the letter or number should be either written in red ink or enclosed in a red square or circle so that it can be found easily. (This applies to both score and parts.)

Students in orchestration classes seldom have any need for more than one copy of a score; but composers frequently do, in order that their music may be made available to several conductors at the same time. The easiest method for making copies of scores, and the one used by most composers today is as follows: The music is written with manuscript ink on special translucent master sheets which can be reproduced by the "Black and White" process (similar to photostating). These thin master sheets, which are available in a variety of sizes and formats designed for various combinations of instruments, can be bought from several firms, three of which are listed on page 293.

Independent Music Publishers
205 East 42nd St.
New York 17, N. Y.

Circle Blue Print Co.
225 West 57th St.
New York 19, N. Y.

National Blue Print Co.
110 West 32nd St.
New York 1, N. Y.

These same firms can make the copies of the sheets and can also supply cardboard or paper covers and spiral binding—or "saddle-stitch" binding for scores of only a few pages. Many blueprint companies in other parts of the country are equipped to make reproductions by the Black and White process, but few sell the blank master sheets or handle covers and bindings.

CONCERNING THE PARTS

Use 12-line or 10-line manuscript paper.

Copy in black ink. Manuscript written in pencil is difficult to read and soon gets smudged. Be sure to make the notes large enough, especially in the parts for such instruments as double bass and tuba, whose players must read from some distance. Also, allow enough room so that the notes are not crowded. Leger lines should be the same distance apart as the lines in the staff.

Ordinarily the part for each wind instrument is written on a separate sheet. However, it is possible to write each pair of woodwinds or brass on one sheet, usually with a separate staff for each part. In rare cases where the two instruments play "a 2" much of the time or have very similar parts, it may be practical to write the parts for both on the same staff. In the past, horn parts have usually been written with horns I and II on one sheet, III and IV on another; today it is becoming more and more common to write a separate part for each horn.

For directions on writing percussion parts, see the final portion of the chapter on percussion.

In planning string parts, be sure to remember that you will need only half as many parts as there are players, because two players read from each part. Instead of copying out each individual string part, most composers and arrangers have copies made via the Black and White method of reproduction. This entails making only the original master part for each string group.

Each part must include indications for tempo, dynamics, expression, phrasing, slurring, bowing, and muting—in short, every direction that is necessary in telling the player exactly how the part should sound.

Rehearsal letters or numbers, described in the section on the score, must be shown in each part.

Rests of more than one or two measures are indicated in the following manner:

Ex. 1

Notice that when a rehearsal letter occurs in the middle of a rest, the rest must be divided to show the number of measures before and after the rehearsal letter.   Rests of only one or two measures are often shown by simply putting a whole rest in each measure.

The expression *tacet* (literally translated, "is silent") in a part indicates that the instrument in question does not play for a specified length of time.   For example, if the tuba had nothing to play in the second movement of a particular symphony, we might write, "2nd Movement, tacet" in the part.   Or if it played at the beginning of the movement but had nothing to play for the last 200 bars, we could write, "Tacet to end of movement (200 bars)" rather than bothering to ennumerate the separate rests and rehearsal letters.

Example 1 illustrates the use of "cues" in parts—in this case the fragment of the trombone part included in the trumpet part.   Cues are a great help to the player and one which he has the right to expect. They are most often included just before an entrance after a rest of some length, but they are also useful as "landmarks" in the middle of very long rests.   One or two bars are usually sufficient for a cue, though longer cues are common.   Be sure to select an important voice that can be easily heard and not a minor part that is apt to be covered up by other instruments.   Cues should be written in small notes with stems in the "wrong" direction to allow for the rests that are included.   If red ink can be used, that will help to distinguish the cues from the notes to be played.   A question that arises here is this: **in writing a cue for a transposing instrument, should the cue also** be transposed or should it be written as it actually is in the score? Both systems have been used, and each has its advantages; but as a general rule the first seems preferable. It should certainly be used in any case where a cued passage may have to be *played* (for example in school orchestra music, where important passages for one instrument are often cued for one or more other instruments, any one of which may substitute if necessary).

Label each part carefully, giving the name of the composition in the middle of the page at the top, the names of the composer and the arranger in the upper right-hand corner, and the name of the instrument that is to play the part (for example, "Clarinet II in B♭") in the upper left-hand corner.

If page turning is involved, copy the part in such a way that there will be a rest of sufficient length to allow for the turn at the bottom of the page. This is more important in wind parts than in string parts, as one of each pair of string players can turn the page while the other continues to play, if necessary. However, that arrangement is better avoided, and rests should be provided at "turning points" whenever possible.

LIST OF FOREIGN NAMES FOR INSTRUMENTS, ORCHESTRAL TERMS

UNLESS one has taken the trouble to learn the Italian, French, and German names for instruments (and the abbreviations for those names) score-reading is likely to degenerate into a kind of guessing game. Of course it is easy enough to guess (correctly) that *Klarinette* means clarinet in German or even that *timbales* is the French name for timpani. But it is also easy to guess, *incorrectly,* that *cors* stands for cornets (instead of horns) or that *tam-tam* is an Indian drum (instead of a gong). And how is one to decipher such names as *Posaunen* (trombones in German) or *piatti* (cymbals in Italian)?

Presumably the student who has covered the material in this book has already learned a good many of the foreign names as he went along. The complete list is given here for purposes of reference or study. Also given are the foreign equivalents of some important terms commonly found in orchestral scores. The blanks in the latter list are caused by the fact that some of the terms are seldom or never used in certain of the languages. Also, there are cases in which the Italian term is used even in French and German scores. For example, one finds *sul ponticello* and *con sordino* in German scores, while such terms as *arco* and *pizzicato* are universal.

NAMES OF INSTRUMENTS

English	Italian	French	German
Piccolo	Flauto Piccolo (or Ottavino)	Petite Flûte	Kleine Flöte
Flute	Flauto	Flûte	Flöte
Oboe	Oboe	Hautbois	Oboe (or Hoboe)
English Horn	Corno Inglese	Cor Anglais	Englisch Horn
Clarinet	Clarinetto	Clarinette	Klarinette
Bass Clarinet	Clarinetto Basso	Clarinette Basse	Bassklarinette
Bassoon	Fagotto	Basson	Fagott
Contra Bassoon	Contrafagotto	Contre-basson	Kontrafagott

English	Italian	French	German
Horn	Corno	Cor	Horn
Trumpet	Tromba	Trompette	Trompete
Trombone	Trombone	Trombone	Posaune
Tuba	Tuba	Tuba	Tuba (or Basstuba)
Timpani (or Kettle Drums)	Timpani	Timbales	Pauken
Bass Drum	Gran Cassa	Grosse Caisse	Grosse Trommel
Cymbals	Piatti	Cymbales	Becken
Snare Drum (or Side Drum)	Tamburo (Militare)	Tambour (Militaire)	Kleine Trommel
Tenor Drum	Tamburo Rullante	Caisse Roulante	Rührtrommel
Triangle	Triangolo	Triangle	Triangel
Tambourine	Tamburino	Tambour de Basque	Schellentrommel
Gong	Tam-tam	Tam-tam	Tam-tam
Castanets	Castagnette	Castagnettes	Kastagnetten
Xylophone	Silofono	Xylophone	Xylophon
Glockenspiel	Campanelli	Jeu de Timbres (or Carillon)	Glockenspiel
Bells or Chimes	Campane	Cloches	Glocken
Celesta	Celesta	Célesta	Celesta
Harp	Arpa	Harpe	Harfe
Violin	Violino	Violon	Violine
Viola	Viola	Alto	Bratsche
Violoncello	Violoncello	Violoncelle	Violoncell
Double Bass	Contrabasso	Contre Basse	Kontrabass

ORCHESTRAL TERMS

English	Italian	French	German
muted	con sordino [1] / con sordini	sourdine(s)	mit Dämpfer (or gedämpft, in horns)
take off mutes	via sordini	enlevez les sourdines	Dämpfer(n) weg
without mute	senza sordino	sans sourdine	ohne Dämpfer
divided	divisi (div.)	divisé(e)s (div.)	geteilt (get.)
divided in 3 parts	div. a 3	div. à 3	dreifach

---

[1] May also be spelled *sordina*, in which case the plural is *sordine*.

English	Italian	French	German
divided in 4 parts	div. a 4	div. à 4	vierfach
in unison	unisono (unis.)	unis	zusammen (or einfach)
a 2	a 2	à 2	zu 2
at (near) the bridge	sul ponticello	sur le cheva- let	sul ponticello (or am Steg)
on the finger- board	sul tasto (or sulla tastiera)	sur la touche	am Griffbrett
with the wood of the bow	col legno	avec le bois	col legno (or mit Holz)
at the point of the bow	punta d'arco	(de la) pointe	Spitze
at the frog		du talon	am Frosch
bells in the air	campane in aria	pavillons en l'air	Schalltrichter auf
half (a string group)	la metà	la moitié	die Hälfte
stopped (as in horns)	chiuso (chiusi)	bouché(s) (sons bouchés)	gestopft
brassy		cuivré	schmetternd
open	aperto (aperti)	ouvert(s)	offen
with soft stick	bacchetta di spugna	baguette d'éponge (baguette molle)	mit Schwamm- schlägel
with hard sticks	bacchette di legno	baguettes en bois	mit Holzschlägeln
change G to F♯	sol muta in fa♯	changez sol en fa♯	G nach Fis umstimmen
near the sounding board (harp)		près de la table	
desk or stand		pupitre	Pult
in the ordinary way (after sul pont., etc.)	modo ordinario	mode ordinaire	gewöhnlich
string	corda	corde	Saite

Note: Nouns are always capitalized in German.

Appendix B

RANGES OF INSTRUMENTS

I N EACH case the limits of the extreme possible range are shown in open notes, the limits of the practical or commonly used range in black notes. These are written ranges.

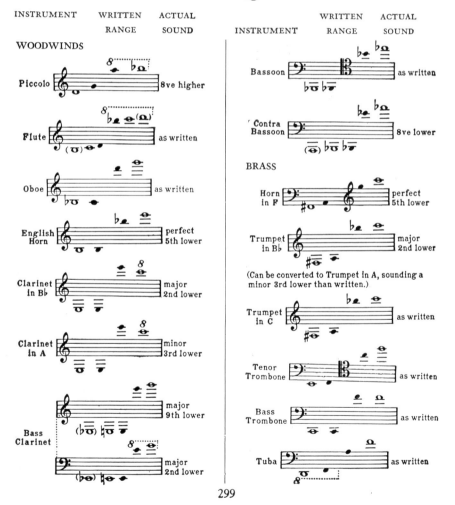

INSTRUMENT	WRITTEN RANGE	ACTUAL SOUND	INSTRUMENT	WRITTEN RANGE	ACTUAL SOUND

PERCUSSION

Timpani — as written

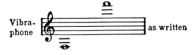

Xylophone — 8ve higher

Glockenspiel — 2 8ves higher

Vibraphone — as written

Bells (Chimes) — 8ve higher

"EXTRAS"

Celesta — 8ve higher

Harp — as written

Piano — as written

Violin — as written

Viola — as written

Cello — as written

Double Bass — 8ve lower

SAXOPHONES

Bb Soprano Saxophone — major 2nd lower

Eb Alto Saxophone — major 6th lower

Bb Tenor Saxophone — major 9th lower

Eb Baritone Saxophone — 8ve & major 6th lower

Bb Bass Saxophone — 2 8ves & major 2nd lower

INFREQUENTLY USED INSTRUMENTS

INSTRUMENT	WRITTEN RANGE	ACTUAL SOUND
WOODWINDS		
Flute in G		perfect 4th lower
Oboe d'Amore		minor 3rd lower
Heckel-phone		8ve lower
Eb Clarinet		minor 3rd higher
Clarinet in D		major 2nd higher
Basset-Horn (in F)		perfect 5th lower
Sarruso-phone		8ve lower

INSTRUMENT	WRITTEN RANGE	ACTUAL SOUND
BRASS		
Trumpet in D		major 2nd higher
Trumpet in F		perfect 4th higher
Bass Trumpet in C		8ve lower
Bass Trumpet in Bb		major 9th lower
Tenor Wagner "Tubas"		major 2nd lower
Bass		perfect 5th lower
STRINGS		
Viola d'Amore		as written

Andersen, Arthur Olaf, *Practical Orchestration,* C. C. Birchard & Co., Boston, 1929. (A highly successful book, usable as either text or reference. It includes numerous examples, chiefly from American works. The exercises in scoring are drawn entirely from Mendelssohn's *Songs Without Words* and Beethoven's Piano Sonatas.)

Berlioz-Strauss, *Treatise on Instrumentation,* Kalmus, New York, 1948 (English translation). (To the original detailed treatise by Berlioz, Richard Strauss has added voluminous comments as well as musical examples drawn largely from the works of Wagner. This massive volume, assembling as it does the combined orchestral knowledge of two of the most important figures in orchestration, contains a wealth of valuable information.)

Collinson, Francis M., *Orchestration for the Theater,* John Lane, London, 1941. (A realistic, well-written work. Although oriented chiefly around English practice, it may prove helpful to readers in other countries as a commentary on this specialized aspect of orchestration.)

Forsyth, Cecil, *Orchestration,* Macmillan Co., New York, Second Edition, 1935. (A thorough and detailed reference book on the individual instruments and their historical backgrounds, written in a witty and highly interesting vein and containing a large number of excellent examples. An important standard work.)

————, *Choral Orchestration,* H. W. Gray Co., New York, 1920. (A rather slim volume, written in the author's usual entertaining style, which discusses certain typical problems encountered in scoring orchestral accompaniments for choral groups.)

Gál, Hans, *Directions for Score Reading,* Vienna Philharmonic Edition, Vienna-New York, 1924. (A pamphlet of pocket-score size which explains the make-up of the orchestra, transpositions, and other points involved in score reading.)

Gevaert, François Auguste, (1) *Nouveau Traité d'Instrumentation,* Lemoine & Cie, Paris, 1885, (2) *Cours Méthodique d'Orchestration,* Lemoine & Cie, Paris, 1890. (Old but still instructive treatises, in French, the first on individual instruments, the second on their use in orchestration.)

Gardner, Maurice, *The Orchestrator's Handbook,* The Staff Music Publishing Co., Great Neck, N. Y., 1948. (A small pamphlet containing ranges, charts, and very brief commentaries on the instruments.)

Heacox, Arthur, *Project Lessons in Orchestration,* Oliver Ditson Co., Philadelphia, 1928. (A concise, highly practical book, well organized for use as a text, which lays considerable stress on problems involved in scoring for school and nonprofessional orchestras. Certain instruments—the piccolo, English horn, bass clarinet, and contra bassoon—are not treated except for a brief note in an appendix.)

302

Jacob, Gordon, *Orchestral Technique,* Oxford University Press, London, 1931. (Extremely well written; concise yet highly informative; on a high level musically; not one of the larger treatises but one of the more successful for classroom use.)

————, *How to Read a Score,* Hawkes & Son Ltd., London, 1949. (A slim pamphlet packed with pertinent and clearly expressed material. Intended principally for the musical amateur who wishes to read scores, this book is less comprehensive and detailed than the same author's *Orchestral Technique.*)

Johnstone, Arthur Edward, *Instruments of the Modern Symphony Orchestra and Band,* Carl Fischer, New York, second revised and augmented edition, 1948. (A manual containing fine pictures of instruments—including some instruments not normally used in either orchestras or bands, such as the zither, dulcimer, harpsichord, and theremin. A short commentary accompanies each picture.)

Kohs, Ellis B., *An Aural Approach to Orchestration,* Musical Mercury, Vol. VI, No. 3–4, March–May, 1939, E. F. Kalmus, New York. (A highly interesting and helpful article which catalogs various combinations of instruments and tells where examples of each may be found in orchestral literature.)

Lockwood, Samuel, *Elementary Orchestration,* George Wahr, Ann Arbor, Michigan, 1926. (A textbook of modest proportions written in a pleasantly informal vein.)

Posell, Elsa Z., *This Is an Orchestra,* Houghton-Mifflin Co., Boston, 1950. (Designed chiefly for readers of pre-college age, this small book provides a brief introduction to orchestral instruments. It is mentioned here because of its excellent pictures of the instruments and because teachers at primary and secondary levels may find it useful in their work.)

Prout, Ebenezer, *The Orchestra* (in two volumes), Augener Ltd., London, 1897. (The first volume is entitled *Technique of the Instruments;* the second, *Orchestral Combination.* Although understandably outmoded in certain respects, this admirably thorough work contains much material that is still applicable today.)

Rimsky-Korsakoff, Nicolas, *Principles of Orchestration,* Kalmus, New York, first published in Europe about 1912. (A large-scale treatise consisting of two sections, the first text, the second full-score examples selected entirely from the author's own works. The book is designed for "those who have already studied instrumentation . . . and who have some knowledge of a number of orchestral scores." One of the most valuable features is the splendid material on various ways of *combining* instruments, a topic treated briefly or not at all in many orchestration books.)

Rogers, Bernard, *The Art of Orchestration,* Appleton-Century Crofts, New York, 1951. (Written by a master of coloristic scoring, this book emphasizes "the special kinship of instruments and color" and draws an analogy between the devices of painting and those of orchestration. The literary style is polished and engaging. Among the many interesting features is a section, illustrated by excerpts from the author's own works, showing the evolution of a composer's score from the first rough sketches to the final realization.)

Skinner, Frank, *Underscore,* Skinner Music Co., Inc., Hollywood, 1950. (Tells in detail how a complete motion picture score is written, arranged, and recorded.)

Widor, C. M., *The Modern Orchestra,* J. Williams, London, 1906. (A large, detailed, and widely used work, now somewhat outmoded in its comments on the technical limitations of instruments.)

Books on the History of Instruments or of the Orchestra

Bekker, Paul, *The Story of the Orchestra,* W. W. Norton, New York, 1936.
Bessaraboff, Nicholas, *Ancient European Musical Instruments,* Harvard University Press, Boston, 1941.
Carse, Adam, *The Orchestra in the XVIIIth Century,* W. Heffer & Sons Ltd., Cambridge, England, 1940.
————, *The Orchestra from Beethoven to Berlioz,* W. Heffer & Sons Ltd., Cambridge, England, 1948.
————, *History of Orchestration,* E. P. Dutton, New York, 1925. (Out of print.)
Coerne, Louis Adolphe, *The Evolution of Modern Orchestration,* Macmillan Co., New York, 1908.
Daubeny, Ulric, *Orchestral Wind Instruments,* William Reeves, London, 1920.
Galpin, Francis W., *A Textbook of European Musical Instruments,* Williams and Norgate Ltd., London, 1937.
Geiringer, Karl, *Musical Instruments,* Oxford University Press, New York, 1945.
Hayes, Gerald R., *Old Instrumental Music* (Book I of series entitled *Musical Instruments and Their Music, 1500–1750*), Oxford University Press, London, 1928.
————, *The Viols and Other Bowed Instruments* (Book II of series listed above), Oxford University Press, London, 1930.
Rensch, Rosalyn, *The Harp,* Philosophical Library, Inc., New York, 1950.
Sachs, Curt, *The History of Musical Instruments,* W. W. Norton, New York, 1940.
Schlesinger, Kathleen, *Instruments of the Modern Orchestra and Early Records of Precursors of the Violin Family* (in two volumes), William Reeves, London, 1910.
Schwartz, H. W., *The Story of Musical Instruments,* Doubleday, Doran & Co. Inc., New York, 1939.

Books on Band Scoring

Adkins, H. E., *Treatise on the Military Band,* Boosey & Co., London, 1931.
Gallo, Stanislao, *The Modern Band,* C. C. Birchard & Co., Boston, 1935.
Hoby, Charles, *Military Band Instrumentation,* Oxford University Press, London, 1936.
Lang, Philip J., *Scoring for the Band,* Mills Music, Inc., New York, 1950.
Miller, Roy M., *Practical Instrumentation for the Wind Band,* William C. Brown Co., Dubuque, Iowa, 1948.
Skeat and Clark, *The Fundamentals of Band Arranging,* Sam Fox, Cleveland, New York, 1938.

Books on Arranging for Dance Orchestra

Cesana, Otto, *Voicing the Modern Dance Orchestra,* Modern Music Publications, New York, 1946.

Diamante, Carlos, *Arranging Latin-American Music Authentically,* King Brand Publications, New York, 1948.

Miller, Glenn, *Glenn Miller's Method for Orchestral Arranging,* Mutual Music Society, Inc., New York, 1943.

Books on Choral Arranging

Davison, Archibald T., *The Technique of Choral Composition,* Harvard University Press, 1945.

Wilson, Harry Robert, *Choral Arranging for Schools, Glee Clubs, and Publication,* Robbins Music Corp., 1949.

INDEX

307